Applied
English
Grammar

APPLIED ENGLISH GRAMMAR

Patricia Byrd
Georgia State University

Beverly Benson
DeKalb College

Heinle & Heinle Publishers
A Division of Wadsworth, Inc.
Boston, Massachusetts 02116 U.S.A.

Vice President and Publisher: Stanley J. Galek
Editorial Director: David C. Lee
Assistant Editor: Kenneth Mattsson
Project Manager: Stacey Sawyer, Sawyer & Williams
Production Supervisor: Patricia Jalbert
Manufacturing Coordinator: Lisa McLaughlin
Text Design: Nancy Benedict
Front Matter Design: Adriane Bosworth
Photo Research: Judy Mason
Illustrations: Susan Detrich
Cover Design and Illustration: Maureen Lauran

Manufactured in the United States of America.

Heinle & Heinle Publishers is a division of Wadsworth, Inc.

Library of Congress Cataloging-in-Publication Data

Byrd, Patricia.
    Applied English grammar / Patricia Byrd, Beverly Benson.
        p.   cm.
    Includes bibliographical references and index.
    ISBN 0-8384-2281-0
    1. English language—Grammar—1950–   2. English language—
  Textbooks for foreign speakers. I. Benson, Beverly. II. Title.
PE1112.B95 1992
428.2′4—dc20   91-43648
                                                    CIP

ISBN 0-8384-2281-0

10 9 8 7 6 5 4 3

CONTENTS

Contents

Contents

Contents

SECTION FIVE   Appendices and Lists   431

••

SECTION SIX   The Grammar Journal   443

••

Crossword Puzzle Answers   460

••

Index   461

••

P R E F A C E

To the Instructor

Our goal has been to write a textbook that will help second-language learners improve their knowledge of English grammar and write more fluently and accurately. We have written this textbook primarily for academic learners planning to attend colleges and universities in the United States, but it may also be useful in other types of programs here and in other countries. We are aware of the difficulty of specifying the English-proficiency level of students caused by the great variety in ESL-program structures in the United States and around the world. This text was prepared for use with students who in many situations would be called "high intermediate to advanced." Typically these students would have TOEFL scores in the 470–500 range (at the beginning of the term) and would usually be expected to continue in ESL study for at least one more term before entering a fulltime academic degree program.

Applied English Grammar has four purposes: (1) to prepare students for advanced ESL, English Composition, or other academic courses, especially courses that emphasize writing and the grammar of written English; (2) to improve students' overall communication skills through an integrated approach to English grammar; (3) to introduce students to an editing system they can use in improving the accuracy of their written English; and (4) to help students improve their learning strategies and skills.

In doing the above, *Applied English Grammar* (1) builds on the prior learning experiences and grammar/writing experiences of the students, (2) focuses on the grammar of written English, and (3) provides a variety of activities and groupings for the instructor who wants to develop a student-centered class. The authors recognize that students bring many different learning styles and preferences to the classroom; variety in materials is necessary for all.

Grammatical Coverage

All of the areas traditional in ESL grammar textbooks are included, but the material has been developed from the point of view of the ESL student who needs to learn to be a more effective writer and editor. Punctuation is included as an important aspect of academic written English.

Appendices at the end of the book list linking verbs, joining words, irregular verbs, modal auxiliaries, and preposition combinations. A detailed index guides the user to appropriate materials.

Format

The organization is nontraditional: six core chapters focus on verbs and time frames; the following ten chapters deal with additional grammar topics of importance to high intermediate/advanced ESL students. Students and instructors are encouraged to complete First Steps (Section One) during the first week of class and to progress chapter by chapter through the core of materials (Section Two), taking time to move into the additional grammar topics (Section Three) as students demonstrate a need or desire for the topics. This plan provides freedom within the text to respond to an immediate communicative need. Flexibility is built in, and students are encouraged to spend time learning something new, or at least approaching the same topic in a different way. Since *Applied English Grammar* is not a beginning grammar textbook, the organization allows for selection of those chapters and parts of chapters most appropriate to the needs of a particular class. Parts of the book can be reviewed quickly or covered in depth, depending on the students. In addition to review, each chapter provides new ideas and new ways of approaching topics students have already studied. Editing (Section Four) of exercise paragraphs and students' own writings is practiced, and a special section, the Grammar Journal (Section Six), provides space for student self-analysis and for plans for study.

Content

Applied English Grammar focuses on the grammar of written English at the high intermediate/advanced level. The need for grammatical knowledge and accuracy is placed within the context of the writing process and the written work of each student using this text. Grammar is explained and illustrated in the context of higher discourse levels. *Applied English Grammar* is organized so that students focus on time frames and contextualized writing, rather than grammar in isolation.

Emphasis is placed on aspects of written English grammar that are writing problems for high intermediate/advanced ESL students. Exercises are frequently contextualized with content worthy of thought and discussion; in fact, discussion questions are included with many exercises. These exercises vary in difficulty and scope.

Terminology and grammatical choices that are likely to be found in courses taught by English as well as ESL faculty are presented. Students can learn the vocabulary they need to discuss their writing and grammar with their teachers.

Teaching and Learning Strategies

A variety of communicative exercises and activities appear throughout the textbook. Some exercises are time consuming and may allow for several possible correct responses. These communicative exercises approximate genuine language use, promote active learning, and build on student interest.

Activities are included to help students learn about their language-learning styles and strategies and to help them become better students and learners.

Applied English Grammar recognizes that students already know a great deal about English grammar. The textbook encourages students to build on prior knowledge.

Control is given to the instructor to select the grammatical areas, exercises, writing assignments, editing exercises, and individual concerns to be covered with a particular group of students.

Exercises include pair and small-group work as well as individual tasks. They range from fill-in-the-blank to open-ended activities. The Grammar Journal helps students identify strengths and weaknesses and fosters student responsibility and self-knowledge.

The Grammar Notebook and the Grammar Journal

In First Steps, students are introduced to the practice of keeping an orderly notebook of the materials that they produce in the grammar/writing course. Only with a collection of such materials easily at hand can students see changes that occur in their own work over the time of the course. In addition to keeping a "Grammar Notebook" or "Portfolio," students are led by the text to carry out activities that reveal their preferred learning styles and strategies. Such self-knowledge can be the foundation for improved learning if students are encouraged to be more thoughtful about their study methods. The Grammar Journal provides a set of activities through which the students can analyze their use of particular aspects of English grammar. These activities are intended as a beginning point for such analysis. Other similar activities can be developed by the teacher to fit the particular students in a class.

In field testing, teachers found that students responded positively to the inclusion in a grammar/writing course of activities that helped them become better learners not just of grammar but of other subjects that they study.

To signal to students the importance of thinking about learning styles, strategies, and skills, the ESL teachers who field tested the materials included time each week for work on the Grammar Journal and other self-analysis activities. In addition, they awarded 10–15% of the final grade for the course for the work done in self-analysis and the development of grammar notebooks or portfolios. Teachers agreed that they indicate to students which activities are valuable through the devotion of class time to such activities and through the giving of grades for such activities. That is, work on study skills had to be included as part of the class itself and not just assigned as homework before students would accept these new tasks as important. Moreover, these tasks were unfamiliar to many students who needed step-by-step help from their teachers in learning how to analyze their own work.

The Grammar Notebooks developed over the two years of field testing into three-ring binders kept by all students. Since few students were accustomed to keeping track of their own work, teachers found that they needed to provide ongoing encouragement and supervision until students became more adept at organizing and analyzing their study. This collection of materials could be used by the students to chart their own progress and to plan for their own learning.

The activity was so successful that teachers began requiring that students purchase for the grammar/writing course not just a copy of the textbook but a three-ring binder with a set of dividers. The notebooks are divided into the sections listed on pages 3 and 4: (1) assignments and other information about this course, (2) class notes, (3) returned test papers, (4) returned writing assignments, and (5) list of words that I want to learn. Teachers from the field testing recommend that all handouts be holepunched for easy placement in the notebooks. One teacher commented that perhaps a handout not worth keeping was a handout not worth doing in the first place. In addition, these teachers advise that all tests be on holepunched paper so that students could more easily keep up with returned examination papers. The Department of Applied Linquistics and ESL at Georgia State University made this holepunching easier by purchasing an electric three-hole punch. Thus, teachers and the ESL program found that some practical changes were necessary to help students have more control over their study.

Instructor's Manual

The Instructor's Manual that accompanies *Applied English Grammar* provides additional suggestions for using this text, including a model ten-week plan for working through the core and an answer key for exercises.

Acknowledgments

It is our pleasure to thank the many friends and colleagues who helped make *Applied English Grammar* possible by contributing their ideas, time, energy, and encouragement. Thanks go to the teachers at Georgia State University who participated in the field testing:

Chris Evans	Mike Oil
Alice Gertzman	Karen Peterson
Pamela Healy	David Robinson
Michele Kuchel	Debra Snell
Alan Mobley	Peggy Swiedler

The following students in the ESL Program at DeKalb College deserve special recognition for providing writing samples used in Section Four, Editing Written English: Edgar M. Ancieta, Steven Chan, Wei C. Chen, Suwan Desit, Farokh Farkhondeh, Kazeem Ajala, Farid M. Khan, Hyun Lee, Sean Lee, Toan Bao Nguyen, Paresh C. Patel, Daniel Tesfaye, Steve Vongsavansack, Chi Xiong, and Joshua S. Yoon.

Graduate students in Patricia Byrd's course on English Grammar and Pedagogical Grammars made many useful observations both about the explanations and about exercises. Most of all we thank the many ESL students who have used these materials and who have provided writing samples that helped us gain a better understanding of the teaching and learning of grammar within the context of written English.

We acknowledge our debt to reference grammars such as Marianne Celce-Murcia and Diane Larsen-Freeman, *The Grammar Book: An ESL/EFL Teacher's Course* and Randolph Quirk, Sidney Greenbaum, Geoffrey Leech, and Jan Svartvik, *A Comprehensive Grammar of the English Language*. Without the work of these grammarians, the writing of teaching grammars would be impossible.

We are also indebted to the scholars who have given us insights into learning styles and skills and into the influences of cultures on the approaches individuals have taken to learning languages. Included among these are Shirley Brice Heath, John C. Condon, Anna Uhl Chamot, J. Michael O'Malley, Rebecca Oxford, Joy Reid, and Fathi Yousef.

While permissions were not needed for the following government documents, we thank their authors for providing us with materials that could be adapted for use by our students.

Black Contributors to Science and Energy Technology. Washington, D.C.: Government Printing Office, undated.

Broughton, Connie. "Serving Refugee Children and Families in Head Start." *Children Today.* Washington, D.C.: Government Printing Office, 1989, 6–10.

Gozdziak, Elzbieta. *Aging: Older Immigrants Find a New Life.* Human Development Services Department of Health and Human Services. no. 359. Washington, D.C.: Government Printing Office, 1989.

Jackson, Geoffrey. "Turkey's Sixth Five-Year Development Plan Offers Promising Opportunities for U.S. Firms." *Business America: The Magazine of International Trade* (June 19, 1989), 18–19. Washington, D.C.: U.S. Department of Commerce.

Newman, Eileen Patz and Dianne D. Odland. "Supermarket Salad Bars—Cost vs. Convenience." *Family Economics Review*, vol. 1, no. 4. Washington, D.C.: Government Printing Office, 1988, 8–10.

Services to the Nation: The Library of Congress. Washington, D.C.: Government Printing Office, 1988.

"The Task Force on Women, Minorities, and the Handicapped in Science and Technology." *Changing America: The New Face of Science and Engineering: Interim Report.* Washington, D.C.: Government Printing Office, 1988.

U.S. Bureau of the Census. "Computer Use in the United States." *Family Economics Review*, vol. 1, no. 4, 19–20. Information was taken from Kominski, Robert. *Computer Use in the United States: 1984.* Current Population Reports, Special Studies, series P-23, no. 155.

U.S. Bureau of the Census. *Rural Farm Population: 1987.* Current Population Reports Series, no. 61. Washington, D.C.: Government Printing Office, 1988.

U.S. Department of the Interior: Bureau of Indian Affairs. *Famous Indians: A Collection of Short Biographies.* Washington, D.C.: Government Printing Office, undated.

U.S. Department of Labor. Bureau of Labor Statistics. "Why People Work." *Exploring Careers*, Bulletin 2001. Washington, D.C.: Government Printing Office, 1979, 2–4.

U.S. Food and Drug Administration. Public Health Services, Department of Health and Human Services. "Anatomy of a Backache," *FDA Consumer*, vol. 23, no. 3, 28–35. Washington, D.C.: Government Printing Office, 1989.

U.S. Food and Drug Administration, Public Health Services, Department of Health and Human Services. "DataPhile: Smoking, Drinking, and Oral Cancer." *FDA Consumer*. Washington, D.C.: Government Printing Office, 1989, 40.

U.S. Food and Drug Administration, Public Health Services, Department of Health and Human Services. "The 'Grazing of America': A Guide to Healthy Snacking," the *FDA Consumer*, vol. 23, no. 2, 8–11. Washington, D.C.: Government Printing Office, 1988.

U.S. Food and Drug Administration. Public Health Services, Department of Health and Human Services. "Kitchen Safety Tips for Seafood," *FDA Consumer: Fishing for Facts on Fish Safety*, vol. 23, no. 1. Washington, D.C.: Government Printing Office, 1989, 25.

Information was used from the following encyclopedias:

Collier's Encyclopedia. 1987 ed.
Encyclopedia Americana. 1983 ed.
The World Book Encyclopedia. 1988 ed.

The definition of *stereotype* used in Chapter 3 was found in the following article:

Simmons, Ozzie. "Stereotypes: Explaining People Who Are Different," in Wurzel, Jaime S. (Ed.), *Toward Multiculturalism: A Reader in Multicultural Education.* Yarmouth, Maine: Intercultural Press, Inc., 1988, 57–66.

Sentence types were illustrated in Chapter 1 with examples from the following source:

Block, Peter. *Flawless Consulting: A Guide to Getting Your Expertise Used.* San Diego, California: University Associates, Inc., 1981.

Permission was granted to use the following materials:

"Emergency Treatment of Burns," Shriners Burns Institute Brochure. Tampa, Florida: Shriners. Undated.

Fitch, Kristine L. "Cultural Conflicts in the Classroom: Major Issues and Strategies for Coping," in Byrd, Patricia (Ed.), *Teaching Across Cultures in the University ESL Program.* Washington, D.C.: NAFSA, 1986, 51–62.

Frost, Robert. "Fire and Ice." From *The Poetry of Robert Frost* edited by Edward Connery Lathem. Copyright 1923, © 1969 by Holt, Rinehart and Winston. Copyright 1951 by Robert Frost. Reprinted by permission of Henry Holt and Company, Inc.

Gamba, Carlos. "The Price of Life." Unpublished manuscript. Atlanta, Georgia: Georgia State University, 1988.

The following people read the manuscript and offered valuable advice and suggestions:

Maria Cantarero (Miami-Dade Community College)
Kathleen Clark (Texas A&M University)
Nancy Fletcher (Texas A&M University)
Patty Freeland (Temple University)
Dennis Godfrey (West Chester University)
Gail Kellersberger (University of Houston)
Ayse Stromsdorfer (St. Louis University)

In October, 1990, the people listed below participated in a focus group discussion in Boston sponsored by Heinle and Heinle. The discussion of issues in the teaching of grammar helped to clarify the purposes and the methods used in the text:

Darlene Larson (New York University)
Virginia Maurer (Brandeis University)
Eileen Prince (Northeastern University)
Ramon Valenzuela (Harvard University)

We are especially thankful for the strong support given by the staff at Heinle and Heinle during the writing as well as the publication of this book. David Lee provided thoughtful and realistic guidance in our discussions of ways to make the materials useful and accessible to teachers as well as to students. Anne Sokolsky and Pat Jalbert led us kindly and promptly through the maze of activities that change a manuscript into a printed textbook.

Finally, we thank Bill Peters for the paragraphs he contributed, the suggestions we have incorporated, and the many hours he spent reading the manuscript. He has continued to be supportive and ready to help us.

To the Student

Applied English Grammar has been designed to help you in your study of English grammar. As a high intermediate/advanced student of English, you already know a great deal about the language, and this textbook will help you become a better writer, editor, and language student.

Each entry in *Applied English Grammar* has explanations and examples. Most entries also have exercises and activities that can be done for practice. There are many exercises and activities to choose from in this book, and many ask you to read, think, talk, write, and edit. It is not necessary to work through *Applied English Grammar* from beginning to end. Because different students have different needs, your needs will determine what activities you do. Sometimes, you and your classmates will be working on different assignments; sometimes, you will be working as partners or in small groups. These decisions are left to you and your instructor, but you should always be concentrating on improving your written English. To find information, you can use the table of contents or the index.

Applied English Grammar will help you learn more about your own English, will encourage you to take responsibility for your learning (especially in Section Six, The Grammar Journal), and will show you how to be analytical about your writing. The major reason for learning about your own English grammar or for becoming analytical is to improve the quality of your written English. The activities will also help you learn about your own preferred learning styles and strategies.

SECTION

ONE

• •

First Steps

Introductory Information about the Course
Introductory Activities
Finding Out about Your English Grammar
Finding Out about Your Learning Styles and Strategies

• • • • • • • • • •

Introductory Information about the Course

Goals for This Course

The materials in this book have been designed to achieve the following goals:

1. To help you learn more about your own English grammar
2. To improve your accuracy in using English grammar, especially in writing for your U.S. college and university courses
3. To teach you methods to use in editing your written English
4. To give you opportunities to improve your English skills inside and outside the ESL classroom

Learning about Your Own English Grammar

Many of the activities in this book are planned to help you learn about your own English grammar. Using this self-knowledge, you can become a more efficient and effective student.

The Grammar Journal

In Section Six, you will be keeping records that will help you learn about your own English grammar. You will also be keeping notes about your plans for improvement and about the progress that you are making. The Grammar Journal will be a history of your progress through this course. It will help you to identify the types of errors you make and will remind you of new grammar points you are learning. Using the Grammar Journal will help you to improve your English.

Keeping a Grammar Notebook

In addition to making entries in the Grammar Journal, you need to keep five other kinds of materials in a separate notebook. Many students find that an efficient way to keep these materials is to use dividers to set up sections for each of the following:

1. **Assignments and Other Information about This Course.** The outline or syllabus for the course along with general information about requirements such as tests and special assignments is kept in this section. You will also keep a record of the work that is assigned by your instructor in this section.
2. **Class Notes.** Notes that you take in class belong in this section.
3. **Returned Test Papers.** Corrected test and quiz papers that are returned to you by your instructor belong in this section. These are important sources of information about your English.

4. **Returned Writing Assignments.** The revised paragraphs and other written assignments that are returned to you by your instructor are kept here. These will be very important for the work that you do in this course. Analyzing your writing will teach you more about your own English grammar.
5. **List of Words That I Want to Learn.** In this section, keep a record of new words that you want to learn. You should put several sheets of blank paper in this section. On each sheet, you can write the new words that you discover and decide to learn as a way of having a more organized approach to learning English. Many students like to alphabetize these sheets of paper: sheet one has words beginning with A,B,C,D; sheet two has words beginning with E,F,G,H; and so forth.

Goals for Your Written English Grammar

In this course, you will do the following things to improve your written English:

1. Learn how to analyze your own sentences.
2. Review familiar grammar items, and learn about new areas of English grammar.
3. Write paragraphs on many topics to learn about the grammar of written English.
4. Learn to edit your own sentences. You will first edit exercises based on the written English of other ESL students. This editing is an important step toward improving your own writing. However, editing other students' English is not the basic purpose of the course. The basic purpose is helping you improve your English grammar and helping you learn to edit your written English.

Goals for Your Spoken English Grammar

In this course you will do the following things to improve your spoken English grammar:

1. Learn how to recognize important differences between spoken and written English.
2. Practice listening as well as speaking both inside and outside the classroom.
3. Observe Americans using English in various contexts outside the ESL classroom.

Introductory Activities

• •

Student Information Sheet

1. Name _____

2. Name you would like to be called in this class _____

3. Home city and country _____

4. Social Security Number or Student Number _____

5. Which of the following do you have? (Check one.)

    _____ an F-1 visa

    _____ other non-immigrant status

    _____ permanent resident status

    _____ United States citizenship

6. Where were you born? _____

7. Where did you graduate from high school? _____

8. What is your native/first language? _____

9. What other languages do you know? _____

10. What countries have you lived in or visited? _____

    _____

11. Have you studied English in the United States? (Circle one.)   yes   no

    Where? _____ When? _____

12. Have you studied English in other countries? (Circle one.)   yes   no

    Where? _____ When? _____

13. Do you plan to earn a university degree in the U.S.? (Circle one.)   yes   no

14. What do you want to major in at this school? _____

_____

15. What areas of English grammar do you already feel confident about? (For example, do you already know the spelling of the past tense form of most irregular verbs or formation of noun plurals?)

_____

_____

16. What areas of English grammar do you want to learn more about? (For example, are you still confused about using the conditional form of the verb?)

_____

_____

17. Why are you taking this course?

_____

_____

_____

18. What do you want to learn in this course?

_____

_____

. . . .

What Do You Want to Know?

With a classmate, add two questions to each category below. The answers will tell you more about this class, its students, and its instructor. As you write your questions, think about the information you want to learn and the correct form of each question. A sample question has been given for each category.

When you have finished writing your questions, be prepared to ask them orally and to write down the answers you receive in the space provided on page 8. If you have asked appropriate questions, you should learn a great deal about this course, your classmates, and your instructor.

What Do You Want to Know about This Course?

1. *Will we have any tests in this course?* _____

2. _____

3. _____

What Do You Want to Know about the Other Students?

1. *What languages do you know?* _____

2. _____

3. _____

What Do You Want to Know about the Instructor?

1. *What other courses do you teach?* _____

2. _____

3. _____

Answers for the Questions

Information about the Course

1. _____

2. _____

3. _____

Information about the Other Students

1. _____

2. _____

3. _____

Information about the Instructor

1. _____

2. _____

3. _____

Partner Introduction

Think about the kinds of information that you would like to know about another student in the class. You might consider asking about previous education, family, native language, and country of birth as well as asking other questions about other kinds of information that you would like to know about the individual. Then, write eight questions that will provide what you consider important information about another person.

1. _____

2. _____

3. _____

4. _____

5. _____

6. _____

7. _____

8. _____

After you have written your eight questions, find a classmate who has also finished writing the questions, introduce yourselves, and ask each other the questions. After you have finished, you will be asked to introduce your partner to the other members of the class and to tell the class something interesting about your partner.

Finally, write a paragraph about your partner using the information you learned from your questions. When both of you finish writing, exchange paragraphs with your partner, and read what your partner wrote about you. Change any information that is not correct. When you have finished reading about yourself, return the paragraph to your partner for additional comments. After making any necessary changes, turn in the paragraph to your instructor.

Finding Out about Your English Grammar

· ·

Diagnostic Paragraph

NAME _____ DATE _____

    Write a paragraph describing your favorite city. In the first sentence you might want to name the city, indicate its location and size, and tell something special about it. Then, describe the city, and tell why it is your favorite city. After you have finished writing, look for mistakes in your paragraph, and correct them. You have 30 minutes.

_____

_____

_____

_____

_____

_____

_____

_____

_____

_____

_____

_____

_____

_____

_____

_____

_____

Diagnostic Test: Grammar Decisions

This test will examine your knowledge of several grammar elements and will check your recognition of standard written English. The sentences in this test were adapted from sentences written by ESL students.

Directions: Read each of the following 65 items, and examine the underlined portions carefully. Each item should be a correctly written sentence. You will be asked to indicate whether each item is correct or incorrect. Use the answer sheet on page 15 to record your answers.

After you have corrected the Diagnostic Test, fill in the record sheet on page 445 of the Grammar Journal. Then, make a list of the areas of English grammar that are especially difficult for you; put that list on page 447 of the Grammar Journal. Finally, think about what you can do to improve your ability to use those areas; put your ideas on page 447 of the Grammar Journal.

1. The dictionary beside the papers on the teacher's desk.
2. Because the weather was cold after the winter storm.
3. After class yesterday, the students met at the library.
4. The library which is located near the tennis court.
5. The student owned many books but never had an English dictionary.
6. Almost everyone had finished the quiz by the time I arrived.
7. I am in the United States since October.
8. While I was waiting for the bus, I finished reading a short story.
9. Before I arrived, I have learned many things about the United States.
10. I am living at 3371 Main Street since August.
11. New York is a hard city to described.
12. She does not need to worry about her grades.
13. These days people want to knew what is going on in other countries.
14. I need to go shopping for a calculator tonight.
15. The car was new, and it was fun to driving it.
16. A new student does not had to declare a major immediately.
17. Some students do not spent enough time studying.
18. He does not speaks good English.
19. When I was in high school, I did not study before exams.
20. This small classroom does not have many desks.
21. He had to study hard last year.
22. I should have studied last night.
23. I can watched television when I finish my homework.
24. After the students finish the exam, they had better check their answers carefully.
25. I should to write my essay tonight.
26. The college has admitted one hundred new students so far this quarter.

27. He <u>has been living</u> here for three months.
28. My trip was interesting because I saw places that I <u>had not saw</u> before.
29. I <u>have not studied</u> English very long.
30. I <u>have took</u> many trips in the past five years.
31. Uniforms <u>are require</u> in many private schools.
32. English <u>is considering</u> the official language in some places.
33. Teachers in my country <u>are allow</u> to discipline students.
34. The museum <u>is filled</u> with paintings and statues.
35. All freshmen <u>are required</u> to take placement exams.
36. If he had not helped me, I <u>would have failed</u> the exam.
37. If I had a two-week vacation, I <u>will go</u> to southern Florida.
38. If a foreigner does not know my native language, he <u>will have</u> many problems in my country.
39. Some students are not allowed to work even if they <u>want</u> to be independent.
40. I <u>would not have taken</u> algebra in college if I had studied it in high school.
41. Some people <u>object to take</u> physical education classes.
42. Many students <u>enjoy to play</u> tennis.
43. After <u>taking</u> the placement test, I ate lunch.
44. Travelers <u>get used to eating</u> different kinds of food.
45. <u>In spite of driving</u> carefully, the bus driver could not avoid the accident.
46. The results of the experiment <u>were</u> published last year.
47. A teacher <u>have</u> time to help all students in a small class.
48. There <u>are</u> many students in the library today.
49. Most people in my country <u>likes</u> to live in large cities.
50. There <u>is</u> many differences between New York and California.
51. Americans have a culture that <u>surprise</u> many visitors.
52. Going to college <u>is</u> expensive.
53. In the United States, school usually <u>start</u> at 8 o'clock.
54. His knowledge about business <u>helps him invest</u> in the right stocks.
55. Everyone who takes calculus <u>needs</u> to have a calculator.
56. Classes started <u>in</u> September 9.
57. I do not know when they <u>got married</u> to each other.
58. It was about 10 o'clock when we arrived <u>in</u> New Orleans.
59. My native language is <u>very different with</u> the English language.
60. Teachers expect students to <u>be responsible of</u> doing their homework.
61. Tuan <u>moved to United States</u> in 1989.
62. <u>At the end of tour,</u> they visited the library and the bookstore.
63. Curtiss Hall <u>is best dormitory</u> on campus.
64. <u>In the front of classroom</u> is the teacher's desk.
65. The trip from New York was <u>a longest trip</u> that I have ever taken.

Diagnostic Test Answer Sheet

NAME _____ DATE _____

If you find a correct sentence, blacken the C; if you find a mistake, blacken the X.

Example: *This grammar class <u>meet</u> for 50 minutes yesterday.*

      (C) **(X)**   (The example sentence is incorrect.)

1. (C) (X)	23. (C) (X)	45. (C) (X)
2. (C) (X)	24. (C) (X)	46. (C) (X)
3. (C) (X)	25. (C) (X)	47. (C) (X)
4. (C) (X)	26. (C) (X)	48. (C) (X)
5. (C) (X)	27. (C) (X)	49. (C) (X)
6. (C) (X)	28. (C) (X)	50. (C) (X)
7. (C) (X)	29. (C) (X)	51. (C) (X)
8. (C) (X)	30. (C) (X)	52. (C) (X)
9. (C) (X)	31. (C) (X)	53. (C) (X)
10. (C) (X)	32. (C) (X)	54. (C) (X)
11. (C) (X)	33. (C) (X)	55. (C) (X)
12. (C) (X)	34. (C) (X)	56. (C) (X)
13. (C) (X)	35. (C) (X)	57. (C) (X)
14. (C) (X)	36. (C) (X)	58. (C) (X)
15. (C) (X)	37. (C) (X)	59. (C) (X)
16. (C) (X)	38. (C) (X)	60. (C) (X)
17. (C) (X)	39. (C) (X)	61. (C) (X)
18. (C) (X)	40. (C) (X)	62. (C) (X)
19. (C) (X)	41. (C) (X)	63. (C) (X)
20. (C) (X)	42. (C) (X)	64. (C) (X)
21. (C) (X)	43. (C) (X)	65. (C) (X)
22. (C) (X)	44. (C) (X)	

Finding Out about Your Learning Styles and Strategies

. . . .

Learning Styles

We use different methods to learn different kinds of things.

1. When we learn a song, we learn the melody by listening to the song being sung or by listening to a record or tape of the song. This type of learning is called the **auditory** style of learning. We can learn by listening.
2. When we learn the names for shapes in geometry, we often learn by looking at pictures or models of the shapes, for example, learning *triangle* by looking at a picture of a triangle. This type of learning is called the **visual** style of learning. We can learn by looking.
3. When we learn a new physical activity such as throwing a ball or doing a dance, we usually learn by doing the physical activity. This type of learning is called the **kinesthetic** style of learning. We can learn by doing physical actions.
4. When we learn how to get around in a new place, we often learn by looking at maps and then by physically going around the new place. For example, in learning about a new school, we can learn to go to the library by looking first at the map and then by walking to the library. This type of learning combines the two styles of **visual** learning and **kinesthetic** learning.
5. In other situations, we learn about a new place by asking for directions and by walking around. This type of learning combines the two styles of **auditory** and **kinesthetic** learning.

Everyone uses more than one way of learning new things. However, we often have one method of learning that we prefer more than the others. Some people are primarily visual learners; they like to see things written down. Other people are primarily auditory learners; they like to have other people tell them new information or tell them how to do something. Still others are very active learners who like to move around when they learn, walking around the room while they recite their lessons.

This information can be important for you as a second language learner for two reasons: (1) If you know about your own preferred method of learning, you can be sure to include that method in your language study. (2) It is possible that you need to expand your learning methods to include more practice with other styles that are especially helpful for learning a new language.

Techniques Used by Visual Learners

1. Studying from vocabulary cards or vocabulary lists

2. Studying by reviewing notes taken in class (working from a visual record of what the teacher said)
3. Associating pictures with new words and making visual connections to new information
4. Reading

Techniques Used by Auditory Learners

1. Saying new words out loud to hear them
2. Listening to teachers without taking notes and remembering the sounds of what was said
3. Studying with other students and repeating main ideas out loud in conversation
4. Tape-recording lectures and classes
5. Listening to records and radio shows

Techniques Used by Kinesthetic Learners

1. Walking around the room while reading or thinking about the materials
2. Using English while doing sports and games
3. Writing and rewriting specific information

Techniques That Combine Visual and Kinesthetic Learning

1. Writing notes in class to see and to get the feel of the information
2. Copying materials from a book or article to see and feel the words
3. Writing marginal notes, making outlines, creating vocabulary cards and lists
4. Using a highlighter to mark important words in a book

Techniques That Combine Visual and Auditory Learning

1. Watching television to combine seeing with listening
2. Writing words and saying them at the same time
3. Reading written materials out loud
4. Saying words out loud while writing them when studying alone; reviewing out loud

Analyzing Your Own Learning Style Preferences

A. Outside of class, learn the following poem, and be prepared to recite the poem at the next class meeting. In class, you will work with another student to carry out the following steps. (1) Decide who will recite the poem first. (2) Then, take turns reciting the poem to each other. (All of the students in the class will be reciting in pairs at the same time.) Continue reciting the poem until both of you have done it exactly correctly. (3) After reciting the poem, explain to each other the methods that you used to learn the poem. Tell each other exactly what you did to learn the words and how you remembered them during the recitation. Take notes on your exact methods. (4) Discuss with your entire class the different methods that were used in learning the poem. (5) Answer the questions on page 448 of the Grammar Journal to keep a record of your understanding of your own learning styles.

Fire and Ice
by Robert Frost

Some say the world will end in fire,
Some say in ice.
From what I've tasted of desire
I hold with those who favor fire.
But if it had to perish twice,
I think I know enough of hate
To say that for destruction ice
Is also great
And would suffice.

B. Here is a map of a small university. Learn the locations of all of the buildings. Then, do the following steps. (1) On a blank sheet of paper, draw the map from memory. Mark all of the buildings on the map. (2) Compare your drawing with the drawing of another student and with the original map. Make any changes that are needed to make your map exactly correct. (3) After drawing and correcting the map, explain to each other the methods that you used to learn the map. Tell each other exactly what you did to learn the information and how you remembered it during the recitation. Take notes on your exact methods. (4) With your entire class, discuss the different methods that were used in learning the map. (5) Answer the questions on page 449 of the Grammar Journal to keep a record of your understanding of your own learning styles.

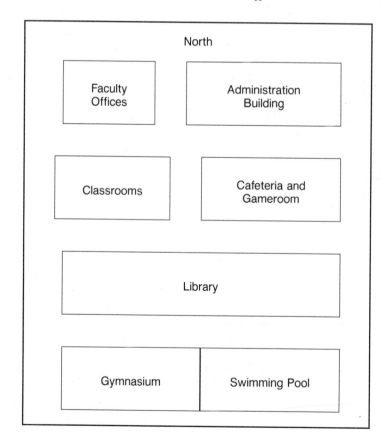

C. You can improve your learning skills by carefully planning to use different learning styles. Talk with another student about activities that you yourselves could use at home to learn the following materials. Try to think of at least three specific actions that you could take. After you have made your lists, compare them to the ideas of the other students in your class. Then, decide if the activities are visual, auditory, or kinesthetic.

The spelling of 10 new irregular verbs   style

1. _____   _____

2. _____   _____

3. _____   _____

The pronunciation of those same verbs   style

1. _____   _____

2. _____   _____

3. _____   _____

The subject-verb agreement rule (putting the -s on present tense singular verbs)   style

1. _____   _____

2. _____   _____

3. _____   _____

Vocabulary to use when buying a car (preparing to talk with a salesperson)   style

1. _____   _____

2. _____   _____

3. _____   _____

Learning Strategies

In addition to having different learning styles, people have different strategies or organized approaches to studying and learning. You can improve your learning by improving your studying in two important ways: (1) making your study more appropriate and (2) making your study more efficient. Researchers have suggested that language learners have two categories for learning new materials: activities that focus on language and activities that focus on other aspects of learning.

Activities Focusing on Language

Language learners study a new language by doing many activities that focus on the new language itself. These activities include the following:

1. Memorizing
2. Making connections between the new language and their other language(s)
3. Using different learning styles to see, hear, and feel the new language
4. Using a good plan of study, including careful and regular review
5. Practicing
6. Thinking about the language, analyzing, and comparing
7. Being an effective student by taking notes, asking questions, summarizing the information, using textbooks effectively
8. Guessing from language and context clues

Activities Focusing on Other Aspects of Learning

Learning a new language has many activities in common with other types of learning, for example:

1. Being a thoughtful and active learner
2. Planning an organized program of study for yourself beyond what any teacher requires
3. Analyzing and evaluating your own learning and progress beyond what any teacher does in a course
4. Being aware of your emotional and physical needs, for example, getting enough rest before an examination, studying in a comfortable and quiet place, or eating a healthy diet
5. Developing social activities that aid learning, including joining clubs at school or meeting native speakers of the language for social and cultural activities

Thinking about Learning Strategies

A. With the other students in your class, discuss the importance of memorizing in language learning. Do you like to memorize new materials? Is that skill valuable for other types of learning? What kinds of things can you memorize in a grammar course? When will memorizing not help in a grammar course?

B. With one or two other students, discuss the steps that each of you takes to memorize new words and information. Compare your list to the lists of other groups of students in your class. Analyze the techniques in terms of visual, auditory, and kinesthetic learning styles. Then, fill in the entry on page 450 of the Grammar Journal.

C. With the other students in your class, list the responsibilities of a teacher to help students learn. Then, list the responsibilities of students for their own learning. What do you think a teacher should do in class to help students? What do you think a teacher should do outside of class to help students? What do you think students should do to help themselves to learn in class? What do you think students should do to help themselves learn outside of class?

D. Working with another student, make a list of two actions that you can take for each of the five "Activities that Focus on Other Aspects of Learning." The actions should be specific things that people can do. After you have compared your list to those of other pairs of students, make a list of the suggestions that you think are especially practical and useful. Keep that list in your Grammar Notebook to use in future discussions of this topic.

SECTION

TWO

English Grammar in Context: Examples, Explanations, Exercises

GRAMMAR CORE

CHAPTER

1

Analyzing Words and Sentences

CHAPTER ORGANIZATION

Parts of Speech
Sentence Parts
    The Basic English Sentence
    Subject, Verb, Object, Complement, and Modifier
    Phrases
    Clauses
Sentence Types by Purposes and Grammatical Structure
Spoken English Compared to Written English
Using Simple Sentences to Make Other Sentences
Simple Sentences
Compound Sentences
Complex Sentences
Compound-Complex Sentences

Parts of Speech

Examine the parts of speech and the sentence parts illustrated in the following sentences:

> *Mazin speaks several languages fluently. He previously studied English in his country. He is also a good athlete. He can play tennis very well.*

Mazin speaks several languages fluently.

Word(s)	Part of Speech	Phrase Type	Sentence Part
Mazin	noun		subject
speaks	verb		verb
several	adjective		
languages	noun		
several languages		noun phrase	direct object
fluently	adverb		adverbial modifier

He previously studied English in his country.

Word(s)	Part of Speech	Phrase Type	Sentence Part
he	pronoun		subject
previously	adverb		adverbial modifier
studied	verb		verb
English	noun		direct object
in	preposition		
his	pronoun		
country	noun		
his country		noun phrase	object of preposition
in his country		prepositional phrase	adverbial modifier

He is also a good athlete.

Word(s)	Part of Speech	Phrase Type	Sentence Part
he	pronoun		subject
is	verb		verb
also	adverb		adverbial modifier
a	article		
good	adjective		
athlete	noun		
a good athlete		noun phrase	complement

He can play tennis very well.

Word(s)	Part of Speech	Phrase Type	Sentence Part
he	pronoun		subject
can	modal auxiliary verb		
play	verb		main verb
can play		verb phrase	complete verb
tennis	noun		direct object
very	adverb or intensifier		
well	adverb		
very well		adverbial phrase	adverbial modifier

Many grammarians classify English words into the nine parts of speech shown in the chart on page 27. You have learned some of these before. Work with the rest of your class to add example words to fill in the blanks in the following chart.

Parts of Speech

....

1. Noun: *book,* _____ , _____ , _____

2. Verb: *run,* _____ , _____ , _____

3. Article: *a,* _____ , _____

4. Adjective: *tall,* _____ , _____ , _____

5. Adverb: *quickly,* _____ , _____ , _____

6. Pronoun: *I,* _____ , _____ , _____

7. Conjunction: *and,* _____ , _____ , _____

8. Preposition: *in,* _____ , _____ , _____

9. Interjection: *Stop!, Watch Out!, Oh!, Oh! No!*

Articles can also be called **determiners** because they are part of a larger group of words such as *this, that, many,* and *much.* More information about determiners can be found in Chapter Nine.

. . . .

Practice with Parts of Speech

A. List the nine parts of speech across the top of a sheet of paper. Underneath the name for each part of speech, write the words from the following list that can be grouped together. Use your dictionary after you have made your decisions, and check your answers.

from	*it*	*so*	*easy*	*oh*	*because*
ouch	*write*	*at*	*easily*	*they*	*borrow*
an	*although*	*a*	*library*	*read*	*but*
she	*expensive*	*in*	*college*	*carefully*	*them*
young	*on*	*and*	*ask*	*quickly*	*intelligent*
student	*the*	*very*	*language*	*excellent*	

B. Add more words to each of the categories on the same sheet of paper you used for exercise A. Then, compare your new list to those of other students in the class. Add to your list any words that you like or that seem important. Keep this list in your Grammar Notebook.

Sentence Parts

Examine the example sentences in this chart.

The Basic English Sentence

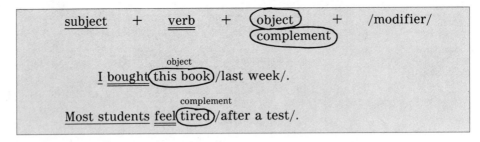

English sentences must have a subject and a verb.	incorrect *Is important for engineers to understand calculus. correct It is important for engineers to understand calculus.
Some verbs must have an object.	incorrect *I buy every morning at the bookstore. correct I buy a newspaper every morning at the bookstore.
Some verbs must have a complement.	incorrect *She feels most of the time. correct She feels happy most of the time.
Other verbs cannot have an object or a complement.	We live in the dormitory.
Many sentences have adverbial modifiers of place, time, manner, or reason.	I will study calculus next year because it is required for engineering students.

An asterisk (*) in front of a sentence means that the sentence is incorrect.

28

Practice with Sentence Parts

Analyze the following example sentences to practice using the marking system and to learn more about English sentence structure.

Many languages <u>*exist*</u> /today/.   *Sarah* <u>*speaks*</u> (three languages.)

Sarah <u>*is*</u> (French.)   *She* <u>*has studied*</u> (English)/for three years/.

1. What parts are underlined with one line? ____Subject____

2. What parts are underlined with two lines? ____verb____

3. What parts are circled? ____Object____

4. What parts are bracketed by slashes? ____Complement____

Subject, Verb, Object, Complement, and Modifier

(Subjects) are <u>nouns and other forms that can function as nouns</u>, such as <u>pronouns, clauses, infinitives, and gerunds</u>. A subject usually comes first in a sentence and is the focus of the meaning. When a simple present tense verb is used, the subject controls the form of the verb.

The subject can be a single word or a combination of two or more words.	*Students take English courses in college.*
	They write essays in their English courses.
	Editing carefully improves their essays.
	How much students improve depends on their desire to write better.
	To be a student is to study.
In this example, the **main subject noun** is *dictionary*. The **complete subject** is the noun phrase *the new dictionary.*	*The new dictionary defines 25,000 words.*
What is the **main subject noun** in this example? What is the **complete subject?**	*On Tuesday, my first class is college algebra.*

Verbs can be a single word or a combination of two or more words.

The verb can be active or passive.

active
Engineers take English courses.

passive
English courses are usually taken during the first year in college.

A verb is often made up of more than one word. The **main verb** is the word *graduate*. The word *will* is called the **auxiliary** or the **auxiliary verb.** The **complete verb** is the verb phrase *will graduate.*

He will graduate next spring.

What is the **complete verb** in each of these examples? What is the **auxiliary?** What is the **main verb**?

She is studying for a test.

We have taken the required English courses.

Direct objects are nouns and other forms that can function as nouns, such as pronouns, clauses, infinitives, and gerunds. A direct object usually comes immediately after the verb.

The object can be a single word or a combination of two or more words.

I lost my grammar book yesterday.

A friend returned it today.

I plan to study for the geometry test.

He enjoys studying in the library.

She said that she plans to major in physics.

Some verbs can have two different objects. The term **indirect object** is used for the receiver of the direct object. In the first example, the direct object is *the dictionary.* The indirect object is *my sister.* Note that a prepositional phrase can be the indirect object.

indirect object   direct object
I gave my sister the dictionary.

direct object / indirect object
I gave the dictionary to my sister.

What is the direct object in this example? What is the indirect object?	*I bought my parents a house.*

What is the direct object in this example? What is the indirect object?	*I found a used dictionary for my brother.*

Complements are many of the same forms that are objects, such as nouns and pronouns. A complement refers back to the subject of the sentence, giving more information about the subject. Linking verbs (words such as *taste* and *feel*) connect subjects and complements. Appendix A gives a list of common linking verbs.

Complements can also be adjectives, infinitives, and prepositional phrases (used as adverbials). Notice that the complement describes the subject; it is linked to the subject.	*My first class is* calculus. *My math book seems* difficult. *My goal is* to improve my writing. *John is* in the computer lab.

Direct objects and complements are alike in that they complete the meaning of certain verbs. They are different in that complements can sometimes be adjectives or prepositional phrases used as adverbials. They are different in that the complement always describes or is linked to the subject.	direct object *I bought **a computer**.* complement *My computer was **a new model**.* complement *My computer was **expensive**.* complement *My computer is **in my bedroom**.*

Modifiers can be single-word adverbs, prepositional phrases, or adverbial clauses. Infinitives are also often used as adverbial modifiers. They provide information about time, place, manner, and reasons. That is, they answer questions such as *when? where? how? why?*

The TOEFL is given /frequently/.

Universities use TOEFL scores /for admission/.

Most ESL students take the TOEFL /before they begin their college or university work/.

The TOEFL is often used /to test English proficiency/.

Modifiers can often be moved to the beginning of a sentence. Time expressions come at the beginning of sentences more than other types of adverbial modifiers.

He studied /in the library/ /**yesterday**/.

/**Yesterday**/, he studied /in the library/.

He ate lunch /in the cafeteria/ /**before he went to the library**/.

/**Before he went to the library**/, he ate lunch /in the cafeteria/.

He sat /with his friends/ /**in the cafeteria**/.

/**In the cafeteria**/, he sat /with his friends/.

Practice with Analyzing Sentences

Mark the complete subjects, complete verbs, objects, complements, and modifiers in the following sentences. Use this marking system whenever you analyze sentences:

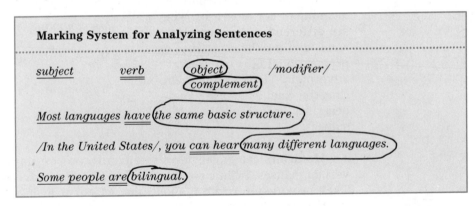

Marking System for Analyzing Sentences

subject   verb   object   /modifier/
                     complement

Most languages have the same basic structure.

/In the United States/, you can hear many different languages.

Some people are bilingual.

1. Throughout history, many people have wanted a universal language.

2. A universal language could aid science, business, and diplomacy.

3. No one proposes the same language.

4. Some people want a new language.

5. Other people want a current language.

6. A universal language could simplify communication among nations and people.

Adapted from *World Book Encyclopedia*, 1988 ed., s.v. "language."

Phrases

A **phrase** is a group of words that work together for one grammatical purpose. There are **noun phrases, verb phrases,** and **prepositional phrases.** A phrase does not have a subject and verb.

noun phrase
*I bought **a used car.***

verb phrase
*He **will buy** a used car.*

prepositional phrase
*She bought a car **from her brother.***

Clauses

A **clause** is a group of words with a subject and verb; a clause is used as part of a sentence. The first example shows an **adverbial clause.** The second example is a **relative (adjective) clause.**

Adverbial and relative clauses are also called **dependent clauses** or **subordinate clauses** because they cannot be used alone; they must be part of a sentence. They cannot be used as independent sentences.

adverbial clause
*I bought a new dictionary **before classes began.***

relative (adjective) clause
*I bought a dictionary **that defines 125,000 words.***

adverbial/subordinate clause
***Although he prefers acting,** he will major in physics.*

relative/subordinate clause
*She met a student **who is a member of the drama club.***

Sentence Types by Purposes and Grammatical Structure

In English, grammarians identify three basic sentence types according to purpose and to grammatical structure. These three basic purposes are to make **statements,** to ask **questions,** and to give **commands.** Questions and commands are formed by making changes in the basic sentence.

Statement

A **statement** is the basic sentence type.

The earth rotates around the sun.

Question

A **question** asks for a response. The basic question types are **Yes-No Questions** and **Information Questions.**

yes-no question
Do you speak French?

information question
Where do you live?

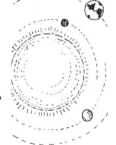

Command

A **command** tells someone to do something.

Open your books to page 71.

. . . .

Practice with Types of Sentences

A. Working with the other students in your class, talk about the correct way to complete the following sentences. Based on your experience and education, where do you expect to use the different sentence types? Circle the letter(s) of the correct answers.

1. Statements are common in _____
   a. spoken English
   b. written English
   c. both spoken and written English

2. Questions are common in _____
   a. spoken English
   b. written English
   c. both spoken and written English

3. Commands are common in _____
   a. spoken English
   b. written English
   c. both spoken and written English

B. Select an article of major importance on the front page of today's newspaper.

1. How many statements can you find? _____

2. How many questions do you see? _____

3. How many commands are given? _____

C. Look at the directions for the Diagnostic Test on page 13.

1. How many statements can you find? _____

2. How many questions do you see? _____

3. How many commands are given? _____

D. Compare the newspaper article that you used in exercise B to the directions that you used in exercise C.

1. How are they different in purpose?
2. How are they different in the kinds of sentences that are used?

Spoken English Compared to Written English

• •

When we write, we are usually more formal than when we speak. Also, in speaking we frequently use short answers and fragments. Fragments are seldom appropriate for written academic English.

Written English uses more formal vocabulary, for example, *discuss* rather than *talk about.*

*In this article, the author **discusses** her predictions for the 21st century.*

*The teacher said, "We need to **talk about** changing the date for the test."*

We are usually required to write complete sentences. Complete sentences are those with subjects and verbs. They can also have objects and modifiers.

Bey studies in the library.

A **fragment** is a part of a sentence; it is an incomplete sentence. In conversations, we often speak in **short answers** or in **fragments.** Such short answers are often given to questions in conversation.

"Why does Bey know so much about the computerized card catalog?"
correct in spoken English
"Because he works in the library."

However, in written academic English such incomplete sentences are very seldom used.

correct in written English
He knows how to use the computerized card catalog because he works in the library.
incorrect in written academic English
*Because he works in the library. He knows how to use the computerized catalog.

. . . .

Practice Comparing Spoken English to Written English

A. Look at this transcript of a conversation that the authors of this book had one morning:

PAT: *"What you doing?"*
BEV: *"Not much. I'm a little tired. Too much work and not enough sleep."*
PAT: *"You ready to finish writing this chapter?"*
BEV: *"Yeah. I can't talk long. Got to get to class early."*
PAT: *"OK. You want to have lunch to talk later?"*

Pat asks three questions in conversational style. Working with another student, compare the grammar of those spoken questions to the grammar of the **complete questions.** Write the complete question in the space provided here.

1. *"What you doing?"* _____

2. *"You ready to finish writing this chapter?"* _____

_____

3. *"You want to have lunch to talk later?"* _____

_____

Bev answers with a mixture of **complete statements** and **fragments.** Which of her answers are complete sentences and which are fragments? Write the fragments in the space given here. Then, write a complete version of each fragment.

Fragment	Complete Sentence
1. *Not much.* _____	*I am not doing much.* _____
2. _____	_____
3. _____	_____
4. _____	_____

B. Are there major differences between the written and the spoken forms of your first or native language? Are these differences similar to the differences between spoken and written English? Discuss the differences in the forms of your native language with other people who speak it. Then, explain some of those differences to the other students in your English grammar course.

Using Simple Sentences to Make Other Sentences

The basic or **simple sentence** can be used to create three other types of sentences: **compound sentences**, **complex sentences**, and **compound-complex sentences**.

Simple Sentences

As you can see in the examples on page 28, a **simple sentence** must have at least a subject and a verb.

The subject and verb can be made up of more than one word. For example, two nouns can be combined with *and* to make the subject, or a noun phrase can be used.

The teacher and the students went to the library.

The expensive new computer is important for my work as a scientist.

In the first example, the **main subject** nouns are *teacher* and *students*. The **complete subject** is *the teacher and the students*. In the second example, the **main subject** is *computer* while the **complete subject** is *the expensive new computer*.

Two or more verbs can be combined to make one verb phrase. The **main verb** is *study*. The **complete verb** is *will study*. The complete verb combines the auxiliary *will* with the verb *study*.

I will study physics next quarter.

In this example, the complete verb is made by combining four main verbs to make the complete verb. No auxiliary is used.

We read, think, write, and study in the library.

Practice with Simple Sentences

A. Analyze the simple sentences below using the marking system in the box:

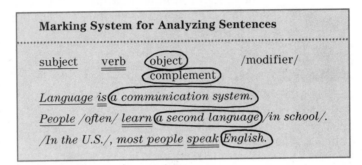

Marking System for Analyzing Sentences

subject   verb   (object)   /modifier/
                   (complement)

Language is (a communication system.)
People /often/ learn (a second language) /in school/.
/In the U.S./, most people speak (English.)

1. Children and adults communicate through language.
2. Most people speak and write at least one language.
3. In the U.S., students often study a second language in school.
4. This second language is usually French, Spanish, or German.
5. Some students study ESL in universities in the U.S.

ESL class in San Juan Capistrano, California

B. Write five simple sentences on a topic of interest to you. It is not necessary to write a complete paragraph, but do write all of the sentences on the same topic. After you have edited the sentences carefully for meaning and grammar, then write the corrected sentences on a separate sheet of paper to keep in your Grammar Notebook.

Compound Sentences

As you can see from the examples, a **compound sentence** is made up of two (or more) simple sentences joined by a comma and a **coordinating word** or by a semicolon. A **transition word** can be used with the semicolon to make clearer the meaning relationship between the two sentences. Examine the examples in the following chart to see how different kinds of punctuation can be used in compound sentences. When you are writing or editing your writing, you might use Appendix B, "Similar Joining Words."

Comma with Coordinating Word

, and	, for	, nor	, yet
, but	, or	, so	

He has a small calculator, **but** he really needs a much better one for his engineering classes.

His first class begins at 8 A.M., **so** he leaves home at 7:30 A.M. to get there on time.

Semicolon

He has a small calculator; he really needs a much better one for his engineering classes.

His first class begins at 8 A.M.; he leaves home at 7:30 A.M. to get there on time.

Semicolon with a Transition Word and a Comma

; also,	; however,	; instead,	; then,
; first,	; in addition,	; on the other hand,	; therefore,
; furthermore,	; indeed,	; second,	

He has a small calculator; **however,** he really needs a much better one for his engineering classes.

His first class begins at 8 A.M.; **therefore,** he leaves home at 7:30 A.M. to get there on time.

Practice with Compound Sentences

A. Many students memorize new information by using **mnemonic devices. Mnemonic** is a word of Greek origin that means "memory." For example, many students have learned which joining words follow a comma by remembering the phrase **FAN BOYS.** This phrase does not really mean anything in American English; you might remember it with a humorous image in your mind of little boys waving big fans shaped like commas. Or, you might think of another mnemonic device that will help you remember the joining words.

The initials F-A-N B-O-Y-S can help you remember the seven coordinating words to use with a comma in a compound sentence. Fill in the remaining six blanks with the coordinating words that begin with each letter.

F = _for_   B = _but_
A = _and_   O = _or_
N = _nor_   Y = _yet_
                     S = _so_

B. To analyze a compound sentence, draw one line under the complete subject of each simple sentence and two lines under the complete verb of each simple sentence. In addition, put + above the **coordinating words** that connect the two simple sentences. For each compound sentence, you should be able to answer the following questions:

(S1)	(1) What is the complete subject of the first simple sentence?
(V1)	(2) What is the complete verb of the first simple sentence?
(End1)	(3) With what word does the first simple sentence end?
(Begin2)	(4) With what word does the second simple sentence begin?
(S2)	(5) What is the complete subject of the second simple sentence?
(V2)	(6) What is the complete verb of the second simple sentence?
(Connect)	(7) What connects the two sentences?

+

Example: *No language is easy to learn, and no language is impossible to learn.*

(S1)	(1) The complete subject of the first simple sentence is *no language.*
(V1)	(2) The complete verb of the first simple sentence is *is.*
(End1)	(3) The first simple sentence ends with the word *learn.*
(Begin2)	(4) The second simple sentence begins with the word *no.*
(S2)	(5) The complete subject of the second simple sentence is *no language.*
(V2)	(6) The complete verb of the second simple sentence is *is.*
(Connect)	(7) The two sentences are connected with *, and.*

Analyze each of the following compound sentences.

1. *The age of the learner often influences second language ability, and a new language is usually easier before the age of 10.*

(S1)	(1) _____	(Begin2)	(4) _____
(V1)	(2) _____	(S2)	(5) _____
(End1)	(3) _____	(V2)	(6) _____
		(Connect)	(7) _____

2. *Young children imitate the language sounds around them, and they learn to speak by listening and by repeating.*

(S1)	(1) _____	(Begin2)	(4) _____
(V1)	(2) _____	(S2)	(5) _____
(End1)	(3) _____	(V2)	(6) _____
		(Connect)	(7) _____

3. *By age 10, a child has learned first language patterns, and a second*
   language requires different patterns.

   (S1)   (1) _____   (Begin2)   (4) _____

   (V1)   (2) _____   (S2)   (5) _____

   (End1)   (3) _____   (V2)   (6) _____

                                    (Connect) (7) _____

4. *Children learn these different patterns easily, so some schools start*
   second language instruction in the primary grades.

   (S1)   (1) _____   (Begin2)   (4) _____

   (V1)   (2) _____   (S2)   (5) _____

   (End1)   (3) _____   (V2)   (6) _____

                                    (Connect) (7) _____

5. *Many adult learners study a second language in college, but they*
   often learn to read and write it first.

   (S1)   (1) _____   (Begin2)   (4) _____

   (V1)   (2) _____   (S2)   (5) _____

   (End1)   (3) _____   (V2)   (6) _____

                                    (Connect) (7) _____

Adapted from *World Book Encyclopedia*, 1988 ed., s.v. "language."

   C. Analyze each of the following compound sentences, and put ++
above the **transition words** that are used to clarify the relationship between the two simple sentences.

(S1)	(1) What is the complete subject of the first simple sentence?
(V1)	(2) What is the complete verb of the first simple sentence?
(End1)	(3) With what word does the first simple sentence end?
(Begin2)	(4) With what word does the second simple sentence begin?
(S2)	(5) What is the complete subject of the second simple sentence?
(V2)	(6) What is the complete verb of the second simple sentence?
(Connect)	(7) What connects the two sentences?

++

Example: *All human beings speak a language; however, they do not speak the same language.*

(S1)	(1) The complete subject of the first simple sentence is *all human beings*.
(V1)	(2) The complete verb of the first simple sentence is *speak*.
(End1)	(3) The first simple sentence ends with the word *language*.
(Begin2)	(4) The second simple sentence begins with the word *they*.
(S2)	(5) The complete subject of the second simple sentence is *they*.
(V2)	(6) The complete verb of the second simple sentence is *do not speak*.
(Connect)	(7) The two sentences are connected with a semicolon, and the transition word *however* is followed by a comma.

---

1. *Linguistics is the study of language; furthermore, linguistics is a new science.*

   (S1)   (1) _____   (Begin2)   (4) _____

   (V1)   (2) _____   (S2)   (5) _____

   (End1)   (3) _____   (V2)   (6) _____

   (Connect)   (7) _____

2. *The ancient Greeks and Romans studied the nature of language;*
however, their studies lacked a scientific system.

(S1)	(1) _____	(Begin2)	(4) _____
(V1)	(2) _____	(S2)	(5) _____
(End1)	(3) _____	(V2)	(6) _____
		(Connect)	(7) _____

Franz Bopp 1791–1867

3. *From the* A.D. *400s to the 1500s, few people questioned the origin of*
language; in fact, the scientific study of language did not start until
the late 1700s.

(S1)	(1) _____	(Begin2)	(4) _____
(V1)	(2) _____	(S2)	(5) _____
(End1)	(3) _____	(V2)	(6) _____
		(Connect)	(7) _____

Jakob Grimm 1785–1863

4. *At that time, Franz Bopp, Jakob Grimm, and Friedrich von Schlegel*
examined several languages; in addition, they identified their
similarities and differences.

(S1)	(1) _____	(Begin2)	(4) _____
(V1)	(2) _____	(S2)	(5) _____
(End1)	(3) _____	(V2)	(6) _____
		(Connect)	(7) _____

Friedrich von Schlegel 1772–1829

5. *During the early 1900s, Ferdinand de Saussure established common elements of all languages; indeed, Bopp, Grimm, von Schlegel, and de Saussure became the first modern linguists.*

Ferdinand de Saussure 1857–1913

(S1)   (1) _____   (Begin2)   (4) _____

(V1)   (2) _____   (S2)   (5) _____

(End1)   (3) _____   (V2)   (6) _____

(Connect)   (7) _____

Adapted from *World Book Encyclopedia*, 1988 ed., s.v. "language."

D. Write five compound sentences on a topic of interest to you. It is not necessary to write a complete paragraph, but do write all of the sentences on the same topic. After you have edited the sentences carefully for meaning and grammar, write the corrected sentences on a separate sheet of paper to keep in your Grammar Notebook for future reference.

Complex Sentences

The following lists contain common subordinating words which introduce adverbial clauses, relative clauses, and noun clauses. They are used to form complex sentences.

Adverbial Clauses				Relative Clauses		Noun Clauses
after	before	since	when	that	who	that
although	even though	unless	where	when	whom	
as	if	until	while	where	whose	
because				which		
adverbial clause *I will study physics **after** I take calculus.* relative clause *I have a dictionary **that** cost $25.* noun clause *I believe **that** my dictionary is easy to use.*						

A **complex sentence** adds a subordinate clause to a simple sentence. The subordinate clause is called a **dependent clause** while the simple sentence is called the **independent clause.** A subordinate or dependent clause cannot be used alone. It cannot be used as a separate sentence. An independent clause is the same thing as a sentence. When you are writing or editing your written English, you might use Appendix B, "Similar Joining Words," to remind yourself of your choices for making complex sentences.

A complex sentence is made up of a simple sentence plus one (or more) subordinate clause(s). **Subordination** means that a sentence becomes a part of another sentence.

Although I speak two other languages, I am studying English because I want to study engineering in the U.S.

Three sentences have been combined to make the example sentence. Sentences 2 and 3 become adverbial modifiers in the combined sentence. They are subordinate clauses in the combined sentence.

sentence #1
I am studying English.

sentence #2
I want to study engineering in the U.S.

sentence #3
I speak two other languages.

In each of the following examples, the dependent or subordinate clause is marked with [ ], and # is put over the subordinating word. Look carefully at the examples given in the following chart. Underline with one line the complete subject of the independent clause and with two lines the complete verb of the independent clause.

\#
<u>Michael</u> <u><u>is studying</u></u> calculus [although he prefers history].

   \#
[Although he prefers history], Michael is studying calculus.

               \#
Michael took notes [when his instructor explained the requirements to pass the course].

   \#
[When his instructor explained the requirements to pass the course], Michael took notes.

   \#
[Because he arrived early], Michael reviewed the chapter to be covered on the test.

         \#
The lecturer [who discussed health] answered many questions.

         \#
The students [who attended the lecture] asked many questions.

. . . .

Practice with Complex Sentences

A. As in the examples, mark each of the subordinate or dependent clauses with [ ], and put a # above the **subordinating words.** In the independent clause, underline the complete subject once and the complete verb twice.

#

[Because communication is important], <u>many people</u> <u><u>study</u></u> *foreign languages.*

Reasons for Studying Foreign Languages

1. Although people learn a second language for many reasons, one important reason is communication.

2. If someone speaks English or Spanish, the person can communicate with millions of people.

3. People can learn about the customs of other people when they learn another language.

4. People who learn another language increase their ability to communicate with others.

5. Many scholars learn several languages because they want to read research in the original language.

Adapted from *World Book Encyclopedia*, 1988 ed., s.v. "language."

B. Write five complex sentences on a topic of interest to you. It is not necessary to write a complete paragraph, but do write all of the sentences on the same topic. After you have edited the sentences carefully for meaning and grammar, write the corrected sentences on a sheet of paper to keep in your Grammar Notebook for future reference.

Compound-Complex Sentences

. . . .

A **compound-complex sentence** is made up of two (or more) simple sentences and one (or more) dependent or subordinate clause(s). See Chapter Ten for additional information on adverbial and relative clauses.

The example begins with a
dependent clause. Then, two
simple sentences are combined.

dependent clause
Because we could not agree on the
same book,
simple sentence (independent clause)
I bought an English-English
dictionary,

and

simple sentence (independent clause)
my brother bought a Spanish-
English dictionary.

A complex sentence becomes a
compound-complex sentence
when a simple sentence is added
to it.

complex sentence
Because it is quiet and
comfortable, I like to study in the
library.
compound-complex sentence
Because it is quiet and
comfortable, I like to study in the
*library, **but I study at home more***
often.

A compound sentence becomes a
compound-complex sentence
when a subordinate clause or a
relative clause is added to it.

compound sentence
Michael plans to be a chemist,
and Grace wants to be a medical
doctor.
compound complex sentence
Although they are both majoring
***in chemistry,** Michael plans to be*
a chemist, and Grace wants to be
a medical doctor.

. . . .

Practice with Compound-Complex Sentences

As in the example, identify the independent clauses and the dependent clauses by putting [ ] around each dependent clause in each
sentence below. For each independent clause, draw one line underneath
the complete subject and two lines underneath the complete verb. Put +
above the **coordinating word,** and put # above the **subordinating word.**

The Indian tribes of North America and South America spoke 2,000
                                        #   +
different languages [when the Europeans arrived], and they

could not communicate with each other.

The Languages of American Indians

1. Although some Indian languages were similar, many were different, and some groups developed writing systems.

2. The Mayan Indians used dots and dashes for numbers, and they created a calendar that was more accurate than the systems of the ancient Egyptians, Greeks, or Romans.

3. The Mayan system of writing had become extinct before the Spaniards arrived, but it was an early system for recording events.

4. The picture writing of the Aztec Indians was in use when the Spaniards arrived in Mexico, and the Spaniards learned to read Aztec writing.

5. Because the Indian tribes spoke many different languages, they needed a way to communicate with each other, so sign language, pictures, smoke signals, and drum beats became popular.

Adapted from *World Book Encyclopedia*, 1988 ed., s.v. "American Indian."

Hopi Indian writing, Arizona

. . . .

Practice with Analyzing Words and Sentences

A. Discussion Assignment: How many different languages are spoken by students in your grammar class? Outside of your ESL classes, do you hear many languages other than English? What are they, and where do you hear them?

Grammar Assignment: Analyze the sentences below. Add [ ] around the words of the subordinate clauses. For each independent clause, mark the complete subject and complete verb. In addition, put a + above the coordinating words that join two simple sentences. Put a # above the subordinating words that connect the dependent clause to the rest of the sentence.

Language

[1]Language is universal in human societies. [2]It allows conversations and written communication over time and distance. [3]People transmit their culture from generation to generation through language. [4]Scholars have identified 3,000 different languages, and many languages have several dialects. [5]Some languages have few speakers, but many

languages have a million speakers. [6]Some languages have millions of speakers; Arabic, Chinese, Hindi, Japanese, Korean, Spanish, and English are popular languages today.

[7]When young children from any language group want attention, they imitate the sounds of the people around them. [8]They build their skill at communication as they learn the sounds. [9]When children go to school at age five or six, they have already learned the patterns of their native language. [10]After they have learned to read and write, children study many subjects, so they can understand the past, present, and future of their world.

Adapted from *World Book Encyclopedia*, 1988 ed., s.v. "language."

B. Decide if each sentence in exercise A is a simple sentence, a compound sentence, a complex sentence, or a compound-complex sentence. How many different types of sentences are used in the composition? Use exercise A to answer the following questions.

1. You will find nouns in many positions in English sentences. They can be **subjects, objects,** and **objects of prepositions.**
   In sentence 3:

   the **complete subject** is ————————————————— ;

   the **direct object** is ————————————————— ;

   the **object of the preposition** *from* is ——————————— ;

   the **object of the preposition** *to* is ——————— , and

   the **object of the preposition** *through* is ——————— .

2. You will find **complete verbs** made of more than one word.

   In sentence 1 the **complete verb** is ————— .

   In sentence 4, the first **complete verb** is ————— , and the second

   complete verb is ————— .

3. There is one **prepositional phrase** in sentence 1.

   There are _____ **prepositional phrases** in sentence 7.

   There are _____ **prepositional phrases** in sentence 9.

4. The **coordinating word** in sentence 4 is _____ .

   The **coordinating word** in sentence 5 is _____ .

5. The **subordinating word** in sentence 7 is _____ .

   The **subordinating word** in sentence 8 is _____ .

   The **subordinating word** in sentence 9 is _____ .

   The **subordinating word** in sentence 10 is _____ .

6. In sentence 6, the first **complete verb** is _____ , and the second

   complete verb is _____ .

7. Sentences _____ , _____ , and _____ are **simple sentences.**

   Sentences _____ , _____ , and _____ are **compound sentences.**

   Sentences _____ , _____ , and _____ are **complex sentences.**

   Sentence _____ is a **compound-complex sentence.**

   C. Discussion Assignment: English has borrowed many words from other languages. For example, *cat* comes from Arabic; *chow* comes from Chinese; and *mosquito* comes from Spanish. Other languages also borrow words from English. Do you know of any words in other languages that are borrowed from English? Why do you think that people borrow words from other languages?

   Grammar Assignment: Analyze the sentences below. Find each independent and dependent clause. Add [ ] around the words of the dependent clauses. Put one line under the complete subject of each independent clause and two lines under the complete verb of each independent clause. Put a + above the coordinating words that join two simple sentences. Put a # above the subordinating words that connect the subordinate clause to the rest of the sentence.

   Exercise D provides additional analysis of the passage.

Language Change

[1]Languages do not remain the same over long periods of time. [2]Changes in grammar, vocabulary, and pronunciation take place in every language. [3]For example, when speakers of different languages meet, new words often enter both languages. [4]When a language adds new vocabulary words, the language changes. [5]When a language adds new meanings to familiar words, the language changes. [6]Most languages change slowly, and people usually do not notice any changes from one year to the next. [7]For example, present-day speakers of English cannot read or understand Old English; people in England spoke Old English 1,000 years ago. [8]Old English is a foreign language to today's English speakers, so students study Old English in the same ways that they study French or German. [9]In modern society, languages will probably continue to change slowly. [10]If a language loses all of its speakers, it will not change anymore. [11]A language without speakers, like Latin, is a dead language.

Adapted from *World Book Encyclopedia*, 1988 ed., s.v. "language."

Old English

Beowulf maþelode,
    bearn Ecgþeowes:
"Ne sorga, snotor guma;
    selre bið æghwæm
þæt he his freond wrece,
    þonne he fela murne.
Ure æ ghwylc sceal
    ende gebidan
worolde lifes; wyrce se
    þe mote
domes ær deaþe; þæt bið
    drihtguman
unlifgendum æfter
    selest.
Aris, rices weard, uton
    raþe feran
Grendles magan gang
    sceawigan.
Ic hit þe gehate, no he
    on helm losaþ,
ne on foldan fæþm, ne
    on fyrgenholt,
ne on gyfenes grund, ga
    pær he wille.
Ðys dogor þu geþyld
    hafa
weana gehwylces, swa
    ic þe wene to."

D. Using the passage in exercise C, answer the following questions:

1. You will find nouns in many positions in English sentences. They can be **subjects, objects,** and **objects of prepositions.**
   In sentence 1:

   the **complete subject** is _____ ;

   the **complement** is _____ ;

   the **object of the preposition** *over* is _____ , and

   the **object of the preposition** *of* is _____ .

2. You will find **complete verbs** made of more than one word.

   In sentence 6, the **complete verb** is _____ , and the second

   complete verb is _____ .

   In sentence 9, the **complete verb** is _____ .

3. There are ___*2*___ **prepositional phrases** in sentence 1.

   There are _____ **prepositional phrases** in sentence 2.

   There are _____ **prepositional phrases** in sentence 8.

4. The **coordinating word** in sentence 6 is _____ .

   The **coordinating word** in sentence 8 is _____ .

5. The **subordinating word** in sentence 3 is _____ .

   The **subordinating word** in sentence 10 is _____ .

6. Sentences _____ , _____ , _____ , and _____ are **simple sentences.**

   Sentences _____ and _____ are **compound sentences.**

   Sentences _____ , _____ , _____ , and _____ are **complex sentences.**

   Sentence _____ is a **compound-complex sentence.**

E. Working with another student, find examples of each type of sentence in one of the following sources: a popular magazine, the student newspaper, or a textbook for a course in your major field of study. Write these examples on a sheet of paper to keep in your Grammar Notebook. Be sure to record the exact source for each quotation: the name of the writer, the publication, the date/place of publication, and the page numbers.

Examples of Sentence Types from a Published Source

Simple sentence: "*Any form of humor or sarcasm has some truth in it.*"   (page 1)

Compound sentence: "*Sometimes the consultant's client is a single individual, but at other times the client may be a group, a department, or a whole organization.*"   (page 2)

Complex sentence: "*When you are asked directions and you tell someone to get off the bus two stops before you do, you are acting as a consultant.*"   (page 1)

Adapted from Block, Peter. *Flawless Consulting: A Guide to Getting Your Expertise Used.* San Diego, California: University Associates, Inc., 1981.

F. As a review, turn to the Diagnostic Test on page 13, and look closely at items 1–5. Compare your answers today with your answers from the first week of this course.

C H A P T E R

2

Past Time Frame

Time Frames

· ·

Grammarians have developed a system to explain the use of English verbs. This system shows that English speakers choose verbs based on the central time of the event that they are explaining. For example, if you are telling a story about something that happened to you when you were a child, the central focus of the story is in past time. Most of the verbs will be in the simple past tense. You might add some information in the past perfect verb form. You might use one or two verbs in the past progressive for two things that happened at the same time. You might use a simple present tense to explain a general truth meaning that you think the story illustrates.

The time frames that will be explained and practiced in this book include the following:

1. the past time frame in Chapter Two
2. the general truth time frame for expressing habits or explaining generalizations in Chapter Three
3. the present time frame in Chapter Four
4. the future time frame in Chapter Six

When you write, you must first decide about the time context in relation to your topic. After you decide on the central time focus, you have made your verb choices simpler. In each time frame, you will generally use only a limited number of different kinds of verbs.

Time Focus	Primary Verb for Central Meaning	Other Verbs for Related Times
Past Time	Simple Past Tense	Past Perfect Past Progressive Present Perfect
General Truth	Simple Present Tense	Present Perfect
Present Time	Present Progressive Simple Present Tense	Present Perfect
Future Time	Modals (especially *will*) Simple Present Tense Present Progressive	

The Forms of English Verbs

The English verb system uses two different methods to make different verb meanings.

Word Change The form of the verb itself can be changed.	He ***writes*** *with a pencil in ESL class.* *She **wrote** a research paper on a typewriter last week.*
Word Combination Other verbs are formed by making combinations of words for different meanings: for example, *is writing, has written, will write*, and so forth. An auxiliary is combined with a form of a main verb. The auxiliary verbs include *be, have,* and the modals.	*He **is writing** a letter now.* *She **has written** her mother every week so far this year.* *We **will write** the report tomorrow.*

Verb Choices for Definite Past Time Meaning

In this chapter, you will work with the **past time frame.** You will practice talking and writing about past time events that occurred at a specific time. When you are writing about definite past time, the basic verb form is the simple past tense. However, you can also use other verbs for special meanings. For example, the past perfect and the past progressive forms of the verb are used to add different kinds of meanings in past time communication. One use of the present perfect is also explained in this chapter.

George Washington

*George Washington **was** the military leader of the American Revolution. He **led** the fight against England. Before he **became** a general, he **had been** a surveyor and **had participated** in mapping the American wilderness. While he **was waiting** for the British to attack, General Washington **worked** to build a stronger colonial army.*

John F. Kennedy

*John F. Kennedy **was** the 35th president of the United States. Before he **became** president, he **had graduated** from Harvard University and **had been** in the United States Navy. While he **was serving** in the navy in World War II, he **injured** his back during an attack.*

1. **Simple Past.** The central event is described using the simple past tense forms of the verb. The simple past tense describes actions or activities that began and ended in the past.

   *George Washington **was** the military leader of the American Revolution. He **led** the fight against England.*

   *John F. Kennedy **was** the 35th president of the United States.*

2. **Past Perfect.** Things that happened before that central time use the past perfect. The past perfect describes actions or activities that were completed before another action or activity in the past.

   *Before he became a general, George Washington **had been** a surveyor and **had participated** in mapping the American wilderness.*

   *Before he became president, Kennedy **had graduated** from Harvard University and **had been** in the United States Navy.*

3. **Past Progressive.** The past progressive describes actions or activities that happened at the same time in the past. The past progressive is rarely used in simple sentences; it is usually used in contrast with another verb in a complex sentence.

   *While he **was waiting** for the British to attack, General Washington **worked** to build a stronger colonial army.*

   *While Kennedy **was serving** in the navy in World War II, he **injured** his back during an attack.*

Simple Past Tense

. . . .

Simple Past Tense/Regular Verbs
For **regular verbs,** the simple past is made by adding -ed to the simple present tense: *walk* becomes *walked.*

*Everyday, he **walks** to the library to study.*

*Yesterday, he **walked** to the library to study.*

*Two of his friends **walked** to the library with him.*

Simple Past Tense/Irregular Verbs
The simple past tense has only one form for all subjects except for the two forms of *be* (*was* and *were*).

*She **was** in the computer lab all afternoon.*

*They **were** in the library until 5:00 P.M.*

For **irregular verbs,** the simple past is made by a change in spelling (and pronunciation) of the basic verb. Irregular verbs are listed alphabetically in Appendix C.

*Usually, she **writes** her essays at home.*

*She **wrote** her research paper in the library.*

*Her friends also **wrote** their papers there.*

. . . .

Practice with the Simple Past Tense

A. Irregular verbs are verbs that do not follow the regular pattern of forming the past and the past participle with -ed. Irregular verbs are words like *write (wrote, written)* or *buy (bought, bought)* or *let (let, let).* The irregular verbs are a problem for many ESL students. You must learn the meanings as well as many different forms, pronunciations, and spellings. Appendix C has an alphabetized list of the most common irregular verbs. Before doing any exercises in this chapter with the irregular verbs, you would probably benefit from looking over the list of irregular verbs in Appendix C. Try putting a sheet of paper over the list to cover all but the first form; write the other three forms on the paper, and then check to see which ones you misspelled. Then, turn to page 451 in the Grammar Journal to analyze your use of irregular verbs. You can improve your skills at language learning by studying the materials provided in First Steps on learning styles and strategies. Discuss those ideas with your classmates to think of effective ways to learn new verbs.

B. One of the interesting powers of the human mind is to think about something while we are busy doing something else. Have you ever tried to solve a problem and could not but found that the answer was clear when you woke up the next morning? Or, have you ever had the experience of not knowing the answer to a test question until right after you walked out of the classroom? This exercise is designed to help you find out what you already know about irregular verbs by doing part of the work and then putting the activity aside for a while before completing it. Begin by writing these headings across the top of a sheet of lined paper:

"Simple Form"	"Simple Past"	"Past Participle"	"*ing* Form"
write	*wrote*	*written*	*writing*

Then, write as many other irregular verbs as you can remember in five minutes. You should include any verb that you can think of even if you cannot think of all of its forms. Give the sheet of paper to your instructor. Do some other activity for at least 30 minutes. Then, get the sheet back from your instructor, and take another four or five minutes to add any other verbs that you have remembered.

C. For practice with irregular verbs, you might enjoy doing this crossword puzzle. For each clue, write the correct past tense form in the answer spaces either across or down as appropriate. After completing the puzzle, turn to page 460 to see the answers.

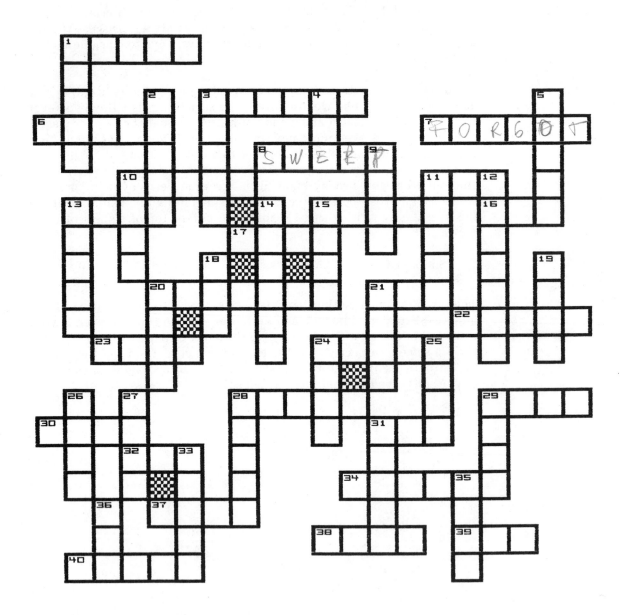

Across Clues

1. to pay out money
3. to put over a surface
6. to use up
7. to not remember
8. to clean with a broom
10. to locate
11. to grip with teeth or jaws
13. to move rapidly
15. to make marks with pen or pencil
16. to own
17. to arrive
20. to carry
21. to not lose
22. to select
23. to send out a force of air
24. to send through the air
28. to give
29. to move smoothly along a surface
30. opposite of to take
31. opposite of to stand
32. to give food
34. to battle
37. to remove from the possession of another person
38. to move through the air
39. to show the way
40. to take illegally

Down Clues

1. opposite of to stay awake
2. opposite of to sit down
3. to move rapidly in an arc
4. to consume food
5. to locate
9. to have a test
10. to move down
11. to start
12. to have an idea
13. to not open
14. to get a disease
15. to cry
18. to receive something
19. to require an amount of money
20. to lose blood
21. to have on clothing
24. to say something
25. to move in a direction
26. to go under
27. to depart
28. to consume a liquid
29. opposite of to open
31. to say words
33. to control a car
35. to have in one's arms
36. to be the correct size

D. For practice with irregular verbs, you might enjoy doing this crossword puzzle. For each clue, write the correct past participle in the answer spaces either across or down as appropriate. After completing the puzzle, turn to page 460 to see the answers.

Across Clues
- 2. begin
- 5. build
- 7. bleed
- 8. feed
- 11. win
- 12. run
- 14. break
- 16. draw
- 18. get
- 19. ring
- 20. catch
- 23. come
- 24. drive
- 25. deal
- 26. cost

Down Clues
- 1. know
- 2. bite
- 3. go
- 4. dig
- 6. fly
- 7. blow
- 9. drink
- 10. bring
- 13. fall
- 14. buy
- 15. eat
- 16. do
- 17. sing
- 20. choose
- 21. have
- 22. feel

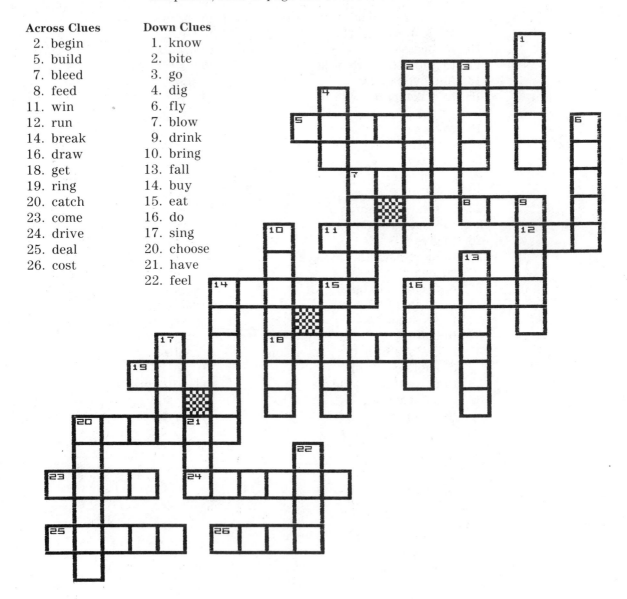

E. Discussion Assignment: Why is mail so important for people as individuals? Why is having a good mail service important for a country? How is mail delivered to individuals in modern times? How is mail sent from one city to another in modern times? You might understand this paragraph better if you look at a map of North and South America and find the locations mentioned to understand the distances involved.

Grammar Assignment: Complete the following paragraphs by providing the correct form of the verb. In the first paragraph, a verb is provided in parentheses for each sentence. In the second paragraph, verbs must be selected from the word list at the end of the paragraph.

Early Mail Service in the United States

The discovery of gold in California in 1848 __*brought*__ settlers from
(bring)
the East Coast to the West Coast of the United States. Within a few

years, the population of California _____ drastically, and
[1](increase)

settlers _____ better mail service from their families and
[2](demand)

friends in the East. Stage coaches _____ the mail, but
[3](carry)

they _____ slow and took several weeks to reach the
[4](be)

West. Ships from New York also _____ the mail around
[5](carry)

South America, but this journey _____ even longer.
[6](take)

In 1860, the Pony Express _____ to deliver mail across
[7]

the country. Riders _____ St. Joseph, Missouri, on the
[8]

Pony Express passing a stage coach in the West

first part of the journey to California. Men on fast horses

_____ in relays day and night at top speeds for ten to

$_9$

fifteen miles across the country. A new rider _____ ready

$_{10}$

at each of the nearly two hundred stations along the route. The mail

_____ two thousand miles away in Sacramento ten days

$_{11}$

later.   [Word List: *arrive, be, begin, leave, ride*]

The riders _____ day and night. Horses and men

$_{12}$

_____ out quickly, and Pony Express riders frequently

$_{13}$

_____ physical danger when they _____

$_{14}$ $_{15}$

through Indian attacks. Unfortunately, the Pony Express only

_____ for nineteen months. The government

$_{16}$

_____ to give financial help to the company, and in 1861

$_{17}$

the completion of the first transcontinental telegraph line at Salt Lake

City, Utah, _____ the end of the Pony Express.

$_{18}$

[Word List: *last, mark, meet, refuse, ride, ride, wear*]

Adapted from *World Book Encyclopedia*, 1988 ed., s.v. "pony express."

F. Discussion Assignment: Why do refugees and immigrants come to the United States? What is the difference between the categories *refugee* and *immigrant*? Was Astor an immigrant or a refugee? How did he make so much money? Would his approach work in modern times? Would you recommend his methods?

Grammar Assignment: In the first paragraph, fill in the blank with the correct form of the verb in parentheses. In the second paragraph, select the verb with the correct meaning from the list below, and put the correct form of that verb in the blank in the appropriate sentence.

The Richest Man in the United States

John Jacob Astor _____ his home in Germany and

^{1}(leave)

_____ in America in 1783 after the American Revolution.

^{2}(arrive)

He _____ the fur-trading business and

^{3}(learn)

_____ his own fur-gathering expeditions in New York

^{4}(start)

State. By 1800, Astor _____ a quarter of a million dollars.

^{5}(have)

In 1808, he _____ the American Fur Company and

^{6}(form)

_____ his fur-trading business into the Northwest

^{7}(extend)

25

Territory and the Louisiana Territory. Astor also _____
[8](enter)
the Oriental trade business and _____ American furs for
[9](trade)
Oriental silk, tea, and glassware.

He _____ most of his profits from the fur and
[10]
Oriental trade business in farm lands, and within a few years, he

_____ the property of present day New York City. When
[11]

he _____ in 1848, he _____ the richest
[12]   [13]

man in America. His real estate holdings and property rentals

_____ more than $20 million. John Jacob Astor
[14]

_____ much of this money to libraries, universities, and
[15]

charities across the United States.   **[Word List: *be, donate, die, invest,***

***own, total*]**

Adapted from *Collier's Encyclopedia*, 1987 ed., s.v. "Astor, John Jacob."

G. Discussion Assignment: *Bell* is an everyday word in the United
States as part of the name for most telephone companies. What is the
name of the telephone company in the place where you are studying
English? The telephone has become essential in the United States for
personal and professional reasons. What are some of the ways in which
telephones are used? Like John Jacob Astor, Alexander Graham Bell was
an immigrant to the United States. How were their lives and their purposes in life different? Do you admire one person more than the other?
Why?

Grammar Assignment: In the first paragraph, fill the blank with the
correct form of the verb in parentheses. In the second paragraph, select
the verb with the correct meaning from the list below, and put the correct form of the verb in the blank in the appropriate sentence.

Alexander Graham Bell: Educator and Inventor

Alexander Graham Bell _____ an inventor, a scientist,
[1](be)
and an educator. He _____ the University of Edinburgh
[2](attend)
and _____ for his grandfather, a speech teacher, and his
[3](work)
father, a speech teacher and writer. In 1870, he _____ to
[4](immigrate)
Canada with his parents and _____ in Ontario where he
[5](settle)
_____ at several schools for the deaf. He
[6](teach)

_____ a school in Boston in 1872 to train teachers in his
[7](start)

method. He _____ a professor of speech and vocal
          [8](be)

physiology at Boston University from 1873 to 1877. During that time, he

_____ with a device for transmitting several telegraph
[9](experiment)

messages at once over a single wire and _____ his work
                                        [10](continue)

with the deaf.

Later, he _____ the principles of the two experiments
          [11]

and _____ the basic principle of the telephone. In March
    [12]

1876, he _____ the telephone and _____
         [13]   [14]

intelligible words. The money that he _____ from his
                                      [15]

telephone _____ his future experiments. He
          [16]

_____ the photo-phone, a device to transmit speech along
[17]

a beam of light, and an electric probe for surgery, a forerunner of the

X ray. In the 45 years after the invention of the telephone, Bell

_____ many years of service to the deaf. In later years,
[18]

he _____ the telephone because it _____
   [19]   [20]

his experiments.   [Word List: *combine, develop, dislike, finance, give,*
interrupt, invent, patent, receive, transmit]

Adapted from *World Book Encyclopedia*, 1988 ed., s.v. "Bell, Alexander Graham."

H. Write a paragraph about the first day in this class. Describe what
you saw, felt, did, and thought. After you are satisfied with the organization and meaning of the paragraph, edit it carefully for verb choice
and form. Use the editing method presented in Section Four of this book.

I. Write a paragraph that tells what you did yesterday. Describe
what you saw, heard, felt, did, and thought. After you are satisfied with
the organization and meaning of the paragraph, edit it carefully for verb
choice and form. Use the editing method presented in Section Four of
this book.

Past Perfect

. . . .

The past perfect verb form is used in a past time context to emphasize that something happened before the basic past time.

Formation

The past perfect is formed by combining the past of *have* with a past participle. It is important to spell the past participle correctly. Appendix C can be helpful when you edit your writing to check the spelling of irregular verbs.

*Majid **had eaten** dinner before he studied.*

*Maria and Petra **had studied** together before they went to the movie.*

Meaning

First, the students took the test. Second, Tuan arrived. This use of the past perfect emphasizes that Tuan missed the midterm examination.

*The students **had** already **taken** the midterm exam by the time Tuan **arrived.***

First, the teacher reviewed the material for the test. Second, the students took the test. This example could be a little confusing because the second thing that happened is given in the beginning position.

*Before the exam, the teacher **had reviewed** the material.*

. . . .

Practice with the Past Perfect

A. A past perfect verb can be used to emphasize that one action was completed before another action in the past. Mark each of the following sentences to show which happened first and which happened second as is done in the examples.

       2nd   1st
Before I came to class, I had studied the assigned chapter.
   2nd   1st
I came to class after I had studied the assignment.

1. I had eaten dinner before I did my homework.

2. Before I watched television, I had studied for the test.

3. I had turned off the television before I went to bed.

4. After I had gone to bed, I turned on the radio.

5. I went to sleep after I had listened to the radio for one hour.

6. By the time that I woke up, the radio had played all night.

B. Using exercise A as a model, write your own examples to illustrate the use of the past perfect to emphasize that one thing happened before another thing in the past. Then, ask another student to mark the sentences to show which event was first and which was second. Check the analysis to see if you need to make any changes in your sentences to clarify which event happened first. Check the spelling of the past participles using Appendix C. Then, write your corrected list of example sentences on a sheet of paper to keep in your Grammar Notebook for future reference.

C. Write five sentences to explain what you had already done today before class began. After you have corrected the sentences, copy them on a sheet of paper. Then, compare your day to that of other students. If you want to learn any of the verbs used by other students, add them to the list in your Grammar Notebook.

D. Discussion Assignment: Is tourism important to your country? What kinds of things seem to interest tourists? What plans do you know about for attracting tourists to the city where you are now living? It might help in understanding this reading to look at a map of the United States. Where is South Dakota? Why might that state have problems if it wants to make money from tourism?

Grammar Assignment: Underline each complete verb with two lines. Why do you think the writer made these choices? What time frame do you expect in a composition that begins with the words *in 1923?*

Mount Rushmore

[1]In 1923, Doan Robinson, a historian from South Dakota, proposed a plan to increase tourism in the remote western state. [2]He visualized a giant sculpture on the side of a mountain in the Black Hills of South Dakota. [3]Gutzon Borglum had completed the statue of Abraham Lincoln for the United States Capitol in Washington, D.C., a few years before. [4]Robinson asked the famous sculptor to construct his dream. [5]Borglum

decided to build a memorial to honor four famous United States presidents: George Washington the "Father of the Country," Thomas Jefferson the "Expansionist," Abraham Lincoln the "Preserver of the Union," and Theodore Roosevelt the "Protector of the Working Man." [6]The giant carving took fourteen years to complete. [7]The four 60-foot-high heads are visible for miles, and tourists from everywhere in the world visit the monument.

Adapted from *Encyclopedia Americana*, 1983 ed., s.v. "Mount Rushmore National Memorial" and "Gutzon Borglum."

Mount Rushmore

E. Discussion Assignment: Many countries in the Western Hemisphere remember Christopher Columbus because of his role in their history. You might ask students in your class who are from North, Central, or South America to tell you what they have learned about this explorer. You might look at a map of the world (see p. 365) to better understand the journeys that he made from Spain to Central America. For many Native Americans, Columbus is not a hero but a villain. Why might their attitudes be different from those of people of European heritage?

Grammar Assignment: What time frame do you expect for a composition about someone who lived 500 years ago? What verb forms could be used? Fill in each blank with the correct form of each verb. For the last two paragraphs, select a verb from the Word List at the end of each paragraph that fits the meaning of the sentence; make sure to put the verb in the correct form. Before filling in the blank spaces in the final paragraph, think about the meanings of the verbs listed at the end. What do these verbs suggest about the end of Columbus's life?

Christopher Columbus: A Life of Change and Disappointment

Christopher Columbus first _____ to sea at the age of
                                    1(go)
19, and he _____ his life in sea explorations and battles.
              2(spend)
He _____ to reach the Orient by sailing westward from
      3(want)
Europe; however, he first _____ to convince a monarch to
                               4(need)
finance his voyage. Before Ferdinand and Isabella of Spain

_____ to finance his famous voyage, Columbus
5(agree)
_____ King John II of Portugal for help, but the king
6(ask)
_____ him.
7(refuse)

Seven years later, on August 3, 1492, Columbus _____
                                                        8
from Palos, Spain. He _____ a squadron of three ships: the
                          9
Santa Maria, the Nina, and the Pinta. After he _____ at
                                                      10
the Canary Islands for water and repairs, he _____ west
                                                   11
for more than three weeks. When he _____ the island of
                                         12
San Salvador on October 12, 1492, he _____ the native
                                           13
inhabitants "Indians." He _____ to Spain as the hero who
                               14
_____ a New World.   **[Word List: *call, command,*
15
discover, reach, return, sail, sail, stop]**

However, Columbus's early fame _____ ; his last three
                                       16
voyages _____ a series of financial and political
            17
disappointments. Officials who were his enemies _____
                                                       18
him on another voyage, and on his final voyage, he _____
                                                         19
mutiny, Indian attacks, treacherous storms, and jealousy from the
Spanish governor. He _____ most of his former prestige
                          20

and authority by the time he _____ on May 20, 1506.
21

[Word List: *arrest, be, die, face, not last, lose*]

Adapted from *World Book Encyclopedia*, 1988 ed., s.v. "Columbus, Christopher."

Past Progressive

The past progressive verb form is made by combining a past form of *be* (*was* or *were*) with an *-ing* form of the verb. Another name for the past progressive is the past continuous.

Formation

Past progressive requires subject-verb agreement. See "agreement" on page 104 in Chapter Three.

*She **was writing** her report when the computer **broke**.*

*They **were writing** their report when the computer **broke**.*

Meaning

The past progressive verb form can be used in the past time frame to emphasize that something happened at the same time as something else.

*The students **were taking** their final exam when they **heard** a loud noise. While their teacher **was talking** to another teacher about the noise, the lights **went** out. The students **sat** quietly in the dark while their teachers **were discussing** the problem. It **was raining** heavily when everyone **went** home.*

Practice with the Past Progressive

A. A past progressive verb is used with action verbs to emphasize that two things happened at the same time in the past. In the space provided below, write examples to explain the things that were happening when class began today. Your sentences should describe the things that people were doing: talking, writing, studying, and so forth.

When Class Began Today

1. *When class began, I was talking with a friend.*

2. When class began, my teacher _____

3. When class began, _____

4. When class began, _____

5. When class began, _____

B. Compare the verbs that you used in exercise A with those used by other students in your class. In the space provided below, make a complete list of the verbs that were used to describe the actions people do in a classroom. Circle any of the verbs that are new to you. Discuss with your class ways that you can add these words to your vocabulary.

When Class Began Today

1. _____	6. _____	11. _____
2. _____	7. _____	12. _____
3. _____	8. _____	13. _____
4. _____	9. _____	14. _____
5. _____	10. _____	15. _____

C. Discussion Assignment: Why do people become famous? What kind of people are famous in the United States? What makes people famous in other cultures? Some Americans are remembered because they became very wealthy. What do you think about money as a basis for fame?

Grammar Assignment: What time frame do you expect to find in a composition about a person who lived in the 19th century? What verb forms might be used? Fill in each blank with the correct form of each verb.

Andrew Carnegie: A Famous American Immigrant

In 1848 at the age of 12, Andrew Carnegie _____ from
                                              [1](emigrate)
Scotland with his family to Allegheny, Pennsylvania. By the time he

_____ Thomas A. Scott, a railroad superintendent with
[2](meet)
the Pennsylvania Railroad, he _____ in a cotton factory
                                  [3](work)
and a telegraph office. However, while he _____ for Scott,
                                              [4](work)
Carnegie _____ how to invest money. With money that he
          [5](learn)
_____ from Scott, Carnegie _____ shares of
[6](borrow)   [7](purchase)
Adams Express Company stock, and he _____ to invest
                                        [8](continue)
his money in railroads, oil, bridges, and iron manufacturing. By the time

he _____ 30, he _____ almost all of his
      [9](be)   [10](devote)

attention to the rapidly expanding iron industry. During the next 20

years, he _____ his business into a unit that controlled
          [11]transform)

the raw materials, transportation, manufacturing, and distribution of

steel. In 1901, he _____ Carnegie Steel to the United
                    [12](sell)

States Steel Corporation. After he _____ at 65, he
                                    [13](retire)

_____ the rest of his life giving away his fortune. He
[14](spend)

_____ the Carnegie Endowment for International Peace,
[15](establish)

the Carnegie Foundation for the Advancement of Teaching, and the

Carnegie Institution of Washington, D.C. He also _____ ,
                                                  [16](build)

many public libraries for towns and universities across the United

States.

Adapted from *Encyclopedia Americana*, 1983 ed., s.v. "Carnegie, Andrew."

Time Expressions Often Used in the Past Time Frame

Expressions such as the following are often used with the simple
past tense, the past perfect, and the past progressive forms of the verb.

Past		
ago	*(three days ago, two weeks ago, a year ago, a few minutes ago)*	He **studied** English in Minneapolis three years ago.
earlier	*(earlier today, earlier this week, earlier this month)*	I **finished** the research paper earlier this week.
in	*(in 1970, in 1776, in March, in [an earlier year or month])*	I **took** my first English course in 1985.
last	*(last night, last Monday, last month, last year)*	I **completed** the chemistry project last Monday.
yesterday	*(yesterday morning, yesterday evening, the day before yesterday)*	They **attended** a concert yesterday.

Past Perfect

....

after   ***After** he **had eaten** dinner, he **drove** to campus.*

before   ***Before** he **drove** to campus, he **had eaten** dinner.*

by the time   ***By the time** that he **finished** his paper, everyone **had gone** home.*

Past Progressive

....

while   *While I **was driving** to campus, I **saw** an accident.*

          *While I **was driving** to campus, I **was listening** to the radio.*

Practice with Past Time Expressions

A. Circle the time expressions that indicate the past time in the following sentences.

Changes in Rural America

1. The number of people who lived in rural areas of the United States in 1987 was 63.9 million, or 27% of the total U.S. population.
2. Before 1930, farm residents had represented 30% of the total population.
3. This proportion fell to 15% in 1950 and to 5% in 1970.
4. Of all farm families, 16% had incomes below the poverty level last year.
5. While the incomes of farm families were declining earlier this decade, the median age of farm residents was increasing.
6. The U.S. Bureau of the Census published this information a few years ago.

Adapted from U.S. Bureau of the Census. *Rural and Rural Farm Population: 1987.* Current Populations Report Series, no. 61. Washington, D.C.: GPO, 1988.

B. Combine these sentences using *after, because, before,* or *while.* You can use the same words more than one time. You will need to change many of the verb forms when you combine the sentences. After editing your sentences, write them on a sheet of paper to keep in your Grammar Notebook for future reference.

Sara took college algebra. Then, she took trigonometry. (before)

Sara had taken college algebra before she took trigonometry.

1. Farid lost his grammar book. He bought a new one.
2. I slept for two hours yesterday afternoon. Then, I felt better.
3. One student took the TOEFL four times. Then, he came to the United States.
4. Seetha drove to class this morning. She listened to the news.
5. Students registered for classes last week. They completed application forms and took placement tests.

Present Perfect: Indefinite Past Time in the Past Time Frame

The present perfect verb form is used to refer to indefinite past time. The present perfect is used for the same indefinite past time meaning in other time contexts. (See page 100 and page 135 for examples of these uses.)

Formation

The present perfect is made of *have* + the past participle. Subject-verb agreement rules must be followed.

*He **has** already **taken** calculus.*

*They **have studied** for the test.*

*Using laptop computers on airplanes **has become** a common practice.*

Use

Present perfect is used to introduce a past time topic with an indefinite meaning.

present perfect for indefinite past time
*Have you **taken** English 101 yet?*

past tense for definite past time
*I **took** it last year, and it **was** really difficult.*

The present perfect is often used to introduce past time information. After the writer is sure that you understand the topic, he or she changes to the definite past tense.

*This company **has had** a short but successful history. The president **started** the business in 1975 with an initial investment of $5,000. By 1980, the company **was** worth $5,000,000.*

Meaning

Definite means the speaker is focusing on a specific time in the past. The present perfect cannot be used for a specific time in the past.

incorrect
*The president has started the business in 1975.

correct
The president started the business in 1975.

The **indefinite** past time means that the event happened in the past "sometime before now."

Have you ever visited Paris?

Present perfect refers to an event that happened at an unknown or unspecified time in the past. It can be used to refer to something that happened only once, to something that was repeated, or to something that started long ago and continues to the present time.

I have been to San Francisco once.

I have visited New York many times.

I have lived here in Cleveland since I was born.

Time Expressions with the Present Perfect

Since and *for* are frequently used in the adverbial modifier of time.

We have lived here since 1980.

We have lived here for over 10 years.

Other time expressions often used with present perfect verbs include *already, recently,* and *yet.*

I have already taken algebra.

I have recently taken physics.

Note that *yet* is used in negative statements and in questions. It is not used in positive statements.

I have not taken calculus yet.

Have you taken calculus yet?

incorrect
*I have taken algebra yet.

correct
I have already taken algebra.

Practice with the Present Perfect

A. In the blank space in each sentence, write the present perfect form of the verbs in parentheses.

1. Paresh _____ many part-time jobs.   (hold)

2. He _____ a cashier at K-Mart.   (be)

3. He _____ as a server at an Indian restaurant.   (work)

4. He _____ books and mail for the campus library.   (deliver)

5. However, Paresh _____ very much   (make, not)
   money at these jobs.

6. He _____ a part-time job that pays   (have, not)
   enough to send him to college.

7. He _____ unhappy and worried recently.   (be)

8. He _____ the "help wanted" ads in the   (read)
   Atlanta Constitution.

9. He _____ several letters to prospective   (write)
   employers.

10. Many students _____ the same   (have)
    experience.

B. Write five sentences that answer these questions: What interesting places have you visited? What interesting things have you done on vacations and other trips? Use the present perfect verb form, and do not mention a specific time. For example,

I have visited Disney World.

I have toured the capital cities of ten different countries.

Disney World, Florida

C. Add a specific month and year to each sentence that you wrote in exercise B. Be sure to change the verbs as you rewrite the sentences. You are answering the questions: When did you visit that place? When did you have that interesting experience? For example,

I visited Disney World in 1990.

I was in Washington on September 14, 1989, and in Paris in October of that same year.

D. Examine the verbs in the following sentences. Did the activity in each sentence take place at a specific past time (simple past tense) or did it take place at an indefinite past time (present perfect verb form)?

Example: *Barnabas flew to Dallas last month.*   (time = *specific*)

He has already been in New Orleans.   (time = *indefinite*)

1. He has also traveled to Florida several times in the past few years.   (time = _____)

2. He went to California last winter.   (time = _____)

3. While he was in California, he went to Disneyland.   (time = _____)

4. Ladan has been to California recently.   (time = _____)

5. She has traveled to Florida twice.   (time = _____)

6. She returned from Orlando yesterday.   (time = _____)

E. Complete the following sentences using present perfect verb forms or simple past tense. Your sentences should be meaningful, and the verb forms should be correct. Describe your ESL class. Share your description with other students in your class, and make any necessary changes in the grammar or the information.

This ESL Class

1. Yesterday, this class _____ .

2. _____ recently.

3. Last Friday, _____ .

4. _____ the day before yesterday.

5. _____ yet.

6. _____ three times.

F. Fill in each blank with the correct form of the verb in parentheses; choose either the present perfect verb form or simple past tense. Circle the time expression in each sentence.

Space Travel

1. Several human beings _____ in space since the first
   (travel)

   manned space flight on April 12, 1961.

2. On that day, Soviet cosmonaut Yuri Gagarin _____ the
   (become)

   first person to travel in space when he _____ a single
   (make)

   orbit around the earth.

3. John H. Glenn, Jr., the first American in orbit, _____
   (circle)

   the earth three times on February 20, 1962.

4. During the years that followed these first space explorations,

   many flights _____ people into orbit around the
   (carry)

   earth.

5. The first human beings on the moon _____ astronauts
   (be)

   Neil A. Armstrong and Edwin E. Aldrin, Jr. They

   _____ on the moon on July 20, 1969. Other
   (land)

   astronauts _____ six moon landings between 1969
   (make)

   and 1972.

6. The United States _____ the first U.S. manned space
   (launch)

   laboratory in 1973. The Skylab I Space Station _____ .
   (orbit)

   about 270 miles above the earth. It _____ when it
   (disintegrate)

   reentered the earth's atmosphere in 1979.

7. In the 1970s, U.S. engineers and scientists _____ a
   (develop)

   reusable manned spacecraft.

8. U.S. astronauts John W. Young and Robert L. Crippen

    _____ a new era in space exploration on April 12,
    (begin)

    1981, when they _____ off in the first space shuttle,
                        (take)

    Columbia.

9. Since 1961, the United States and the Soviet Union

    _____ a number of spacecraft into solar orbit for the
    (launch)

    purpose of expanding their knowledge about the moon, the planets,

    and the stars.

10. For the past ten years, the exploration of space _____
                                                           (provide)

    knowledge about the universe. Scientists _____
                                                  (perform)

    experiments on the moon, and space probes _____
                                                   (photograph)

    distant planets.

Adapted from *World Book Encyclopedia*, 1988 ed., s.v. "space travel."

Picture of Mars taken by Viking 1 Orbiter on June 18, 1976

Practice with the Past Time Frame

A. Reread the short paragraphs about George Washington and John F. Kennedy on pages 56–57. Write a similar paragraph about the life of an important person who is no longer alive. The person could be a hero from your culture or country. Or, the person could be someone that you are especially interested in. The paragraph should tell your reader four things: (1) Who was this person? (2) What did he or she do that was important? (3) What had the person done before the heroic action? (4) What two or more things happened at the same time in this person's life? After you have revised the paragraph to have it factually correct, edit the verbs carefully. Then, share the paragraph with the rest of your class.

B. Working with other students in your class, decide on and circle the best answer to complete each of the following statements:

1. When communicating about a past experience, which verb form would you expect to use most frequently?
   a. the simple past tense
   b. the past progressive form
   c. the past perfect form
   d. the present perfect form
2. Which verb form(s) involve(s) subject-verb agreement? (If you are not sure, see page 104 in Chapter Three.)
   a. the simple past tense
   b. the past progressive form
   c. the past perfect form
   d. the present perfect form
3. Which verb form(s) usually need(s) two actions to express the appropriate meaning?
   a. the simple past tense
   b. the past progressive form
   c. the past perfect form
   d. the present perfect form
4. When communicating about two things that happened in the past, which verb form do you use to show the action that happened first?
   a. the simple past tense
   b. the past progressive form
   c. the past perfect form
   d. the present perfect form
5. Which verb form is frequently used with *while?*
   a. the simple past tense
   b. the past progressive form
   c. the past perfect form
   d. the present perfect form

6. Which verb form is frequently used with *since?*
   a. the simple past tense
   b. the past progressive form
   c. the past perfect form
   d. the present perfect form

C. Circle the time expression in each sentence. Then, write the letter of the best answer in the blank at the beginning of each sentence:

_____ 1. Jose _____ to the library last night.
   a. went   c. has gone
   b. had gone   d. was gone

_____ 2. Before he went to the library, Jose _____ supper.
   a. eat   c. has eaten
   b. had eaten   d. was eating

_____ 3. While he _____ to the library, Jose met three classmates.
   a. was walked   c. has walked
   b. had walked   d. was walking

_____ 4. He _____ to them when it started to rain.
   a. was talked   c. has talked
   b. talks   d. was talking

_____ 5. The rainstorm _____ within five minutes.
   a. ended   c. has ended
   b. ends   d. was ending

_____ 6. Before the rainstorm ended, everyone _____ wet.
   a. get   c. has gotten
   b. had gotten   d. was getting

_____ 7. Jose _____ home after the storm had ended.
   a. went   c. has gone
   b. had gone   d. was going

_____ 8. He _____ on the interstate highway when another storm began.
   a. drove   c. has driven
   b. was driven   d. was driving

____ 9. When Jose turned on his television in his home, he ____ about
the possible tornado in his area.

    a. learned   c. has learned

    b. had learned   d. was learning

____ 10. Jose was glad that he ____ to return home.

    a. was decided   c. has decided

    b. had decided   d. was deciding

D. Discussion Assignment: Of all the many refugee and immigrant groups to come to the United States, only African-Americans were forced to come here against their own desire. Working with the other students in your class, discuss as much as you know about the history of African-American people. Why were they brought to the U.S.? When were they freed? What is the "civil rights movement," and when did it occur? Why are the achievements of the people described in the following paragraphs so remarkable?

Dr. Martin Luther King leads 300 civil rights marchers on their march from Selma to Montgomery, Alabama, in March 1965.

Grammar Assignment: Underline each complete verb with two lines, and then answer the following questions for each paragraph:

1. How many complete verbs did you find?
2. How many irregular verbs did you find?
3. Which words did you need to look up in your dictionary to find their meanings?
4. Discuss with your classmates ways in which you can learn new vocabulary. Use the materials on learning styles and strategies in First Steps to suggest specific actions you can take to improve your English.

Garrett A. Morgan, 1877–1963

[1]Garrett A. Morgan received wide recognition for his contributions to public safety. [2]Firemen in many cities in the early 1900s wore the safety helmet and gas mask that he had invented. [3]He himself used the mask to rescue men after a gas main had exploded in a tunnel under Lake Erie. [4]After this disaster, the city of Cleveland honored him with a gold medal for his heroic efforts. [5]In 1923, Morgan received a patent for another new concept—a traffic signal to regulate vehicle movement in city areas. [6]Men systematically raised "Stop" and "Go" signs at intersections to improve traffic safety. [7]The automatic light signal in use today replaced Morgan's device.

Frederick M. Jones, 1892–1961

[1]Frederick M. Jones held more than 60 patents in a variety of fields, but refrigeration was his specialty. [2]In 1935, he invented the first automatic refrigeration system for long-haul trucks. [3]Later, he adapted the system to a variety of other carriers, including ships and railway cars. [4]His invention eliminated the problem of food spoilage and changed America's eating habits. [5]In addition, Jones developed an air-conditioning unit for military field hospitals, a portable X-ray machine, and a refrigerator for military field kitchens in World War I. [6]After the war, he worked as a garage mechanic and developed a self-starting gasoline motor. [7]In the late 1920s. Jones designed a series of devices for the movie industry; he adapted silent movie projectors to accommodate talking films and developed the box-office equipment that delivers tickets and automatically returns change.

Katherine Johnson, 1918–

[1]Katherine Johnson is an aerospace technologist at the National Aeronautics and Space Administration's Langley Research Center, Hampton, Virginia. [2]She is a mathematician and physicist. [3]She has

worked on problems of interplanetary trajectories, space navigation, and the orbits of spacecraft. [4]Johnson has analyzed data from tracking stations around the world. [5]She has also studied new navigational procedures to determine more practical ways to track manned and unmanned space missions. [6]For her pioneer work in this field, she was a recipient of the Group Achievement Award as a member of NASA's Lunar Spacecraft and Operations team.

Otis Boykin, 1920–

[1]Otis Boykin has invented a wide range of electronic devices. [2]Many computers, radios, television sets, and other electronically controlled devices use his resistor. [3]In addition, Boykin has developed a control unit for artificial heart stimulators, a variable resistor for guided missiles, a burglarproof cash register, and a chemical air filter. [4]His innovations have had both military and commercial applications. [5]Some have reduced the cost of producing electronic controls for radio and television. [6]At present, people use more than three dozen products with Boykin components throughout the world.

Virgil G. Trice, Jr., 1926–

[1]Virgil Trice has spent almost 30 years in developing nuclear energy. [2]Now, his interest is radioactive waste from nuclear power generation. [3]He has been working in the waste management field since 1971 when he joined the Atomic Energy Commission. [4]In 1975, he transferred to the Energy Research and Development Administration and then to the Department of Energy in 1977. [5]He is responsible for radioactive waste management planning, reporting, and program control: an area important to the future of nuclear power. [6]His career includes teaching part-time as associate professor of Chemical Engineering at Howard University.

Adapted from *Black Contributors to Science and Energy Technology.* Washington, D.C.: GPO, undated.

E. Discussion Assignment: Do you know any people who are American Indians? Have you ever heard the term *Native American* as a name for *American Indians?* What does the new name suggest about the way these people think of themselves? Where do these people live today? What is their legal status in the United States? If you do not know the answers to these questions, you might seek information in a reference book such as the *Encyclopedia Americana* or the *World Book Encyclopedia.*

Grammar Assignment: Complete the following paragraphs by choosing the appropriate verbs from the lists at the bottom of each paragraph.

Geronimo

Geronimo

With the piercing shout of "Geronimo!" today's U.S. paratroopers plummet from their troop-carrying aircraft. The cry _____ the fiery spirit of the last and most feared of Apache war leaders. Geronimo _____ beside Cochise, Victorio, and Mangas Coloradas, but long after these bold chieftains _____ , his name _____ panic in the frontier settlements of the Southwest.   [Word list: *had died, fought, recalls, spread*]

One after another, in the 1860s and 1870s, the Apache tribes capitulated to civilization, _____ their raiding forays into Mexico, and _____ on reservations. The Chiricahua Apaches _____ among the last to defy the U.S. government. These _____ Geronimo's people. Although not born a Chiricahua, he _____ a Chiricahuan woman.

[Word List: *abandoned, had married, settled, were, were*]

He _____ in his middle 40s when the U.S. government
_____ the Chiricahuas from their mountain homeland in
southeastern Arizona to the San Carlos Indian Reservation. Geronimo
_____ a band of rebellious tribesmen who wanted no part
of farming on the parched bottomlands of the San Carlos Reservation.
For the next decade he and a small band of "renegades" alternately
_____ in Arizona and Mexico and then
_____ to reservation restraints at San Carlos.

[Word List: *led, moved, raided, returned, was*]

In the autumn of 1881, Geronimo and other leaders once more
_____ the reservation and _____ to
Mexico. From the Sierra Madre, they _____ their horses
through the settlements of Mexico and southern Arizona, plundering,
burning, and killing. The U.S. Army _____ General
George Crook to Arizona. He _____ an experienced Indian
fighter who believed that only Apaches could catch Apaches.

[Word List: *left, rode, sent, traveled, was*]

Crook _____ Chiricahua scout units and plunged into
Mexico. Crook _____ Geronimo and his band to San
Carlos three times. Finally, to stop Geronimo, the U.S. government
_____ to remove the Chiricahuas from Arizona. The
government _____ nearly all the Chiricahuas—those who
had remained peacefully at San Carlos as well as the hostile Indians—
first in Florida, then in Alabama, and finally in Oklahoma. During this
time Geronimo _____ a Christian and even
_____ in President Theodore Roosevelt's inaugural parade
in 1905. Geronimo finally _____ of pneumonia at the Fort
Sill hospital in 1909.   [Word List: *became, decided, died, enlisted,*
imprisoned, returned, rode]

Adapted from U.S. Department of the Interior: Bureau of Indian Affairs. *Famous Indians:*
A Collection of Short Biographies. Washington, D.C.: GPO, undated.

F. On a sheet of paper, write lists that divide all of the verbs used in "Geronimo" into two groups: regular or irregular. Then, write the basic dictionary form for each of the past tense forms used in the article. For example, the basic form of *abandoned* is *abandon;* the basic form of *were* is *be.* Compare your spellings to those of other students in your class, and make any necessary corrections.

G. Write a paragraph of 10–12 sentences to describe an important person in the history of your culture or your country. If possible, check the facts in the paragraph with another person from your country, or go to the library to check them in an encyclopedia. If you use a written source, be sure to include a reference and to punctuate all quotations correctly. After you have revised the paragraph to make it accurate, underline the complete verb in each sentence. Edit the verbs for correct form and correct spelling. Share your description with the other students in your class so that they can learn more about your people and the history of your culture and country.

H. Complete the following chart with information about five of your classmates. Provide details about what they were doing or where they were ten years ago, five years ago, and last year. Then, use those details to write one sentence about each of their lives. When you have written the sentences, ask your classmates to check the factual accuracy of your sentences. After you have corrected any factual errors, edit the sentences to be sure that you have used the correct verb forms. Write your five sentences on a sheet of paper to keep in your Grammar Notebook. Example: *Manuel **had lived** in Rio before he **moved** to Mexico City. Manuel **graduated** from high school after he **had moved** to Mexico City.*

What time frame should you use for this topic? _____

What verb forms can you expect to use? _____

STUDENT	ten years ago	five years ago	last year
Manuel	lived in Rio	moved to Mexico City	graduated from high school
1. _____			
2. _____			
3. _____			
4. _____			
5. _____			

I. Discussion Assignment: Why are books important? Why do governments sometimes try to control or censor books? What kinds of writing materials do you use? For what different purposes are writing materials used?

Grammar Assignment: Discuss the following questions with the other students in your class. What time frame do you expect to find in a paragraph written about the history of writing? What verb forms might be used? Fill in each blank with the correct form of each verb. What verb forms did you use?

Types of Writing Materials

People _____ their thoughts and actions on many
¹(record)
types of writing materials for thousands of years. Prehistoric writers

_____ pictures and symbols on stones and walls of caves.
²(draw)
About 4000 B.C., the Sumerians _____ marks into soft
³(press)
clay. Then, they _____ the clay. About 3000 B.C., the
⁴(bake)
Egyptians _____ papyrus to use for writing. In the 2nd
⁵(invent)
century B.C., parchment, a specially treated animal skin,

_____ to replace papyrus as the chief writing material.
⁶(begin)
The Romans _____ a new kind of book. Instead of long
⁷(construct)
rolls of papyrus or parchment, the Romans _____ books
⁸(make)
from wooden boards and _____ them together with
⁹(tie)
thongs. After the invention of a brush and a suitable ink, the use of

cloth as writing material _____ popular.
¹⁰(become)
The Chinese _____ with making paper. According to
¹¹(experiment)
Chinese tradition, Ts'ai Lun, a Chinese court official,

_____ paper in A.D. 105. He _____ the
¹²(invent)   ¹³(use)
inner bark of the mulberry tree. Within 500 years, the Japanese also

_____ the craft of papermaking. The use of paper
¹⁴(know)
_____ westward from the Far East by way of Baghdad,
¹⁵(spread)
Damascus, Egypt, and Morocco. The art of papermaking

_____ Europe more than 1,000 years after its invention in
¹⁶(reach)
China. The first major change in the Chinese manual papermaking

process _____ in 1798 when Nicholas-Louis Robert
¹⁷(come)

_____ a machine to make paper in continuous rolls rather
¹⁸(invent)

than sheets. Writing materials _____ during the past
¹⁹(change)

2,000 years.

Adapted from *Encyclopedia Americana*, 1983 ed., s.v. "paper."

J. Discussion Assignment: What stories or information did you learn about the moon when you were a child? Why is the moon important to today's space age?

Grammar Assignment: Discuss the answers to the following questions with the other students in your class: What is the time frame of the following paragraph? What words help you identify the time frame? What verb forms are used?

Then, fill in each blank with the correct form of the verb. In the first paragraph, verbs are provided in each sentence. For the second paragraph, select a verb that fits the meaning of the sentence from the list at the end, and put the correct form of that verb in the blank in the appropriate sentence.

The Moon

The moon _____ men for centuries, and men of many
¹(fascinate)

cultures _____ about it. The Mesopotamians (c. 2200 B.C.)
²(write)

_____ lunar eclipses, and the Babylonians (c. 500 B.C.)
³(record)

_____ the dates of eclipses. Aristarchus (c. 280 B.C.), a
⁴(predict)

Greek astronomer, _____ the moon's distance from the
⁵(measure)

earth, and Posidonius (c. 74 B.C.), a Syrian philosopher,

_____ the moon's influence on the earth's tides. In 1609–
⁶(explain)

1610, Galileo, an Italian scientist, _____ the first practical
⁷(make)

use of a telescope to study the moon.

The modern space age _____ on September 12, 1959,
₈

when the Soviet Union _____ Luna 2, the first man-made
₉

object to land on the moon. Ten years later, on July 20, 1969, astronaut

Neil Armstrong of the United States _____ the first
₁₀

human to walk on the moon. Since that date, astronauts

_____ thousands of photographs of the surface of the
₁₁

moon and _____ samples of moon rocks and soil. These
₁₂

pictures and samples $\underset{13}{\rule{3cm}{0.4pt}}$ scientists enough materials
for years of study and analysis.   **[Word List: *become, begin, gather,*
give, launch, take]**

Adapted from *World Book Encyclopedia*, 1988 ed., s.v. "moon."

K. As a review, turn to the Diagnostic Test on pages 13–14 of First
Steps, and look closely at items 6–10 and 26–30. Compare your answers
today with your answers from the first week of this course.

L. To practice editing someone else's written English, turn to Section
Four. Study the information about editing on page 404, and then do the
editing exercises on page 410.

M. For additional writing topics and the editing summary for this
chapter, turn to Section Four, page 424.

CHAPTER

3

General Truth Time Frame

CHAPTER ORGANIZATION

"General Truth" Defined
Verb Choices for General Truth Meaning
Simple Present Tense Verbs
Present Perfect: Indefinite Past Time in General Truth Contexts
Time Expressions with the Present Perfect
Subject-Verb Agreement
    Rule 1: Basic Agreement
    Rule 2: Compound Subjects
    Rule 3: Subjects with Prepositional Phrases or Clauses
    Rule 4: *There/Here*
    Rule 5: Amounts
    Rule 6: Indefinite Pronouns
    Rule 7: *Either/Or* and *Neither/Nor*
    Rule 8: False Plurals
    Rule 9: Gerunds and Infinitives

"General Truth" Defined

In your university work, you will often write about factual information, theories, and other generalizations: You will communicate about things that are generally true; in other words, you will communicate about **general truth.**

Water freezes at O degrees centigrade.

The sun appears to rise in the east, but in fact it does not.

The economy of a country depends on its political history as well as its natural resources.

Many students study at the library every weekend.

Juan studies for three hours each day.

General truth writing can be personal or nonpersonal. It can be general truth about yourself or other people. It can be about habits and other aspects of everyday life. It can be general truth about the natural world as in scientific and technical writing. For this meaning, the simple present tense is the most commonly used verb form.

My sister likes mathematics.

I study in the library every weekend.

The water source for this city is badly polluted.

Time markers (*each, every*) can be used to communicate about habits.

Paresh studies at the library every night.

Adverbs of frequency are often used with the simple present tense. See page 332 in Chapter Fourteen for more information about these adverbs.

He usually studies in the main reading room.

He never leaves before 10 P.M.

Verb Choices for General Truth Meaning

Simple Present Tense. For general truth meaning, the central information will usually be presented with simple present tense forms of the verb. Look again at the examples that are given at the beginning of this chapter, and discuss with other students in your class the meaning of each. Is it for factual, scientific meaning, or for personal, habitual meaning?

Example	Type of Meaning
Water *freezes* at O degrees centigrade.	_____
The sun **appears** to rise in the east, but in fact it **does** not.	_____
The economy of a country **depends** on its political history as well as its natural resources.	_____
Many students **study** at the library every weekend.	_____
Juan **studies** for three hours each day.	_____

Simple Present Tense Verbs

The six most common meanings of the simple present tense verb form are illustrated below. While the simple present tense has six possible meanings, this chapter will focus only on present tense verbs for academic or personal generalizations.

Generalizations
Simple present tense verbs are used to express general truth, customs, and physical laws. These generalizations include current time personal habits.

*Oil **floats** on water.*

*He **studies** in the library every day.*

Present Time
Simple present tense is used with stative verbs for present time meanings. These verbs cannot usually be used in the progressive verb form.

*Right now I **have** 30 minutes to prepare for the test.*

Future Time
Simple present tense verbs can be used to mean future time for a scheduled event.

*The game **starts** at 3:30 tomorrow.*

Future Time Adverbial Clauses
Simple present tense is used in a subordinate clause when the main verb is in future time.

*When he **finishes** this term, he will be a senior.*

Future Time Conditional Clauses
Simple present tense is used in a subordinate clause when the main clause is future conditional.

*If she **drops** the course, she will not get a tuition refund.*

Will and *Can.* These two modal auxiliaries can be used for general truth meaning as well as for future time meaning. (See Chapter Five for more information on the meanings of the modals.)

*An "empty" gasoline container **will explode** when a burning match is dropped in it.*

*She **can write** computer programs using BASIC.*

· ·

Practice with the General Truth

A. Discussion Assignment: Have you ever seen snow? Have you ever driven a car in snow? What was it like? What are some of the dangers that people face when driving or walking during a snowstorm?

Grammar Assignment: Place double lines under each complete verb and single lines under each complete subject. Then, answer the questions listed below.

Snow Facts

[1]Snow is frozen water vapor in the form of ice crystals. [2]These crystals form in clouds at temperatures below freezing. [3]They are transparent and only a few millimeters in diameter. [4]Four basic types of crystals exist with countless varieties of each type. [5]According to scientists, no two crystals are identical. [6]These tiny crystals bump into each other and stick together to form a snowflake. [7]After it reaches the ground, the snowflake loses its individual shape and becomes granular in form. [8]Falling snowflakes and ground snow are very different in appearance.

1. How many general truth verbs did you find?   _____

2. How many singular verbs did you find?   _____

3. How many plural verbs did you find?   _____

4. The following sentences give additional facts about snow. Complete each sentence with the correct form of the verb in parentheses.

   a. In the north and in the mountains, snow often _____ as individual ice crystals. (fall)

   b. In warmer areas, the crystals _____ snowflakes. (form)

   c. Hundreds of crystals often _____ to form a large snowflake. (combine)

   d. In some areas of the United States, a single snowfall sometimes

      _____ 30 inches in depth. (exceed)

   e. These heavy snowfalls _____ in the Rocky Mountains. (occur)

   f. Snow often _____ transportation problems in these parts of the United States. (create)

Adapted from *Encyclopedia Americana*, 1983 ed., s.v. "snow."

B. Write five sentences to answer the following five questions about your own habits. After editing your sentences, share them with another student to learn more about each other's routines. Make any necessary corrections in your sentences, and put them in your Grammar Notebook to use as examples of general truth writing.

1. What time do you usually get up on weekday mornings?
2. What time do you usually eat supper during the week?
3. What do you bring to class every day?
4. Where do you usually study?
5. Approximately how many hours do you study every week?

C. After doing exercise B, turn to a classmate, and ask your classmate the following questions. Write his or her answers on a sheet of paper. Then, answer these questions as your classmate asks them to you. Check each other's answers to be sure that they are factually correct. Then, edit the sentences that you wrote to give your classmate's answers.

1. What time does your first class begin?
2. How many classes do you have each day?
3. What time do you usually get home after school?
4. What do you do to relax?
5. Approximately how many hours do you study every day?

D. Complete the example sentence, and then write five sentences that describe a typical day in your ESL grammar or writing class. Share your list with the rest of your class. After making any necessary corrections, keep the description of your class in your Grammar Notebook for future reference.

Class begins at _____

E. Write five sentences that describe yourself or one of your classmates (by name). Use simple present tense verbs. Share your list with the rest of your class. After making any necessary corrections, keep the description in your Grammar Notebook for future reference.

F. Think about a typical weekday for you. What do you do every day at the same time? Complete the example sentence, and then write five sentences about a typical day. Share your list with the rest of your class. After making any necessary corrections, keep the description of your daily routine in your Grammar Notebook for future reference.

I usually get up at _____

G. Complete the following sentences to make generalizations. Use simple present verb forms. After editing your sentences to be sure that you have used the correct forms for the verbs, share your generalizations with the rest of your class.

1. My first language _____

2. Sometimes, I _____

3. I usually _____

4. A typical student in my country _____

5. The English language _____

6. My teacher _____

7. My classes today _____

8. Newspapers _____

9. Students at this school _____

10. I never _____

H. With the other students in your class, discuss the answers that all of you gave to numbers 3 and 10 in exercise G. How are your ideas alike and how are they different?

I. Discussion Assignment: What picture do you have in your mind when you hear the word *library*? What activities do you think of when you hear that word? How many different kinds of libraries have you ever visited? Why do you go to the library? What kinds of materials are available to use in the library at your school? How large is that school library? Why would the Congress of the United States need a library?

Grammar Assignment: Place double lines under each complete verb. Then, answer the questions listed below.

The Library of Congress

[1]The Library of Congress in Washington, D.C., is the world's largest library. [2]It serves as the research branch of the Congress and is the national library of the United States. [3]Its collections provide a comprehensive record of the history, knowledge, and cultures of the nation and the world. [4]The Library of Congress complex includes three buildings. [5]The Thomas Jefferson Building is the oldest. [6]The building's Great Hall includes marble columns, murals and mosaics, statuary, and stained glass. [7]The Main Reading Room houses a collection of 45,000 reference books and desks for 212 readers. [8]Sculptures on the large bronze doors of the John Adams Building represent 12 historic figures. [9]They include Ts'ang Chieh, Chinese patron saint of pictographic letters; Cadmus, legendary Greek inventor of the alphabet; and Sequoyah, the American Indian inventor of an alphabet for the Cherokee language. [10]The white marble James Madison Memorial Building more than doubles the library's space. [11]The library has 20 million books and pamphlets in 60 languages. [12]These materials stretch along 535 miles of shelves.

Adapted from United States. *Services to the Nation: The Library of Congress*. Washington, D.C.: U.S. Government Printing Office, 1988.

1. How many general truth verbs did you find? _____

2. List the verbs that were used with singular subjects.

3. List the verbs that were used with plural subjects.

J. Discussion Assignment: Most people do not think about their teeth until there is a problem or until it is time to visit the dentist. Before reading the following composition about human teeth, talk with other students in your class about these important, if often neglected, parts of the human body. Why are teeth important? What different things can cause people to lose their teeth? Why are dentists so feared?

Grammar Assignment: Place double lines under each complete verb in the composition. Then, answer the questions listed below.

Human Teeth

[1]Human teeth are complex structures. [2]The first set of teeth consists of twenty teeth: there are 10 teeth in each jaw. [3]The primary teeth begin to appear when an infant is approximately six months old. [4]They continue to emerge until the child is approximately two years old. [5]The first permanent tooth usually emerges at the age of six, and a mixture of primary and permanent teeth is present until the child is twelve years old. [6]By the age of twelve, the child usually has 28 of the 32 permanent teeth, and by the age of 21, a person possesses all 32 of the permanent teeth. [7]There is often much variation in time from this average timetable, but time variation is not important. [8]Deviations in the order of sequence of types of teeth often indicate the possibility of future problems.

Adapted from *Encyclopedia Americana*, 1983 ed., s.v. "teeth."

1. List the 10 verbs that were used with singular subjects.

2. List the five verbs that were used with plural subjects.

K. Write five sentences about U.S. customs or habits that you find surprising. Think about things that Americans do differently from people from other countries. Share your statements with the rest of your class. After making any necessary changes, keep your list in your Grammar Notebook for future reference. Example: *In the U.S., few unmarried adults still live with their parents. Many Americans eat catsup with meat or with fried potatoes.*

L. Generalizations about people from other cultures can be negative and inaccurate. These generalizations are called *stereotypes*. Anthropologist Robert Simmons gives this definition of *stereotype* (Simmons 1989, page 59): "A stereotype is an exaggerated belief associated with a category [of people], and its function is to justify conduct in relation to that category." First, look up any of the words in this definition that you are not sure about, or find out their meanings by asking another student for help. Then, discuss with the rest of your class the two subdivisions of the definition to be sure that you all agree on the same definition of this important word.

M. Stereotypes can be dangerous because they keep us from thinking clearly about other people; stereotypes keep us from seeing other people as they see themselves. Here are some examples about the United States that are untrue, negative stereotypes. *American children do not love their parents and do not take care of them when they are old. Americans are superficial and do not have strong friendships. Americans love their jobs more than their families.* The truth is much more complicated. You are probably aware of stereotypes that other people have about your culture and/or home country. Write three of these stereotypes. For each stereotype, write what you think is a more accurate explanation of your culture. After you have revised and edited the sentences, write them neatly on another sheet of paper to turn in to your instructor. How does it make you feel to think about these stereotypes? What can be done to help people understand each other better?

N. Interview a classmate or an American friend to find out what he or she does during a typical weekend. Then, write a paragraph about the typical weekend. After you are satisfied with the organization and meaning of the paragraph, edit it carefully for verb choices and form. Use the editing method presented in Section Four of this book.

O. Interview a classmate or an American friend to find out how he or she celebrates New Year's Day. You might consider asking about any special activities, parties, food, or customs of this holiday. Then, write a paragraph about what you have learned. After you are satisfied with the organization and meaning of the paragraph, edit it carefully for verb choices and form. Use the editing method presented in Section Four.

Present Perfect: Indefinite Past Time in General Truth Contexts

The present perfect verb form can be used to refer to indefinite past time that is related to the general truth information being presented. The present perfect is also used for this indefinite past time meaning in other time frames. See page 75 for the use of present perfect in past time contexts and page 135 for present perfect in present time contexts.

Formation

The present perfect is made of *have* + the past participle. Subject-verb agreement rules must be followed.

*I **have studied** English for a long time.*

*Up to now, we **have studied** three chapters.*

Use

In this example, the present perfect is used to introduce a topic in the past with an indefinite meaning. Then, the speaker changes to the simple present tense for general truth meanings.

*The XYZ Corporation **has existed** for only a short time. Its rise to power **is** an example of the theory that **has** just **been discussed**. Business success today **depends** on a combination of financing and advertising. Such success also **requires** knowledge of the market and considerable good luck.*

Meaning

Definite means the speaker is talking about a specific past time. The present perfect cannot be used for a specific time in the past.

*The ABC Corporation **existed** for only 10 years. (It does not exist now. Simple past tense means that something happened at a definite time in the past—and is over.)*

The **indefinite** past time means that the event happened in the past "sometime before now." It is possible for the action to continue into the future.

*The XYZ Corporation **has existed** since 1980. (It started in 1980 and continues until now.)*

Time Expressions with the Present Perfect

Since and *for* are often used in present perfect sentences. On page 76, examples are also given with the time expressions *already, recently,* and *yet*. Other time expressions are also possible.

Other time expressions that occur with the present perfect are *so far* and *up to now*.

*Margot **has taken** three English courses **so far**.*

*Helen **has taken** two computer courses **up to now**.*

Practice with the Present Perfect

A. Complete the following sentences. Your sentences should be meaningful, and the verb forms should be correct.

1. _____ since I moved here.

2. _____ so far.

3. _____ since _____ (month).

4. _____ since _____ (day).

5. _____ since 7 A.M. today.

6. _____ for three weeks.

7. _____ up to now.

8. _____ for thirty minutes.

B. The following chart provides information about students, their addresses, and the length of time each student has lived at a particular address.

Student	Address	Length of Time There
Suha	1021 Pennybrook Court	3 years
Terry	62 Island Parkway #58	2 months
Chambers	324 Mary Lane	since 1990
Michelle	5222 11th Street	10 months
Khalid	423 Northlake Drive	since 1988
Janty	62 Island Parkway #21	since December

1. Write three sentences about these students, and use present perfect verb forms together with *since* or *for*.
2. Write three sentences using simple past tense verbs together with *ago*.
3. Write three sentences using simple present tense verbs.

C. Discussion Assignment: What information do you know about the moon? Are there any stories about the moon in your culture? Are there any stories in American culture?

Grammar Assignment: What verb form would you expect to use in a sentence beginning *For hundreds of years*? Identify the time frame in this paragraph, and fill in each blank with the correct form of the verb. Select a verb that fits the meaning of the sentence from the list at the end of each paragraph. Some verbs will be used more than once.

The Environment of the Moon

For the past several hundred years, people _____ at the moon and _____ to analyze it. Much of the information about the moon _____ common knowledge. The moon, the earth's closest neighbor in space, _____ the brightest object in the night sky. However, although the moon _____ to shine brightly each night, it _____ off no light of its own. Instead, it _____ light from the sun. From the earth, the moon _____ to be the same size as the sun because it _____ only 240,000 miles away; the sun _____ more than 92,000,000 miles away.

[Word List: *appear, be, gaze, give, reflect, seem, try*]

No life _____ on the earth's closest neighbor; it _____ no air, water, or wind. The temperatures _____ also extreme. During the day, the temperature _____ higher than 212 degrees Fahrenheit, and during the night, the surface of the moon _____ colder than the North Pole. Although these statements _____ common knowledge, space flights and moon landings _____ to seek additional information to explain the mysteries of the earth, the sun, and the other plants.   [Word List: *be, become, continue, exist, have*]

Adapted from *World Book Encyclopedia*, 1988 ed., s.v. "moon."

Subject-Verb Agreement

One of the most important characteristics of the simple present tense is the relationship between a subject and a verb. This relationship is called **subject-verb agreement.** Fill in the blanks in the sentences that follow the examples. One or two sentences in each set will not fit the rule for that set to encourage you to read each sentence carefully.

Rule 1: Basic Agreement

If the subject of a sentence or clause is a singular-count noun, a singular proper noun, a noncount noun, or *he, she,* or *it,* the verb adds *-s.* Provide the correct form of the verb in parentheses to make these general truth and current time habit statements complete:

> *Lam **goes** home after every class.*
>
> *He **studies** English on Monday evening.*
>
> *He **does not go** to class during the day.*
>
> *His teacher's advice **helps** him.*

1. A good home computer _____ at least $1,000.
   (cost)

2. Maria _____ in the library every day.
   (study)

3. Both students _____ Arabic and French.
   (speak)

4. Kazeem _____ that popcorn _____ good when he
   (think)   (taste)

   studies.

5. He _____ the date of the next test.
   (know, not)

Rule 2: Compound Subjects

A compound subject joins two or more nouns, two or more pronouns, or a noun and a pronoun. A compound subject is plural; two or more singular subjects have been combined to make a plural subject. If the subject of a sentence or clause is a compound subject, use the simple form of the verb. Provide the correct form of the verb in parentheses.

> *Joon and Hai **study** English every morning.*
>
> *He and I **sit** next to each other.*
>
> *Ali and I **work** together.*

1. The faculty and staff _____ their cars in the same parking
   (park)

   lot.

2. Algebra _____ the groundwork for calculus.
   (provide)

3. Juan and I _____ at the university cafeteria every day.
   (eat)

4. History and chemistry _____ my favorite subjects.
   (be)

5. Although he enjoys baseball, soccer _____ to be his favorite
   (continue)

   sport.

Rule 3: Subjects with Prepositional Phrases or Clauses

Prepositional phrases and clauses can come between the subject and verb, but they do not influence subject-verb agreement. Provide the correct form of the verb in parentheses.

> *The student in the front row **studies** accounting.*
>
> *The students who are absent today **know** about the test.*

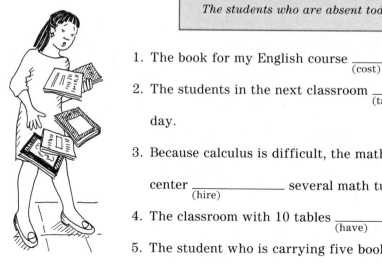

1. The book for my English course _____ $25.00.
   (cost)

2. The students in the next classroom _____ very loudly every
   (talk)

   day.

3. Because calculus is difficult, the math coordinator in the learning

   center _____ several math tutors every term.
   (hire)

4. The classroom with 10 tables _____ 20 chairs in it.
   (have)

5. The student who is carrying five books _____ to need help.
   (seem)

Rule 4: *There/Here*

When the sentence or clause begins with *there* or *here*, the verb agrees with the noun that follows the verb. Although you will often hear Americans violate this rule when they are speaking, it is especially important to follow the rule in your writing. Provide the correct form of the verb.

> *There **are** 20 students in this class.*
>
> *There **is** one student in the front row.*
>
> *Here **comes** Mario; now we can go to the library.*

1. There _____ one book on the desk.
   (be)

2. Here _____ the calculator that you ordered.
   (be)

3. After every computer class, there _____ several students who
   (be)

   stay to work in the lab.

4. Here _____ the books that I need for my report.
   (be)

5. Here _____ the information that I need for my report.
   (be)

Rule 5: Amounts

If a subject indicates distance, time, or amounts of money, the singular form of the verb is used. Often these sentences use forms of *be*. For each sentence below, provide the correct form of *be*.

> *Six hundred miles **is** a long way to drive.*
>
> *Three hours **is** a long test.*
>
> *Sixty dollars **is** too much to pay for a book.*

1. Four miles _____ a long walk to school each morning.

2. Five days _____ a long time to wait for final grades.

3. Two test papers _____ missing from the chairman's office.

4. Six hours of sleep before a test _____ enough for me.

5. Three dollars _____ a lot of money for a package of typing paper.

Rule 6: Indefinite Pronouns

If the subject is a singular indefinite pronoun, the verb adds -s.

> **Singular Indefinite Pronouns**
> ....
>
> *any, anybody, anyone, anything*
>
> *each, either, everybody, everyone, everything*
>
> *neither, nobody, no one, nothing*
>
> *one*
>
> *somebody, someone, something*
>
> ---
>
> *Each student* **needs** *a pen for the test.*
>
> *Neither one* **owes** *any money.*
>
> *Somebody* **needs** *to ask a question.*

1. Everyone _____ the answer to this question.
   (know)

2. Each student _____ a calculator.
   (use)

3. All students _____ a dictionary.
   (need)

4. Neither _____ to choose the essay topic.
   (want)

5. Someone _____ the library every morning.
   (open)

Rule 7: *Either/Or* and *Neither/Nor*

When you use *either/or* or *neither/nor* to form a subject, the word that is closest to the verb controls subject-verb agreement. Provide the correct form of the verb in parentheses.

> *Either the board members or the president* **remembers** *the decision.*
>
> *Neither the president nor the board members* **remember** *the decision.*

1. Neither the students nor their teacher _____ happy about
   $(seem)$
   the test results.

2. Neither the teacher nor the students _____ happy about the
   $(seem)$
   test results.

3. Either history or political science _____ his favorite subject.
   (be)

4. Either the driver or the passengers _____ responsible for
   (be)
   paying the parking ticket.

5. Neither the dean nor the faculty members _____ many
   $(attend)$
   student functions.

Rule 8: False Plurals

Some nouns look like plurals, but they are really singular. The names of many academic disciplines (*mathematics*) and diseases (*measles*) are in this group. Other false plurals include the word *news*. Make a list of the false plurals you already know, and share your list with your classmates.

> *Mathematics* **is** *an important subject for business majors.*
>
> *Measles* **is** *a childhood disease.*
>
> *News* **is** *important.*

Academic Disciplines	Diseases	Others
mathematics	*measles*	*news*

Rule 9: Gerunds and Infinitives

Verbs can be used as nouns either by being changed to **gerunds** (by adding *-ing*) or to **infinitives** (by adding *to*). If the subject of a sentence is a gerund or an infinitive, the present tense form of the verb adds *-s*. See Chapter Sixteen for more information on gerunds and infinitives. Provide the correct form of the verb in parentheses.

> *Choosing a major **takes** thought.*
>
> *To choose a major **takes** thought.*

1. Studying at the library _____ to be a good idea.
   (seem)

2. Jogging and swimming _____ to be my favorite hobbies.
   (continue)

   [Remember Rule #2!]

3. To study _____ not to learn.
   (be)

4. To move to a new city _____ a basic feature of American life.
   (seem)

5. Eating properly and exercising often _____ a student
   (keep)

   healthy.

Practice with Subject-Verb Agreement

A. Analyze your answers to items 46–55 on the Diagnostic Test in First Steps. Then, analyze at least three compositions that you have written in which you have used simple present tense verb forms. Answer the questions on page 453 of the Grammar Journal.

B. After you are certain that you understand each of the basic rules of subject-verb agreement, write one example for each of the nine rules using information from your own life to illustrate each of the basic rules. Exchange your list of examples with another student in the class to have help in checking your accuracy. After making any necessary corrections, record your examples on a sheet of paper to keep in your Grammar Notebook for future reference.

C. Discussion Assignment: Before reading about this particular river, look at a map of the United States to locate the following rivers: the Mississippi River, the Missouri River, the Rio Grande River, and the Columbia River. These rivers are all important to current American economic and political life. Discuss ideas and information that you have about the importance of these rivers.

Grammar Assignment: Complete the following general truth paragraph with simple present tense forms of the verbs in parentheses. Check for subject-verb agreement.

The Mississippi River

The Mississippi River, also called the "Great River,"

_____ the longest river in the United States.
¹(be)

The river _____ at Lake Itasca in the state of
²(originate)

Minnesota. The elevation in Minnesota _____
³(be)

1,670 feet above sea level. The river _____ at
⁴(end)

the Gulf of Mexico where it _____ over half a
⁵(discharge)

million cubic feet of water in the Gulf of Mexico every

second. The Mississippi River system _____
⁶(be)

made up of the Mississippi River and hundreds of tributaries

that feed into it. Major tributaries _____ the
⁷(include)

Missouri River, the Ohio River, the Arkansas River, and the

Red River. The volume of water in the river

_____ as tributaries _____ their
⁸(increase)   ⁹(empty)

water into the Great River from water drained off of more

than 1,150,000 square miles in 31 states.

Adapted from *Encyclopedia Americana*, 1983 ed., s.v. "Mississippi River."

D. Discussion Assignment: The *greenhouse effect* says that the earth is getting warmer. Why is that a problem? Discuss any ideas and information that you have about problems caused by warming climates.

Grammar Assignment: Complete the following general truth paragraph with simple present tense forms of the verbs in parentheses. Check for subject-verb agreement.

The Greenhouse Effect

Scientists _____ an increase in average temperatures
¹(explain)

around the world as the *greenhouse effect*. Greenhouses

_____ glass buildings that _____ people to
²(be)   ³(allow)

grow plants during the entire year. The structure _____
⁴(protect)

plants from bad weather and _____ light, moisture, and a
⁵(provide)

steady flow of heat. The glass walls and roof _____
⁶(allow)

sunlight to penetrate and to heat up the inside. The heat inside a

greenhouse slowly _____ through the roof and walls.
_{7(escape)}
Scientists today _____ the earth as a big greenhouse. The
_{8(picture)}
atmosphere _____ like the glass roof and walls. Sunlight
_{9(act)}
_____ through the atmosphere and _____
_{10(pass)}   _{11(heat)}
the surface of the earth. Similar to the action in a greenhouse, the heat

_____ . Some of the heat, or infrared radiation,
_{12(rise)}

_____ through the atmosphere to outer space, but carbon
_{13(pass)}
dioxide, ozone, and water vapor in the atmosphere _____
_{14(absorb)}
some of it and _____ it back toward the earth to warm
_{15(send)}
the surface even more. The amount of carbon dioxide in the atmosphere

_____ when fossil fuels like coal, oil, and natural gas
_{16(increase)}
_____ and _____ carbon dioxide. According
_{17(burn)}   _{18(release)}
to scientists, if the amount of carbon dioxide in the atmosphere

continues to increase during the next century, the earth's average

temperature might rise by as much as 10 degrees Fahrenheit.

Adapted from *World Book Encyclopedia*, 1988 ed., s.v. "greenhouse" and "greenhouse effect."

E. Discussion Assignment: The world is constantly changing, but change upsets many people. Why is change so difficult? What things are changing in your life right now? How can people best deal with change?
    Grammar Assignment:

1. What time frame should you use for this topic?
2. Why?
3. Using the verbs listed at the end, add verbs to the sentences, and then check your verb choices with a partner. Some verbs are used more than one time.
4. Which sentences need verbs with -s endings?

Changes in Family Relationships in Refugee and Immigrant Families

[1]In traditional Asian societies, the social position of the elderly

_____ generally very high, both in the society at large and

within the family unit. [2]In extended Indo-Chinese families, the elderly members _____ "the pillars" of the clan. [3]They

_____ other family members a sense of continuity,

strength, and support. [4]The elders _____ great respect.

[5]They _____ the cultural values and traditions to their

children and grandchildren.

[6]However, in the United States, school-age children, who usually

assimilate language and culture faster than their parents and

grandparents, often _____ themselves in the unusual role

of interpreting that language and culture to their elders. [7]At the same

time, the older individuals suddenly _____ students. [8]The

role reversal _____ very difficult to accept for both the

older and the younger generation, and it often _____

intergenerational tensions.   [**Word List: *be, become, cause, find, give,***

receive, transmit]

Adapted from Gozdziak, Elzbieta. *Aging: Older Immigrants Find a New Life.* Human
Development Services, Department of Health and Human Services Publication no. 359.
Washington, D.C.: GPO, 1989.

F. Analyze the sentences in the paragraph in exercise E by sentence
type (simple, compound, complex, or compound-complex).

Sentence 1 is _____   Sentence 5 is _____

Sentence 2 is _____   Sentence 6 is _____

Sentence 3 is _____   Sentence 7 is _____

Sentence 4 is _____   Sentence 8 is _____

Practice with the General Truth Time Frame

A. Discussion Assignment: Do you eat a balanced diet? Write down
everything that you ate yesterday, and see if you had something from
each of the food groups listed on the next page.

Grammar Assignment: Use a highlighter to mark the verbs in each sentence.

How many subjects required a verb with -s? _____

How many plural subjects are used? _____

Healthy Eating

[1]No single food supplies all of the essential nutrients in the amounts that the body needs, so it is important, especially for growing children, to eat a variety of foods. [2]Eating foods from each of the following four food groups daily helps to ensure a balanced diet:

Meat, Poultry, Fish, Eggs

Milk and Milk Products (dairy)

Breads and Cereals (grains)

Vegetables and Fruits

- fruits and vegetables;
- meat, poultry, fish, eggs, and dried beans and peas;
- milk and cheese; and
- whole-grain breads and cereals.

[3]Bread, cereals, and other grain products provide B vitamins, iron, protein, and fiber. [4]Fruits and vegetables are good sources of vitamin A, vitamin C, folic acid, fiber, and many minerals. [5]Meats, poultry, fish, eggs, and dried beans and peas supply protein, iron and other minerals, as well as several B vitamins. [6]Milk and cheese are major sources of calcium—very important in the diets of children and teenagers. [7]Storing as much calcium as possible in the bones in younger years helps to prevent osteoporosis later in life.

[8]Although people benefit from snacking, we often fall into the habit of constantly eating the same foods. [9]Snacks sometimes even replace,

rather than supplement, regular meals. [10]And snack foods often do not provide the variety of nutrients that we need. [11]For example, a soda that replaces milk at lunch reduces the amount of calcium in the person's diet. [12]Therefore, those of us who like to snack on soft drinks need to have a cheeseburger, rather than a plain burger, with our drinks. [13]A slice of cheese pizza is another good snack that adds calcium to the diet. [14]Because of the high stress in their lives, students, especially, need to remember to have a balanced diet even if it is high in snack foods which are eaten between classes or on the way to work.

Adapted from U.S. Food and Drug Administration. Public Health Service, Department of Health and Human Services. "The 'Grazing of America': A Guide to Healthy Snacking." *FDA Consumer*, vol. 23, no. 2. Washington, D.C.: GPO, 1988.

B. Discussion Assignment: What does the word *work* mean to you? What work do you do right now? What work do you think you will do in the future? Number each of the explanations given in the passage for the reasons people work: How many are listed? What others can you suggest? Why do people stop working?

Grammar Assignment: Write in the space provided the correct form of the verb in parentheses.

Why Do People Work?

A person _____ for all kinds of reasons. Most people
1(work)
_____ , first and foremost, to make money. They
2(work)
_____ to be able to buy necessities like food, clothing, and
3(work)
a place to live. They _____ , too, for the money to buy
4(work)
leisure and convenience goods like cars, stereo equipment, movie tickets, and sporting equipment. The list of things that people

_____ to spend money on _____ very long
5(like)   6(be)
indeed. People also _____ money for major expenditures—
7(need)
education, travel, medical bills, and retirement. For many people, work

_____ a means of earning a living and nothing more.
8(be)
There _____ nothing wrong with that, but there
9(be)
_____ other satisfactions that _____ from
10(be)   11(come)
working.

Socializing with other people _____ to be an
_{12(seem)}
important part of work for many people. They _____
_{13(make)}
friends and _____ new people. Satisfaction from seeing
_{14(meet)}
the results of their efforts _____ another reason for
_{15(be)}
working. Many jobs and careers _____ creation of
_{16(involve)}
products. Carpenters, jewelers, mechanics, and chefs

_____ the pleasure of making things for other people's
_{17(have)}
approval and use. Other people _____ for ways to express
_{18(look)}
their creative abilities. Some of these people _____ a
_{19(find)}
place in the glamourous and often insecure world of dance, music, art,

fashion, writing, or publishing. Some people _____ a job
_{20(want)}
that _____ them to be physically active all day long.
_{21(permit)}
Others _____ ways to work outdoors.
_{22(seek)}

A third reason for working _____ to help other
_{23(be)}
people. Some people _____ jobs that _____
_{24(choose)}   _{25(give)}
them a chance to do something useful for society. Many people

_____ a strong desire to put their talents and efforts into
_{26(have)}
something that _____ the common good. Police officers,
_{27(promote)}
teachers, medical doctors, and wildlife conservation officers

_____ just a few of the people who _____
_{28(be)}   _{29(work)}
for society as a whole.

Self-esteem _____ an important reason for working.
_{30(be)}
People _____ to feel that their work _____
_{31(need)}   _{32(be)}
worthwhile. These people _____ with their work. Many
_{33(identify)}
other people _____ that work _____ so
_{34(think)}   _{35(be not)}
important. They _____ elsewhere for the feeling that
_{36(look)}
their lives _____ worthwhile. They _____
_{37(be)}   _{38(find)}
their happiness with their families and friends and their hobbies and

leisure activities.

Adapted from U.S. Department of Labor. Bureau of Labor Statistics. *Exploring Careers.*
Bulletin 2001. Washington, D.C.: GPO, 1979.

C. Discussion Assignment: Why do researchers study topics like the one in the following passage? The U.S. government warns citizens about health dangers. Have you seen any of these warnings about smoking? about drinking alcoholic beverages? about drugs? Where did you see them? Do you think it is the business of the government to interfere in the lives of individual citizens?

Grammar Assignment: Use a highlighter to mark the verbs in all dependent and independent clauses in "Smoking, Drinking and Oral Cancer."

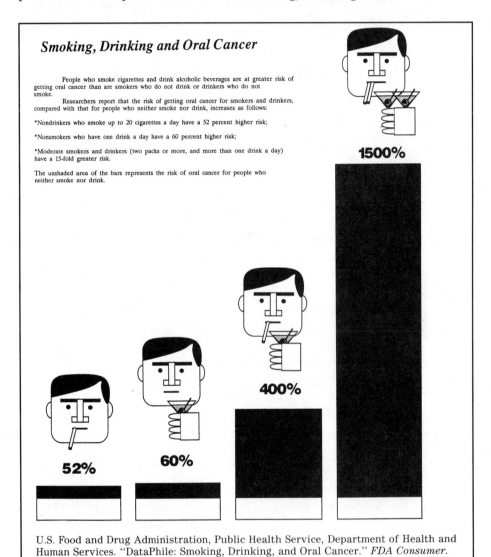

Smoking, Drinking and Oral Cancer

People who smoke cigarettes and drink alcoholic beverages are at greater risk of getting oral cancer than are smokers who do not drink or drinkers who do not smoke.

Researchers report that the risk of getting oral cancer for smokers and drinkers, compared with that for people who neither smoke nor drink, increases as follows:

*Nondrinkers who smoke up to 20 cigarettes a day have a 52 percent higher risk;

*Nonsmokers who have one drink a day have a 60 percent higher risk;

*Moderate smokers and drinkers (two packs or more, and more than one drink a day) have a 15-fold greater risk.

The unshaded area of the bars represents the risk of oral cancer for people who neither smoke nor drink.

1500%

400%

52% **60%**

U.S. Food and Drug Administration, Public Health Service, Department of Health and Human Services. "DataPhile: Smoking, Drinking, and Oral Cancer." *FDA Consumer*. Washington, D.C.: GPO, 1989, 40.

How many subjects required a verb with -*s*? _____

How many plural subjects are used? _____

D. Discussion Assignment: Do you like to play games? What kinds of games do you prefer? Do you like word games or action games? Are crossword puzzles popular in your country? Have you ever played one in English? You might enjoy working the crossword puzzles on pages 60 and 62 in Chapter Two and on page 324 of Chapter Thirteen.

Grammar Assignment: Mark all the complete verbs for each sentence in the following passage by underlining them twice. To analyze the kinds of verbs used by the writer, list the forms on the chart given on the next page. Discuss with the other students in your class the uses of the different verb forms in the article: why does the writer use simple present tense in some sentences but other verb forms in different sentences?

Crossword Puzzles

[1]Crossword puzzles <u>are</u> popular word games throughout the world. [2]They <u>are</u> a combination of black and white squares. [3]The answers to numbered word clues provide the letters that fill the blocks. [4]A person who wants to solve a crossword puzzle writes each letter of the answer in the row of empty squares which starts with the same number as the number of the clue. [5]Besides the clues, solvers can use the letters from one word to guess the letters of the missing words. [6]An American journalist developed the first crossword puzzle in 1913. [7]It appeared in the Sunday edition of the New York *World* newspaper on December 21, 1913. [8]The game fascinated Americans, and crossword puzzles were soon appearing in other newspapers in the United States. [9]In 1924, the first book of crossword puzzles appeared, and the new fad spread to other countries and other languages. [10]Crossword puzzle books and dictionaries became popular gifts in the 1920s. [11]Today, crossword puzzles appear in many languages throughout the world. [12]Since 1913, many games have become popular, but crossword puzzles have continued to remain popular and to become more challenging. [13]Their popularity will probably continue for many more years.

Adapted from *Encyclopedia Americana*, 1983 ed., s.v. "crossword puzzle."

Verb Forms Found in "Crossword Puzzles"

Put in the appropriate column the verbs that you identified in "Crossword Puzzles." The first two sentences are done for you.

Simple Present Tense	Simple Past Tense	Modal with Verb	Present or Past Perfect	Present or Past Progressive
1. *are*				
2. *are*				
3.				
4.				
5.				
6.				
7.				
8.				
9.				
10.				
11.				
12.				
13.				

E. Use the information provided in the following chart to write 10 sentences about Turkey. Compare your sentences to those of other students in your class. Together select the most interesting 10 sentences that make up a description that would be helpful to someone who does not know anything about that country. Edit the sentences carefully, especially for subject-verb agreement. After editing the sentences, keep them in your Grammar Notebook for future reference.

Turkey at a Glance

Population:	52.8 million
Population growth rate:	2.8 percent
Area:	766,640 sq. km.: slightly larger than Texas
Religion:	Moslem (98 percent)
Government:	Parliamentary democracy
Language:	Turkish
GNP per capita	$1,292
Foreign visitors (1988)	4.17 million
Composition of GNP (1988)	
Agriculture	16 percent
Industry	34 percent
Construction	4 percent
Trade	18 percent
Transportation	10 percent
Exports (1988)	$11.6 billion
Imports (1988)	$14.3 billion
Composition of Imports	
Investment goods	27.8 percent
Raw materials	64.4 percent
Consumer goods	7.8 percent
Natural resources	coal, chromite, copper, boron, oil
Agricultural products	cotton, tobacco, cereals, sugar beets, fruits, and nuts
Industry (types)	textiles, processed foodstuffs, iron and steel, cement, and leather goods

Jackson, Geoffrey. "Turkey's Sixth Five-Year Development Plan Offers Promising Opportunities for U.S. Firms." *Business America: The Magazine of International Trade* (June 19, 1989), 19. Washington, D.C.: U.S. Department of Commerce.

F. In the reference area of your library, find an up-to-date chart or table with information about your country similar to that provided about Turkey. A reference librarian can help you find such information in publications of the United Nations. If you are from Turkey, find information about another country that interests you. Bring a photocopy of the chart or table to class. Prepare 10 sentences about your country based on the factual information that you found in the chart or table. After you have revised and edited the sentences carefully, write them on a sheet of paper. Include a complete reference to the source of your information. Then, share your information with another student from a different country. Be sure to keep your own information in your Grammar Notebook for future reference.

G. Consider the strengths and weaknesses of the school (or city) where you are now studying. You might consider tuition, housing and food, transportation, course selection, facilities, cultural adjustments, recreational opportunities, or anything else you choose. Write a paragraph to explain these strengths and weaknesses. After you are satisfied with the organization and meaning of the paragraph, edit it carefully for verb choice and form. Use the editing method presented in Section Four of this book.

H. Think about a typical day in your life. Then, write a paragraph that describes such a day. After you are satisfied with the organization and meaning of the paragraph, edit it carefully for verb choice and form. Use the editing method presented in Section Four of this book.

I. For additional writing topics and the editing summary for this chapter, turn to Section Four, page 425.

CHAPTER

4

• •

Present Time Frame

CHAPTER ORGANIZATION

Verb Choices for Present Time Meaning
The Grammar of the Present Progressive
The Meaning of the Present Progressive
The Grammar of Stative Verbs
　　Have as a Stative Verb
　　Be as a Stative Verb
Stative Verb Groups
Time Expressions for Present Time Meanings
Present Perfect: Indefinite Past Time in Present Time Contexts

• • • • • • • • • • • • •

Verb Choices for Present Time Meaning

The most frequently used verb forms for present time meaning are the **present progressive** and the **simple present tense.**

These two verb forms have very different meanings and cannot be substituted for each other.

general truth
*Most students **go** through a difficult transition when they graduate from high school and enter a university.*

present time
*Anna, a freshmen, **is** now **going** through the transition from being a high school student to being a university student.*

Present Progressive
The present progressive verb form describes **actions** or situations in progress at the moment of speaking.

present time: active
*You **are reading** this example right now.*

Present Tense (Stative Meaning)
The simple present tense verb form is used with a special group of verbs to describe **states of being** rather than actions.

present time: stative
*He **feels** tired right now because he stayed up late studying for the test.*

For most verbs, the most common meaning of simple present tense is "general truth" or "habitual action."

general truth
*In the U.S., all students **study** English.*

For most verbs, the most common meaning of the present progressive verb form is "present time event."

present time
*You **are studying** English this term.*

Students in U.S. colleges and universities rarely write about present time personal events except in ESL and in freshman English classes. If you take a writing course, you might be assigned to write about personal topics that may require the use of the present progressive verb form to describe present time events. In other classes, most writing is about the past or about general truth. However, "A View of the United States in the Late Twentieth Century" on page 138 illustrates present-time writing on a non-personal subject.

The Grammar of the Present Progressive

The **progressive verb form** combines *be* with the *-ing* form of the verb. It can be either present tense or past tense. (The past progressive is explained on pages 57 and 71 in Chapter Two.) Another name for the progressive is the **continuous** verb form.

Compare the verbs in the two examples. Both refer to the present time. Notice that subject-verb agreement must be followed.

*He **is studying** architecture now.*

*He and his friend **are studying** architecture at the same university.*

Practice with the Present Progressive

To find out if you have any problems with spelling the *-ing* form of the verb, write the correct *-ing* form for each of the following verbs. You can use your dictionary and Appendix C to check your answers. What can you do to improve the accuracy of your spelling?

1. finish _____	10. work _____
2. try _____	11. remember _____
3. come _____	12. enjoy _____
4. help _____	13. plan _____
5. decide _____	14. sleep _____
6. open _____	15. complete _____
7. beg _____	16. ride _____
8. begin _____	17. solve _____
9. start _____	18. rain _____

19. write   _____

20. read   _____

21. watch   _____

22. draw   _____

23. date   _____

24. hide   _____

25. study   _____

26. make   _____

27. hop   _____

28. answer   _____

29. stop   _____

30. run   _____

31. buy   _____

32. become   _____

33. sit   _____

34. consider   _____

35. hope   _____

36. travel   _____

The Meaning of the Present Progressive

The **present progressive** can be used for the following meanings. The use of present progressive for future time is explained on page 169 in Chapter Six.

Present Time Action
The present progressive is used for actions in progress at the present time.

present time
You **are reading** this sentence now.

present time
You **are studying** English this term.

Repeated Present Time Actions
The present progressive form of some verbs means a repetition of an action in present time.

present time
He **is tapping** his pencil on the desk.

Future Time
The present progressive can be used for future time actions. A time word is usually used to make the future time meaning clear.

future time
They **are buying** a new computer tomorrow.

Practice with the Meaning of Present Progressive

A. Complete the following sentences about your classmates; the information should be true at the present time.

My Classmates

1. _____ is living at _____ .

2. _____ is working at _____ .

3. _____ is talking to _____ .

4. _____ is sitting beside _____ .

5. _____ is writing in *Applied English Grammar*.

6. _____ is sitting in front of _____ .

B. Write ten sentences that answer the following ten questions about what you are doing right now. After editing your sentences for verb form and spelling, put them in your Grammar Notebook to use as examples.

My Current Actions

1. Where are you sitting?
2. What are you doing?
3. What are you thinking about?
4. What are you doing with your right hand?
5. What are you writing?
6. What are you wearing?
7. What student are you sitting beside?
8. Where is your teacher standing?
9. What are you studying?
10. Where are you living?

C. Write five questions for the following five answers. Turn to Chapter Seven if you have problems with the grammar of questions.

Questions

1. Answer: Bridget is sharpening her pencil now.

   Question: *Who* _____?

2. Answer: Twenty students are currently studying *Applied English Grammar*.

   Question: *How many* _____?

3. Answer: Sean is studying physics this term.

   Question: *What* _____?

4. Answer: Tuan is working in the library today.

   Question: *Where* _____?

5. Answer: Cynthia is coughing right now.

   Question: *What* _____?

D. Write sentences to answer the following questions using the present progressive verb form. Discuss your answers with the rest of your class. Then, make any necessary corrections in your sentences.

Right Now

1. What are you thinking about "at this moment"?

   At this moment, I am thinking about verbs. _____

2. What are you doing "right now"?
3. Think about a friend who is not in the classroom. What is this friend "probably" doing "right now"?
4. What courses are you taking "this term"?
5. Where are you planning to go "this summer"?
6. What is your teacher doing "right now"?

E. Pretend you are sitting in a library and observing several students. Use the correct form of each verb to describe what you see. Compare your answers to those of other students in your class, and make any necessary corrections.

The Library

1. Magid *is looking for* ____ a book on pollution.   (look for)

2. Toan _____ to a reference librarian.   (talk)

3. Sylvia _____ Maria with her report.   (help)

4. Two students _____ together for the   (study)
   vocabulary test.

5. Sonia and Kinfe _____ newspapers.   (read)

6. Mahmoud _____ the microfilm reader.   (use)

7. Four students _____ at one table.   (sit)

8. Everyone _____ very hard.   (work)

F. Complete the sentences with the verbs in parentheses. Choose between the simple present or the present progressive verb forms. Discuss the reasons for your choices with the other students in your class.

Comparisons

1. Mazin eats____ lunch in the student cafeteria every day.

   He is eating____ lunch there right now.   (eat)

2. Tuan _____ to school now.

   He _____ to school every day.   (drive)

3. David usually _____ tea with his lunch.

   He _____ tea right now.   (drink)

4. Maria _____ her homework now.

   She frequently _____ her homework on the bus.   (do)

5. Mohammad _____ in the front row every

   day. He _____ in the front row now.   (sit)

G. Complete the sentences with the verbs in parentheses. Choose between the simple present or the present progressive verb forms. Discuss your reasons for your choices with your classmates.

Contrasts

1. Tuan always _____ Vietnamese when he is

   at home, but right now he _____ English.   (speak)

2. Sara _____ calculus now, but she

   _____ English every weekend.   (study)

3. Emmanuella and Zubair seldom _____

   together; however, they _____ together   (work)
   right now.

4. Jean always _____ math problems quickly,

   but this time, he _____ a problem slowly   (solve)
   and with difficulty.

5. Bachir usually _____ two novels every

   week; however, he _____ only one novel   (read)
   this week.

H. Complete the sentences with the verbs in parentheses. Choose between the simple present or the present progressive verb forms. Discuss your reasons for your choices with your classmates.

Carol and Sylvia

1. Carol _____ hard every day.   (study)

2. She _____ three classes this term.   (take)

3. She _____ every day with an 8 A.M. class.   (begin)

4. She _____ in her math class right now.   (sit)

5. Carol and Sylvia _____ an English grammar   (have)
   class at 1 P.M. every day.

6. They _____ passive voice this week.   (study)

7. Carol and Sylvia _____ to their last class   (walk)
right now.

8. After their last class, they always _____ to   (go)
the library to study.

I. An action in the future can also be expressed by using the present progressive verb form. A future time expression is needed to indicate future meaning.

*Cristina is taking chemistry **next term**.*

*They are attending a lecture **tomorrow**.*

Identify which sentences express a future action (future) and which sentences express an action going on right now (present).

I am taking a test tomorrow.   *future*_____

I am writing a grammar exercise right now.   *present*_____

Mohammad and Rudy

1. Mohammad is sitting in the cafeteria alone.   _____

2. He is writing an essay.   _____

3. He is leaving for class in 10 minutes.   _____

4. Rudy is taking swimming lessons right now.   _____

5. He is going swimming tomorrow.   _____

J. Look around your classroom, and describe (by name) what five classmates are doing right now. Share your five sentences with the rest of your class. After making any necessary changes, keep your sentences in your Grammar Notebook for future reference. Example: *Larissa is looking for a pen at this moment.*

K. Go to the student cafeteria, and write five sentences that describe the actions of the people you see. Use the present progressive verb tense. Share your five sentences with the rest of your class. After making any necessary changes, keep your sentences in your Grammar Notebook for future reference. Example: *One student is paying for his food right now.*

The Grammar of Stative Verbs

· ·

The adjective **stative** refers to "states of being" in contrast to actions. The difference in meaning between stative and non-stative can be seen in the difference between the verbs *love* (a state of being) and *walk* (an action).

Stative verbs use simple present tense to mean present time. The hamburger is not doing anything.

present time state of being
*This hamburger **seems** expensive.*

Non-stative verbs use present progressive to mean present time. You are doing the action of reading.

present time action
*You **are reading** this example.*

It is more accurate to think of stative as a kind of meaning that a verb can have. For example, *taste* has two different meanings.

This is a state-of-being meaning. The soup is not doing anything.

present time state of being
*The soup **tastes** good.*

The cook is doing an action.

present time action
*The cook **is tasting** the soup.*

Have as a Stative Verb

Have can also be used for either an active or a stative meaning.

Ownership is seen as a fact. It is complete and not in process.

*He **has** a computer.*

The trouble is a fact of his life. It is a general truth statement about his ability to do calculus.

*He **has** trouble with calculus.*

The trouble is not complete, but is an action going on right now in the present time. He is taking calculus and not doing very well in the course.

*He **is having** a lot of trouble with calculus.*

Be as a Stative Verb

The most commonly used stative verb is *be*.

Generally, the simple present tense is used for present time meanings.

correct
*He **is** a student.*
incorrect
*He is being a student.

When selecting the verb form, you must consider whether the meaning refers to an action or to a state of being. The list of **stative verbs** can serve as a guide to help you make your choice, but you cannot use it without thought.

The verbs listed in the following chart are usually used for stative meanings.

Stative Verb Groups

1. verbs of the five **senses**	*appear*　　*see* *feel*　　　*smell* *hear*　　　*taste* *look* (when it means "appear")
2. verbs for **mental states**	*believe*　　*remember* *doubt*　　　*suppose* *imagine*　　*think* *know*　　　*understand* *mean*　　　*wonder* *recognize*
3. verbs to describe **emotions**	*appreciate*　*love* *desire*　　　*need* *dislike*　　　*prefer* *hate*　　　　*seem* *like*　　　　*want*
4. verbs of **ownership, possession,** 　　or **relationship**	*belong* *contain* *have* *own*
5. verbs for **measuring**	*cost* *equal* *measure* *weigh*

Practice with Stative Meanings

Complete the sentences with the verbs in parentheses. Choose between the simple present (for stative or for general truth meanings) or the present progressive verb forms (for present time actions).

Different Students

1. Right now, Tai *is reading*___ the *New York Times*, but he
   (read)

   does not understand it. Many words _____ very
   (read)   (be)

   difficult.

2. Right now, Sonia _____ in the back row of a history
   (sit)

   class. Because she _____ glasses but does not wear
   (need)

   them, she _____ trouble reading the writing on the
   (have)

   blackboard.

3. Right now, Mansoo _____ about his family. Although he
   (think)

   has not seen them in eight months, he _____ that they
   (believe)

   are healthy and happy.

4. Andrew _____ Miami. Although he lived in San Diego
   (like)

   for most of his teenage years, he _____ Miami to San
   (prefer)

   Diego. He _____ to stay in Miami forever, but he
   (want)

   _____ to go to college in Atlanta for one year.
   (plan)

5. Twenty students _____ in class right now. They
   (be)

   _____ a test. One student _____ absent.
   (take)   (be)

Time Expressions for Present Time Meanings

· ·

The following words are frequently used with the present progressive verb form.

at the moment	*Seetha is sitting in class* **at the moment.**
currently	*She is* **currently** *studying verb meanings.*
now, right now	*She is using her textbook* **right now.**
this week, this month	*She is studying present time* **this week.**
today	*She is writing a paragraph* **today.**
Time markers (*now, at this moment*) can be used to identify actions that are happening right now.	*Juan is reading this example* **right now.**
Time markers such as *today, this morning,* or *this week* are used for current times larger than just the present moment.	*He is studying English grammar* **this term.** *He is living in the U.S.* **this year.**

· ·

Practice with Present Time Meaning

A. In the space provided here, write sentences about your activities. Compare your answers to those of other students in your class. How are your lives alike? How are they different?

1. _____ this week.

2. _____ today.

133

3. _____ right now.

4. _____ this month.

5. _____ at this moment.

B. Complete the following sentences with the verbs in parentheses. Circle the time expressions.

1. Juan _____ this page right now.
   (read)

2. He _____ English grammar at the moment.
   (study)

3. Larissa and Maria _____ calculus together this
   (take)

   term.

4. They _____ beside each other today in ESL class.
   (sit)

5. Juan, Larissa, and Maria _____ to study at the
   (currently, plan)

   library later today.

C. Write the time expression that best completes each sentence. Use each expression twice in this review of time expressions.

   a. *for 30 minutes*   c. *right now*   e. *yesterday*
   b. *every day*   d. *since last week*

1. We ate lunch in the student cafeteria _____ .

2. The student behind me has had a cold _____ .

3. I try to study for five hours _____ .

4. My roommate has watched television until midnight

   _____ .

5. I took a midterm exam _____ .

6. My roommate is studying _____ . In fact, he has

   not moved _____ .

7. We eat lunch in the student cafeteria _____ .

8. I am working on a grammar exercise _____ , and I

   have worked on verbs _____ .

Present Perfect: Indefinite Past Time in Present Time Contexts

The **present perfect** verb form can be used to refer to indefinite past time that is related to the present time. The present perfect is also used for this indefinite past time meaning in other time frames. See page 75 for the use of present perfect in past time contexts and page 100 for present perfect in general truth contexts.

Formation

The present perfect is made of *have* + the past participle. Subject-verb agreement rules must be followed.

*Alexios **has studied** French for two years.*

*He and his sister **have visited** France.*

Use

Present perfect is used to introduce a topic in the past with an indefinite meaning. Then, the speaker changes to the present progressive for present time meanings.

*The university **has offered** computer courses for 10 years. Currently, the Computer Science Department **is discussing** major changes in the courses. The professors **are meeting** each week, and students **are waiting** to learn about changes in requirements.*

Meaning

Definite means the speaker is talking or writing about a specific time in the past. The present perfect cannot be used for a specific time in the past. The action was completed in the past and cannot continue in the present.

*The university **offered** Greek courses for 10 years but stopped teaching the courses in 1975. (The university taught Greek courses from 1965 to 1975 and does not offer Greek courses now.)*

The **indefinite** past time refers to a period of time that began in the past and has not stopped. It is possible for the action to continue into the present. The past time is thought of as related to present time.

*The university **has offered** ESL for 10 years. Over 200 students are taking ESL this year. (The university started ESL courses 10 years ago and continues them now.)*

Practice with the Present Perfect

A. Discussion Assignment: How did the universe begin? When did it begin? How can we find out these answers? Have you ever heard of the Hubble telescope or the U.S. space shuttle? Do you believe in spending billions of dollars to find out more about our universe?

Grammar Assignment: Place double lines under each complete verb. Why do you think the writer made these choices? Then, answer the questions after the paragraph.

Our Universe and Its Creation

[1]Since human beings first turned their eyes toward the glittering sky, they have searched for answers to questions about life and the beginnings of life. [2]In the past few years, the stars have yielded some of their secrets; however, they have not given us all of the answers to our questions. [3]Today's theory of an expanding universe best fits what scientists have already observed. [4]The first hint of this theory came from Edwin Hubble's discovery in 1929 that galaxies are moving away from us. [5]In Hubble's explanation, all the major objects in the universe are speeding away from one another. [6]Arno Penzias and Robert Wilson won the Nobel Prize in Physics in 1978 when they aimed a huge satellite radio antenna skyward and detected a faint signal that came uniformly

The Great Galaxy in Adromeda

from all parts of the sky. [7]Although most astronomers today believe in Hubble's explanation for a big bang beginning of the universe, many are still arguing over basic details, such as how old the universe is. [8]They are waiting for the Hubble telescope and a series of space probes to provide answers to their questions.

Adapted from Cook, William J., and Joannie Schrof. "Journey to the Beginning of Time," *U.S. News & World Report* (March 26, 1990): 54.

1. How many present perfect forms did you find?   _____

2. How many present tense forms did you find?   _____

3. How many present progressive forms did you find?   _____

4. How many past tense forms did you find?   _____

B. Discuss the following chart with the other students in your class. How does the chart work? What type of information is given?

ESL 085 Advanced Reading

Student Name	Title of Book Assigned	Author	Pages Read by Today	Total Pages in Book
Suha	*The Red Badge of Courage*	Crane	97	109
Terry	*Moby Dick*	Melville	22	114
Chambers	*Moby Dick*	Melville	81	114
Michelle	*The Red Badge of Courage*	Crane	43	109
Khalid	*A Tale of Two Cities*	Dickens	97	140
Janty	*A Tale of Two Cities*	Dickens	40	140

C. Using the information from the chart in exercise B, write three sentences using present perfect verb forms (for indefinite past time meaning), three sentences using present progressive verb forms (for present time actions), and three sentences using simple present tense (for general truth or stative meanings). Provide as much information as possible in each sentence. After editing your sentences, share them with other students in your class. Make any necessary changes, and then keep the example sentences in your Grammar Notebook for future reference.

Suha has read 97 pages of The Red Badge of Courage *by Crane, but Michelle has read only 43 pages.*

Suha and Michelle are reading The Red Badge of Courage.

Suha needs to read 12 pages of her novel, but Michelle has 66 pages of hers to read.

Practice with the Present Time Frame

A. Analyze the answers that you gave on the diagnostic paragraph, the diagnostic test, and any other writing that you have done recently about present time events. Did you have any problems with present progressive, present tense, or stative verbs? What kinds of problems did you have? Analyze your knowledge of and use of these verb forms in the space provided on page 454 of the Grammar Journal.

B. Discussion Assignment: Americans are supposed to like change and not to be interested in the past. However, people also say that change is difficult and hard on their nerves. What is your attitude toward change? Do you value the past of your family and/or your culture? Do you agree that Americans seem to like change? What evidence can you give for your opinion?

Grammar Assignment: This passage illustrates the use of the present progressive for writing that is impersonal and academic. Underline each complete verb twice. Use the chart given after the paragraph to list the different types of verbs that are used. Why does the author change from one type to the other?

A View of the United States in the Late Twentieth Century

[1]Our advanced industrial nation is changing. [2]Our society is changing: more people are old, fewer people are young, and more come from minority groups. [3]Our industry is changing: we are no longer the world economic leader; instead, we are a competitor with other

industrial nations. ⁴Our education system is changing: although our colleges and universities are crowded, they are becoming more and more dependent on foreign students and faculty. ⁵Our public school education system has reached a crisis state in which U.S. students do not score as high as students from other countries. ⁶Our present scientific and engineering workforce—the foundation for U.S. technological, economic, and military leadership—is weakening due to retirements and declining student interest. ⁷One of America's most urgent tasks is to strengthen our science and engineering workforce. ⁸Our educational system from prekindergarten through the Ph.D. is failing to produce the workers that we need to meet future demand. ⁹Indeed, unless parents, schools, colleges, professional societies, industry, state legislatures, federal agencies, the president, and Congress agree, our science and engineering workforce will continue to have problems, and the prospects for maintaining an advanced industrial society will decrease.

Adapted from The Task Force on Women, Minorities, and the Handicapped in Science and Technology. *Changing America: The New Face of Science and Engineering: Interim Report.* Washington, D.C.: GPO, 1988.

Verb Forms	Examples from the Paragraph
1. _____	_____
2. _____	_____
3. _____	_____
4. _____	_____
5. _____	_____

C. Write a composition about changes that are occurring in someone or someplace that you know about. You could write about changes in yourself, in your family, in your culture, in your city, or in your school. Be sure to give specific examples for each of the changes that you discuss. You might share your first draft with another student to see if he or she has any questions about your ideas or your examples. After you have revised the composition for meaning, then edit the verbs carefully for form and spelling.

5

Modals

CHAPTER ORGANIZATION

"Modal Auxiliary Verb" Defined

The nine words in the chart are called the **modal auxiliary verbs.** They are listed in pairs of related words. Only *must* does not have a related word. Other words such as *have to* and *ought to* have similar meanings. They will also be presented in this chapter. The traditional definitions used for each of the modal auxiliaries are given in Appendix D.

can	could
may	might
shall	should
must	—
will	would

The Basic Grammar of the Modal Auxiliaries

Formation
For its basic form, the modal auxiliary combines with the simple form of a verb without *to*.

correct
He can speak French.

Three Common Errors
One of the most common errors for students is to add the unnecessary *to*.

incorrect
He can ̶t̶o̶ speak French.

Subject-verb agreement does not apply to modal auxiliaries.

incorrect
He can̶s̶ speak French.

Two modals cannot be used together in the same verb phrase.

incorrect
He will c̶a̶n̶ be able to speak Spanish next year.

Words with Similar Meanings

English has other words that have almost the same meaning as some of the modals; grammarians call these verbs **semi-modals** or **paraphrastic modals.** These synonyms are very important because of their frequent use in spoken and written English.

Synonyms for the Modals

Modal	Semi-Modal (Synonym)	Traditional Definition
can	*be able to*	"ability" or "possibility"
should	*ought to*	"duty" or "obligation"
should	*had better*	"strong advice"
must	*have to*	"necessity" or "requirement"

Ought to and *had better* are not usually used in formal written English, but they are often used in speaking and in informal writing.

Dr. Jones said, "You **ought to be here early for the test.**"

Maria said, "You **had better return** the book to the library today, or you **will have to pay** a fine."

Have to and *be able to* are useful synonyms for *must* and *can*, especially for combining with the basic modals. Remember you cannot combine two modals; however, you can combine a semi-modal with a modal.

He **might be able to attend** the conference.

You **could have to retype** the whole paper.

Practice with *Have To* and *Be Able To*

Write five sentences about results of your university education using combinations of modals with *have to* and *be able to*. Use several different modals for different meanings. Share your examples with the other students in your class to learn about their plans and expectations for their education. After you have revised and edited the sentences, write them on a sheet of paper to keep in your Grammar Notebook for future reference. The following are examples of the kinds of sentences that you might write:

1. *I should be able to speak English better.*
2. *I should be able to get a very good job.*
3. *I will have to give up my independence when I return to live with my family.*

4. *I want to live in California, but I could have to work in my father's business in New Jersey.*
5. *I might be able to go to graduate school, but on the other hand I might need to work for a few years to have enough money for the rest of my education.*

The Modal Auxiliary System

When English speakers use one modal, they are thinking about it in relation to the other modals. To use the modals accurately and fluently, you should think about them as a system.

In addition to future time meanings, modals are used for two major types of meaning: (1) to give advice and ask permission and (2) to guess and to predict. The modals can be ranked from weaker to stronger for each meaning. Each of these systems is discussed in detail later in this chapter.

Using Modals to Give Advice

When people give advice to friends, they often use the modals. When someone asks, "*What should I do?*" our answers frequently include various modals for these meanings: the answer gets stronger as you move down this list from *can* to *will*.

Meaning System for Giving Advice

Situation: You ask for advice about courses to take next term: "*What courses should I take next term?*"

143

Modal	Meaning	Example
can, could, may, or *might*	"These are your choices; these are possible."	*Your advisor states your choices: "You **can take** physics or astronomy. Either of these is fine."*
should or *ought to*	"I advise this; it is a very good idea."	*A good friend says: "You **should take** astronomy; the teacher is really interesting. I liked the course a lot and really recommend it."*
must or *have to*	"You really have no choices because of law or other necessity."	*Your advisor says: "Everybody **has to take** English 101. Also, you **must pass** the university's writing examination before you can graduate."*
will†	"You do as I tell you."	*Your advisor says: "It doesn't matter what you want to do. You **will take** physical education next quarter."*

†Note: This meaning of *will* is grammatically possible but is so strong and potentially rude that it is rarely used.

Should and *Must* for Recommendations

In addition to their future time use, modal auxiliaries are often used to communicate about ethical and moral topics. People make recommendations on the basis of their own personal and cultural values. These recommendations communicate people's understanding of the right or wrong thing to do in particular situations. Very often these duties and obligations are discussed using *should* or *must.*

Should refers to advice and recommendations.	We **should go** to the library before class.
	You **should get** plenty of rest before a test.
Must is used for required actions and very strong advice.	Students **must pay** tuition by the first day of class.
	You **must not smoke** in the library.

Must is often used in contrast to *should* to discuss whether an action is a necessity or only a very good idea.

*In many countries, people say "children **must obey** their parents," not "children **should obey** their parents."*

. . . .

Practice Using Modals to Give Advice

A. With the other students in your class, discuss advice to give a friend who says to you each of the following sentences:

1. *"I don't know how to spell my teacher's name, and I need to write her a note."*
2. *"I don't know the telephone number of the foreign student advisor."*
3. *"I have a sore throat."*
4. *"I feel sleepy."*
5. *"I have an algebra midterm test tomorrow."*
6. *"I don't know what to have for lunch."*
7. *"I have lost my textbook for this course."*
8. *"I think my roommate cheated on his final examination."*
9. *"I think my roommate stole some money from my billfold."*
10. *"I overslept this morning and missed my first class."*
11. *"This library book was due last week."*
12. *"I have lost my driver's license."*
13. *"I am really frightened about taking the TOEFL test."*

B. Most U.S. colleges and universities have student handbooks that list the rules of student conduct. Analyze a section of the student handbook at your school. What modals are used? How strongly stated are the various rules for student conduct? Are any of the rules a surprise to you?

C. Discussion Assignment: What advice has your family given you to stay healthy? What advice do you hear on radio or television? What advice do you give your friends about having good health?

Grammar Assignment: What verbs do you expect a writer to use for that purpose? Find all of the modal auxiliaries. Would you change any of them to make the meaning stronger or weaker?

Suggestions for Keeping Your Body Healthy

[1]Would you like to live a longer life? [2]To live longer, you must keep your body healthy, and I have some suggestions for you. [3]First, you must eat healthy foods that will provide necessary protein, vitamins,

and carbohydrates. [4]You should not eat food that contains a great deal of fat and cholesterol because they clog your arteries and cause heart attacks. [5]Proper diet can help to keep your body healthy. [6]The second important requirement is regular exercise. [7]You must exercise every day. [8]You might jog or lift weights to keep your body healthy and active. [9]The third and most important point is not to take illegal drugs. [10]Drugs might ruin your life and the lives of your family. [11]You should not smoke, and you should not take heroin, LSD, or cocaine. [12]By keeping your body healthy now while you are young, you could live longer, and you might enjoy life more.

D. Work with another student, and write five sentences that give advice about learning English to share with students in a lower-level ESL class. Underline the modals, revise them for meaning, and then edit them for form and spelling. You might prepare a handout or a booklet to give to other students.

E. Work with another student, and prepare a list of five sentences about things that are required in the United States (*must*) and another five sentences about things that are a good idea (*should*). Underline the modals, and edit them for meaning, for form, and for spelling. Then, compare your list with those of others in the class. Do you agree or disagree with their sentences?

F. Working with other students from your country, talk about the advice you might give to Americans who want to visit your country. You could give advice and recommendations about such topics as what to see, where to stay, how to travel, what clothes to take for particular seasons of the year, what special events to try to see, and what to expect. Decide what topic you want to give advice about, and write a 10–12 sentence paragraph about that topic. When you finish writing, underline the modals, revise them for meaning, and then edit them for form and spelling. Use the Editing Checklist on page 414 to do a thorough editing job.

Can and *May* for Asking and Giving Permission

Can and *may* are used to ask for permission and to give permission. (For information on using modals in questions, see pages 182 and 188 in Chapter Seven.) Selection of the correct word depends on your relationship to the person with whom you are communicating. Choice of either *can* or *may* also depends on your personality (formal or informal) and your age (older people tend to be more formal than younger people). For example, in these relationships, you would probably choose these modals:

1. A person asking permission of a friend: *"Can I . . . ?"*
2. A person giving permission to a friend: *"You can . . . "*

3. A younger person asking permission of a formal older person: *"May I . . . ?"*
4. A formal older person giving permission to a younger person: *"You may . . . "*

5. A student asking permission of a formal teacher: *"May I . . . ?"*
6. A formal teacher giving permission to a student: *"You may . . . "*

7. A student asking permission of an informal teacher: *"Can I . . . "*
8. An informal teacher giving permission to a student: *"You can . . . "*

Practice Using Modals to Give Permission

A. Watch a courtroom television show. How does the judge give permission? How do the defendants, plaintiffs, and lawyers ask for permission? What modals do you hear them using?

B. Talk with your instructor about his or her preferences for the way that you ask permission in his or her classes.

C. Discuss with other students in your class the questions that you could use in each of the following situations. If possible, include some American students in the discussion.

1. You need change to buy a newspaper from a machine on the street. You go into a nearby shop to ask the clerk for change.
2. You want to talk with your instructor about your midterm grade. You stay after class to ask for an appointment.
3. Your American roommate likes to keep the window open in the bedroom, but you are getting a cold and do not feel very well. You ask for permission to close the window.
4. You are on the bus riding to school. The window is open next to your seat. You want to close the window, but you do not know if the other person in your seat would agree. You ask for permission to close the window.
5. You are visiting the home of your roommate's parents. You ask for permission to use their telephone.

Using Modals to Communicate about Guesses

Imagine this scene: you and some friends are in the cafeteria. An older stranger who is wearing a long white jacket over his clothes enters the cafeteria. You say to your friends, "Who is that?" Then, you start to make guesses based on your knowledge of the school, the cafeteria, and the kinds of clothes that people wear in those places.

Not being sure, the speaker has these choices: *may, might, could.*	*"He <u>might</u> be a surgeon. They wear white jackets. But why would a medical doctor come in here?"*
Since the speaker has strong evidence and feels very sure he is right, his choice is *must.*	*"He <u>must</u> be on the faculty— maybe in chemistry. Only students and faculty members ever come to this cafeteria."*
This speaker is disagreeing with the second speaker. She is suggesting that *may, might* or *could* is a better word choice. She thinks that *must* is too strong.	*"But he <u>could</u> be a student. We have lots of older students at this university."*

In life, people often talk and write about things that they are not entirely sure about. English speakers use the modals to indicate their level of certainty. If they are absolutely sure, they will probably use a general truth present tense verb. If they are quite certain, but do not have complete evidence, they will usually use *must.* At the other extreme, if they are very uncertain, they use *could, may,* or *might.*

System for Expressing Guesses

Modal	Meaning
could, may, or *might*	"reasonable explanation"
should	"very good explanation"
must	"strong explanation" or "little doubt"

. . . .

Practice Using Modals to Make Guesses

A. Bring photographs taken from popular magazines to class. Select scenes that are interesting to you or that you do not understand. Be sure to remove any words that would identify the people in the scene. Work with another student to analyze each photograph that you have brought. Who are the people in the photograph? What is the purpose of the photograph? What is happening? Be careful to select modals based on your certainty about your analysis.

B. With another student, go to a library, a cafeteria, a store, or anywhere that you can observe people whom you do not know. Select one person who is interesting to you. Write a description of the situation and of the person's appearance. Then, make guesses about such areas as the person's occupation, age, interests, family, and reasons for being in the situation. For example, if you see a woman with a plain gold ring on her left ring finger, your guess might be that "*she must be married.*" If you see a man with a dark tan, your guess might be that "*he might be an athlete*" or "*he might work outside.*" What verbs do you expect to use in the first section of the description? What verbs do you expect to use in the second part of the description?

C. Share the description that you wrote in exercise B with the rest of your class. At first, give them only the description and see what guesses they make about the person that you saw. Then, share your own guesses with the class.

Modals for Future Time Meanings

. . . .

All of the modal auxiliaries can be used to talk or write about the future. Each of the modals has a meaning that combines future time with some other meaning. While the most commonly used verb for future time is *will*, all of the others can be useful when you communicate about the future. Communicating about future time is presented in Chapter Six.

Should is used to communicate about future obligations or duties. In this sentence, the writer uses *should* to communicate about future time responsibilities.

*In the 21st century, the United States **should take** greater responsibility to decrease global pollution.*

Might is used to communicate about future probabilities with low expectations.

*Mary is not sure about her plans for next year. She **might go** to graduate school in California.*

149

Practice Using Modals for Future Time Meanings

A. Working with another student, prepare five sentences about the future of the world. You can write about war, peace, space travel, pollution, disease, or any other topic that you think will be important in the future of human beings on this planet. You will be making predictions about the future of the world and using different modals. Then, compare your list to those of others in the class. Write the five sentences you think are the most important and the best written on a sheet of paper. Then, underline the modals, revise them for meaning, and edit them for form and spelling. Use the Editing Checklist on page 414. Keep your predictions in your Grammar Notebook for future reference.

B. Write a paragraph of 10–12 sentences in which you make predictions about your own future or the future of your family. What *might* it be like? What *should* it be like? What *will* it be like? What *could, should, must, will* you do now to make the future the way that you describe it? When you finish writing, underline the modals, revise them for meaning, and then edit them for form and spelling. Use the Editing Checklist on page 414.

Modals for Past Time Meanings

Modals are not just for future time meanings. When you are communicating about past time events, you can add the various meanings of the modals.

Examples of Modals for Past Time Meanings	
could + verb for past time abilities	*When I **was** a child, I **could run** faster than anyone in my class.*
would + verb for past time habits	*When I **was** a child, I **would visit** my grandmother every Sunday.*
modal + *have* + past participle for things not done	*I **should have sharpened** my pencil before class started, but I **forgot**.* *I **could have taken** the driving test yesterday, but I **did not have** enough time to do it.*

modal + *have* + past participle for guesses about the past	*Juan **might have gone** to the party, but I **did not see** him there.* *She **must have taken** algebra in high school because she **is taking** calculus now.*

Could and *Would* for Past Time Meanings

Only *could* and *would* have past time meanings when combined with a simple form of the verb. They both refer to things that were true in the past but that are no longer true.

Could means "past time ability" or "past time possibility."	*When I **was** a child, I **could speak** French. Now, I have forgotten how to speak French.* *I live on campus in a dormitory now and must clean my own room. When I lived at home, I **could depend** on my mother to clean my room.*
Would means "past time habit."	*When I lived in Florida, I **would go** to the beach every summer. Now, I live in Colorado and go to the mountains.*

Can and *Could* to Mean "Ability"

Can and *could* are used to communicate about abilities and skills.

Can is used for present time skills and abilities.	*Jorge **can play** the guitar.* *Monika **can sing** beautifully.*
Could is used for past time skills and abilities that have been lost.	*I **could run** quickly when I was younger; now I prefer to walk.*

Past Time Meanings for Other Modals

For the other modals and for other meanings of *would* and *could*, you can make a past time meaning by combining the modal with *have* + the past participle. These combinations are usually used to communicate about something that did not happen in the past. The basic meaning of the modal is combined with the meaning of "past time" and "did not happen."

Could have is used to mean that "there was an opportunity but it was not taken."

I **could have gone** to the party last night, but I was sick. I am sorry that I missed the fun, but I was too sick to leave my apartment.

Should have is used to mean that "there was an obligation or a duty, but it was not done."

I **should have studied** for the test, but I had to go to work. Therefore, I earned money to pay for my classes, but I did not learn as much as I wanted to learn from my classes. Isn't life strange?

Would have is used to mean that "there was something I wanted to do or had promised to do but did not do."

I **would have helped** with the project, but I was out of town. Therefore, I did not help with the project, and I feel very bad about disappointing my friends. But I had to help my sister move to a new apartment.

Had To and *Must Have* for Past Time Meanings

Must and *have to* have the same meaning for future time, present time, and general truth sentences.

Students **must pay** tuition on time.

Students **have to pay** tuition on time.

For past time meaning, *must* + *have* + past participle is used to make a guess about a past time action.

Maria is a good student, but she failed the test. What happened? I do not know the answer. But I have an idea that I think is the correct explanation. She **must have been** sick. She looked like she felt bad during the test.

For past time meaning, *had to* + verb is used for rules and obligations.

The instructor did not give us a choice. The students **had to take** the examination on the day after the holiday.

Practice with Past Time Meanings for Modals

A. Write two of your own examples for the past time meanings of *could* (past time ability and past time possibility) and *would* (past time habit). For example: *When I was in my country, I would eat dinner with my whole family every night.* Share your examples with the other students in your class to be sure that they are grammatically correct. After making any necessary changes, put the correct sentences in your Grammar Notebook to keep for future reference.

B. Write two examples from your own experience using *could, should,* or *would* for past time things that you did not do. Check these examples with other students in the class to be sure that they are grammatically correct. In each example, tell what happened: (1) what was supposed to happen, (2) what really happened, and (3) what you think or feel about the situation. Here is an example: *I would have taken the midterm exam on the right day, but my car broke down on the way to school. I spent the morning getting my car towed to the garage and repaired. I am very worried about what my teacher will do about giving a make-up test.* After editing your sentences, write them on a sheet of paper to keep in your Grammar Notebook for future reference.

C. Write five sentences about what you *could do* when you were a child and *cannot do* now. Then, write five sentences about what you *can do* now that you *could not do* when you were a child. Revise the sentences to have the correct meaning. After you have written the ten sentences, underline each verb twice. Then, edit the verbs for form and for spelling. After editing the sentences, write them on a sheet of paper to keep in your Grammar Notebook for future reference. Finally, compare the changes in your life to the changes in the lives of other people in your class. What similarities and differences do you notice? Do you think that some changes seem to occur in the lives of all human beings as they become adults?

D. Using the information from exercise C, work with the other students in your class, and write five sentences to describe things that people could do as children that they cannot do as adults. After editing the sentences, write them on a sheet of paper to keep in your Grammar Notebook for future reference.

E. Write five sentences about what you *should do* during the next four or five weeks; write about your duties and obligations in the near future. Then, write five sentences about what you *should have done* within the past four or five weeks, but did not do. Revise the sentences to have the correct meaning. Then, underline each verb twice, and edit the verbs for form and for spelling. After correcting the sentences, share them with the other students in your class. Make any necessary changes, and write the sentences on a sheet of paper to keep in your Grammar Notebook for future reference.

F. Working with another student, write five sentences about what you *must do* to earn a degree at your school. Then, write five sentences about what you *had to do* to apply and register at your school. Revise the sentences to have the correct meaning. After you have written the ten sentences, underline the verbs. Then, edit the verbs for form and for spelling. Write the corrected sentences on a sheet of paper to keep in your Grammar Notebook for future reference.

G. Write a paragraph of 10–12 sentences in which you describe a bad decision you made in the past. What was the decision? Why did you make that decision? What should you have decided instead? What could you have decided? What would you rather have decided? When you finish writing, underline the modals. Revise the sentences to have the correct meaning. Then, edit them for form and for spelling. Keep the edited paragraph in your Grammar Notebook.

Negative Meanings of *Have To* and *Must*

In the negative, *must + not* is used to give rules and requirements.

*Students **must not talk** during examinations.*

In contrast, the negative of *have to* means that something is not required. It means the opposite of *must + not*.

*You **do not have to use** a pen on the test; you can use a pencil.*

Note that *have to* uses the auxiliary *do* to form the negative.

*Tuan **does not have to pay** tuition because he has a scholarship.*

*Tuan **does not have to take** a foreign language course because he already speaks three languages.*

*Tuan and his sister **do not have to work** because their father has a very good job.*

Practice with Negative Meanings of *Have To* and *Must*

A. Add *must not* or *do/does/did not have to* in each of the following sentences.

Final Exams

1. Students _____ be absent for the final exam because

   there is no make-up; a student who is absent receives an F.

2. Each final exam session lasts for two hours, but students

   _____ stay the entire time. If they finish early, they

   can leave.

3. They _____ bring dictionaries to the final exam, but if

   they bring dictionaries, they can use them.

4. A student _____ use a bilingual dictionary; only

   English-English dictionaries are permitted.

5. A student _____ look at another student's paper during

   the exam; looking at someone else's paper is considered cheating.

6. Some final exams have extra credit exercises, but a student

   _____ do the extra credit to receive an A on the exam.

7. Students _____ write their exams in pen, but papers

   that are written in pen are easier to read than papers that are

   written in pencil.

8. Students _____ use their textbooks during many final

   exams. Textbooks and notes are prohibited.

   B. Working with the other students in your class, write four rules
for proper student behavior. Make two of your rules negative and two of
them positive. After editing the rules carefully, write them on a sheet of
paper to keep in your Grammar Notebook.

C. Students usually have many questions about examinations. Working with the rest of the students in your class, make a list of questions to ask your instructor about the final examination for this course. After editing the questions, write them on a sheet of paper. Then, discuss your list with your instructor, and write the answers to the questions on the same sheet of paper. Keep the questions and their answers in your Grammar Notebook. Typical questions include the following: Do we have to have a final examination? Do we have to write in ink?

Will and *Can* for General Truth Meanings

When you write about general truth topics, you can use at least two of the modals. Both *can* and *will* are often used for general truth meanings.

You know already that *can* is used to talk about skills and abilities; these are general truth topics. They have the same meaning as simple present tense.

*She **can speak** German.*

*He **can play** tennis well.*

*She **speaks** German.*

*He **plays** tennis well.*

In addition, *will* can be used for exactly the same meaning as simple present tense. These sentences have the same meaning. *Will* does not refer to future time here.

*Oil **floats** on water.*

*Oil **will float** on water.*

Practice with *Will* and *Can* for General Truth Meanings

A. Interview another student in your class to find out about his or her abilities and skills. Write six sentences to describe those abilities. Use *can* for three and simple present tense for three. First check the accuracy of your statements with the person you interviewed. After you make any necessary corrections, share your information with the rest of the class. Then, write the corrected sentences on a sheet of paper to give to the student that you interviewed. Keep the sheet of paper about yourself in your Grammar Notebook.

B. Working with another student, decide on the meaning of *will* in each of these sentences. Does it mean "future time"? Does it mean "general truth"? Write either *future* or *general* in the space provided after each sentence.

1. The moon will rise tomorrow night at 8:31 P.M. _____

2. Prices will increase whenever demand is high and supply is low.

   _____

3. Prices will increase next Monday. _____

4. Combustion will cease without oxygen. _____

5. Greed will often overcome honesty. _____

6. The library will be closed on Tuesday because of the holiday.

   _____

7. Librarians will offer help to any student with a research question.

   _____

8. The library will move to a new building next year.

   _____

9. The library will not be open on Sunday mornings. _____

10. Water will freeze at 32 degrees F. _____

Using Modals to Give Indirect Commands

Because people in the United States value informality and equality, even people with authority will often speak indirectly to give commands. Teachers will speak indirectly to students; employers will speak indirectly to employees. This indirectness can be confusing because a command can be given without sounding like a command. Modals play a large role in this spoken indirectness.

Should is used with the meaning of *must*.	*An employer says, "You **should arrive** at work no later than 8:30 A.M."*
Might is used with the meaning of *must*.	*A teacher says, "You **might study** Chapter Five for the test."*

Could is used with the meaning of *must.*	*A supervisor says, "You **could retype** that report to make it look better."*
Would is used with the meaning of *must.*	*A doctor says, "It **would be** a good idea for you to lose some weight."*

Similarly, people in the United States often use *would* and *could* in questions to make polite suggestions and requests because these modals are felt to be more indirect and because a question is more indirect than an imperative command. These words are more conditional in their meaning and offer the appearance of choice to the individual. The strength of the request depends upon the power of the person making the request. Use of these modals also depends upon the formality of the relationship and the situation.

Formal Suggestion	
Formal polite requests and suggestions are often made using *would.*	*Would you please close the door?* *Would you mind handing me that dictionary?*
Informal Suggestion	
In less formal situations such as talking with friends, the command form is used to make requests and suggestions. A polite tone of voice prevents the request from sounding like an order. Words like *please* and *thank you* are often used.	*Close that door, please! Thanks.* *Hand me that dictionary, please. Thanks.*
Formal Offer	
A formal polite offer is often made with *would.*	*Would you like some coffee?*
Informal Offer	
Other types of questions are also polite but less formal.	*We have some coffee. Do you want some?*
Formal Question about Preferences	
Polite requests and questions about preferences are often made with *would rather.* In this use, *would rather* means "prefer."	*Would you rather go to lunch at 12:30 or 1:00?* *I would rather have chicken for dinner than lamb.*

Practice Using Modals for Polite Requests

A. Write two of your own examples for each of the following uses of *would:* (1) polite requests and questions and (2) questions about preferences. Share your examples with other students in your class to be sure that they are grammatically correct. After you have written, revised, and edited the sentences, record your examples on a sheet of paper to keep in your Grammar Notebook. On that same sheet of paper, write your answers to the questions that you have written. When do you hear Americans using such questions? Do you ever use them? In what situations do you use them? Discuss your answers with the other students in your class.

B. Work with another student to decide on polite questions to fit the following situations. Discuss your answers with the rest of the class. This is the basic problem: you need to borrow a pen to take notes in class because your pen has just run out of ink. What question do you ask? And how do you ask it?

1. Class has not yet started. You ask a good friend who speaks your native language. She or he is sitting next to you.
2. Class has not yet started. You ask a good friend who does not speak your language. She or he is sitting next to you. Your friend's English is not very good.
3. Class has not yet started. You are sitting on the front row. The instructor has noticed that you have a problem.
4. Class has not yet started. The only person near you is an older woman student from a country different from yours. You think that her English is pretty good.
5. Class has already started, and the instructor is explaining an exercise. You ask a good friend who is sitting next to you. Your friend does not speak your native language.
6. Class has already started, and the instructor is explaining an exercise. You ask a good friend who is sitting next to you. Your friend is from your hometown and is someone whom you have known all of your life.
7. Class has already started, and you are doing an exercise with a group of other students. You ask a student in the group. He is an older man whose English does not seem as good as yours, but he seems very kind.

C. Discussion Assignment: How do you expect teachers to treat students? What words do you expect teachers to use when they make assignments? Have you ever had the experience of not understanding what the teacher wanted you to do? What happened? What do you think was the problem?

Grammar Assignment: Find the two statements used by the American ESL teacher that were misunderstood by her students. Discuss ways that the teacher could have made her statements clearer. With another student, write sentences that communicate her meaning in a clearer way. Share those sentences with your class.

Cultural Differences in the ESL Classroom

[1]The importance that North Americans place on indirect expression of authority is a frequent barrier to communication—both linguistically and culturally. [2]When an American teacher tells an ESL student at a program in the United States, "You might move your chair over here close to me so you won't be tempted to talk to Jose" that student rarely understands the message: "Stop talking to Jose."

[3]Teachers should word their orders as orders, not requests. [4]Then, the grammatical structure is more comprehensible, and the students recognize the statement as one requiring a specific response rather than truly offering a choice. [5]This lack of communication became clear to me when I urged a group working on a project to stop gossiping and get down to business. [6]I said, "You should stop visiting and get down to work. [7]You won't get anything done before class is over." [8]The students smiled politely and nodded at me; the gossip continued, and nothing was done that day. [9]I was furious; the students were puzzled by my anger. [10]They had understood the words completely; what had *not* been communicated was my demand that they do something different from what they were doing. [11]The students honestly felt that I was offering a suggestion, which they were free to act on or to ignore as they saw fit.

[12]I now think that ESL teachers must make their expectations clear at the beginning of the term or assignment, even if they seem obvious to the teachers. [13]While teachers must respect the dignity of their students, they must also be sure that they have clearly communicated their orders and instructions.

Adapted from Fitch, Kristine L. "Cultural Conflicts in the Classroom: Major Issues and Strategies for Coping," in Byrd, Patricia (Ed.) *Teaching Across Cultures in the University ESL Program.* Washington, D.C.: NAFSA, 1986, 51–62.

Shall in American English

In the United States, *shall* has three important uses. However, this modal is probably not used as much as *will, can, should,* or *must.*

Formal Agreement
In spoken English, *shall* is a formal way of seeking agreement and more often used in questions than in statements. Usually the speaker expects agreement.

An instructor says to the class, *"**Shall** we begin now?"*

Introductions
In written academic English, *shall* is often used in an introduction to explain the content of a book or article.

*In Chapter Six, we **shall** discuss the implications of management theory on actual business practice.*

Famous Songs and Statements
In the United States, *shall* is associated with several famous songs and statements. An influential song of the civil rights movement of the 1960s is still well known today.

*The students sang "We **Shall** Overcome."*

Americans still use a phrase made famous in World War II by General Douglas MacArthur when he left the Philippines. Americans use this as a statement of determination.

*"I **shall** return."*

A famous song from the play *The King and I* is "**Shall** We Dance?" This phrase can still be heard in the United States. The Joker used the phrase in the 1989 *Batman* movie when he began to dance with Batman's girlfriend!

*"**Shall** we dance?"*

Modals in Passive Sentences

Modals can be used in passive sentences. Since passive is discussed in detail in Chapter Eleven, only a few examples are given here. The passages in the exercise illustrate the use of modals for passive meanings.

The modals have the same meanings when they are combined with the passive. They are used to talk about abilities, advice, obligations, and so forth. However, the emphasis is on the process or action rather than on the person who did the action.

The basic grammar of modal passives is modal + *be* + past participle.	*The research papers **should be finished** by next week.* *All fees **must be paid** before the second day of class.*

Practice with Modals in Passive Sentences

The modal + passive combination is used in the following information about safe storage and cooking of fish. Use a highlighter to mark each example of modal + passive.

Storage of Seafood

Seafood should always be refrigerated at 35 to 45 degrees Fahrenheit or frozen at zero degrees Fahrenheit until preparation time. Because many refrigerator-freezer compartments do not reach zero, seafood should not be stored in them for as long as in a separate freezer. It is a good idea to check actual freezer and refrigerator temperatures from time to time with a thermometer.

Cooking Methods for Seafood

Almost any fish can be baked, broiled, poached, steamed, or fried. Some people would rather bake fatty fish and poach or steam lean fish. Fish fillets and steaks can be broiled or barbecued. Shrimp can be simmered 3 to 5 minutes, depending on the size and quantity.

Adapted from U.S. Food and Drug Administration. Public Health Services, Department of Health and Human Services. "Kitchen Safety Tips for Seafood." *FDA Consumer: Fishing for Facts on Fish Safety,* vol. 23, no. 1. Washington, D.C.: GPO, 1989, p. 25.

Practice with Modals

A. Fill in the blanks with modals that explain the classroom etiquette you follow in this class. Be ready to explain why you chose a particular modal. Add additional sentences that describe your particular class.

1. Students _____ borrow a pen or pencil from a classmate during the class.

2. Students _____ whisper to each other when the teacher is talking.

3. Students _____ bring the textbook to class every day.

4. Students _____ use a bilingual dictionary.

5. Students _____ use an English-English dictionary.

6. Students _____ sit wherever they want.

7. Students _____ knock on the door before they enter the classroom, if they are late.

8. Students _____ attend every class.

9. Students _____ pay tuition before they can attend this class.

10. Students _____ hand in written homework.

11. Students _____ copy someone else's paper.

12. Students _____ make up assignments or tests if they are absent.

13. Students _____ stand up when they answer questions.

14. Students _____ learn to be tolerant of other classmates' cultures.

15. Students _____

16. Students _____

B. Discussion Assignment: Do you eat any differently now that you live in the United States? Do you eat any differently now that you are in college? How would you describe "the American way of eating"? What does the word *grazing* mean?

Grammar Assignment: Provide an appropriate modal in the blanks below. Be ready to explain why you chose a particular modal and to identify other modals that might also be effective.

163

The American Way of Eating

"Grazing" could be the new American way of eating, according to nutritionists. "Since everyone is always rushing around in a hurry these days, there is often no time for three square meals. So, grazing, or snacking on mini-meals, has become important," says Marilyn Stephenson, a registered dietitian and assistant to the director, Office of Nutrition and Food Science, Food and Drug Administration. Grazing could be a way of filling in those necessary calories and nutrients that you _____ otherwise miss because of incomplete or skipped meals. Done wisely, grazing is not only good for you, it _____ also be fun, too.

Adult Grazing

Adults _____ be more careful than children about snacking. Because of different energy needs, adults need fewer calories to maintain their bodies. Fat and high levels of cholesterol are risk factors for heart disease. Also, a high dietary fat intake _____ lead to certain types of cancer. According to the American Heart Association and the National Cancer Institute, Americans _____ reduce their fat intake to about 30 percent of their total calories. In addition, popular snack foods, such as chips and packaged popcorn, _____ contain up to 950 milligrams of sodium per serving. *Dietary Guidelines* recommends no more than 1,100 to 3,300 milligrams a day. High blood pressure _____ be a result of excessive sodium. Therefore, older adults _____ watch their sodium intake because of the prevalence of high blood pressure and heart disease in their age group.

Teenage Grazing

Although teenagers _____ benefit from snacking, they often fall into the habit of eating the same snack foods, and sometimes these snacks even substitute for, rather than supplement, regular meals.

These snack foods _____ not provide the variety of
nutrients that are found in regular meals. For example, a soda that
replaces milk at lunch _____ reduce the amount of
calcium in the diet. Parents _____ encourage teenagers
who like to snack on soft drinks to have a cheeseburger rather than a
plain hamburger with their drinks. A slice of cheese pizza
_____ add calcium to the diet. Snacking
_____ be a potential asset to a teenager's diet, but it
_____ also be a liability if it results in too many calories.
Instead, parents _____ encourage sensible snacking.

Changing one's snacking habits _____ take some
practice. Nutritious snacks are not as tasty and satisfying as traditional
ones, such as candy and potato chips. However, snackers
_____ become aware of the nutrition content of their
snack foods by reading labels for ingredient and nutrient content.

Adapted from U.S. Food and Drug Administration. Public Health Services, Department of
Health and Human Services. "The 'Grazing' of America: A Guide to Healthy Snacking."
FDA Consumer, vol. 23, no. 2. Washington, D.C.: GPO, 1989.

C. Discussion Assignment: Why did you decide to come to college?
Why did you decide to come to a U.S. college? What educational goals do
you expect students from the United States to have?

Grammar Assignment: Decide whether to use *should* or *must* in the
following sentences. Be ready to explain your modal choices.

A Goal for the United States

The United States _____ adopt the following goal: all
children born today will have a quality mathematics and science
education and the opportunity to participate in the science and
engineering workforce to their fullest potential. Americans
_____ find ways to bring many more young people into
engineering and science fields. These young people _____
receive sound mathematics and science instruction in school, aspire to
college, qualify for these majors at college, and complete their degrees.

More baccalaureates _____ stay on as graduate students,
as postdoctorals, and as teachers of future science and engineering
students. Changing the mathematics and science interest and
achievement of a generation of students is a huge task. Americans will
have to make some changes.

To raise levels of mathematics and science achievement by minority
students, educational reform _____ target the 25 largest
minority school districts. Such districts _____ undertake a
system-wide assessment of mathematics and science education. The
federal government _____ establish a competitive grants
program for school districts to implement these plans.

The maximum number of students—especially minority and female
students—_____ take college-track mathematics and
science. High schools _____ require three years of
mathematics including precalculus and plan to require four years,
including calculus, as soon as possible. Three years of laboratory science
and one year of computer science _____ be high school
graduation requirements.

Adapted from The Task Force on Women, Minorities, and the Handicapped in Science and
Technology. *Changing America: The New Face of Science and Engineering: Interim Report.*
Washington, D.C.: GPO, 1988.

D. You need to know about any problems that you might have with
using the modals. These little words are extremely important for accuracy and fluency in English. Questions are provided on page 455 in the
Grammar Journal for you to analyze your use of modals.

E. To practice editing someone else's written English, turn to Section
Four. Study the information about editing on page 404, and then do the
editing exercises on page 414.

F. For additional writing topics, and the editing summary for this
chapter, turn to Section Four, page 426.

6

Future Time Frame

CHAPTER ORGANIZATION

Future Time Choice
Basic Future Time Verb Choices
Verb Forms Used to Indicate Future Time
Future Time Adverbs and Adverbial Modifiers
Speaking about the Future
Writing about the Future

Future Time Choice

· ·

When talking or writing about the future, you have many different choices in English. The purpose of this chapter is to help you explore those choices and add to your ability to communicate about future time.

Changing America: The Workforce

*Changing demographics **will** markedly affect the future workforce in the United States. Of the new workers entering the labor force by the year 2000, only 15 percent **will** be white men. The rest **will** be either white women, members of minority groups, or immigrants. Between 1980 and 2000, the 18- to 24-year-old segment of the U.S. population **is going to** decline by 19 percent while the overall population **will** increase by 18 percent. By 2010, one in every three 18-year-olds **will** be black or Hispanic.*

Changing America: New Technology

*By the year 2015, there **will** be new technology in medicine, and there **will** be cures for diseases such as AIDS, cancer, and diabetes. People **will** be living longer. Our transportation system **will** have changed tremendously. People **will** be able to travel to distant places in less time than they can travel ten miles today. Technology in the schools **is** also **going to** change. Students **will** not have to attend school; instead, they **will** study at home with computers and video cassettes. In the future, people's lives **will be** easier.*

Adapted from The Task Force on Women, Minorities, and the Handicapped in Science and Technology. *Changing America: The New Face of Science and Engineering: Interim Report.* Washington, D.C.: GPO, 1988.

Basic Future Time Verb Choices

· ·

These are your primary verb choices when communicating about future time.

Modal Auxiliaries
Although *will* is the most frequent modal for simple future time, all of the other modals can be used for future time for special meanings.

modal
*We **will have** a test on Friday.*

modal
*We **might go** to a movie after the test.*

Be Going To + Verb
This verb form has the same meaning as *will*. It is frequently used in conversations to talk about planned actions.

be + going + to + verb
We ***are going to have*** a test on Friday.

Present Progressive
This verb form is used for scheduled events. Usually an adverbial of time is used with the present progressive for future time meaning. Only action verbs are used.

present progressive
We ***are taking*** a test on Friday.

present progressive
They ***are moving*** to a new apartment next week.

Simple Present Tense
This verb form is used for scheduled events. The verbs often used include *arrive, be, begin, close, end, leave, open,* and *start*.

present tense
The test ***is*** on Friday.

present tense
The new movie ***starts*** at 6:30 P.M. tomorrow.

Simple Present Tense
in Clauses
See Chapter Ten and Chapter Fifteen for more information on clauses.

adverbial clause
When the test is over, we will go home.

conditional clause
If you fail ***the final examination,*** you will fail the course.

Verb Forms Used to Indicate Future Time

When communicating about the future, writers often put the information in the context of what happened in the past or of what is generally true.

Past
The writer describes the past and then gives implications for the future.

In the early 19th century, the U.S. ***was*** first an agricultural society, and then it ***became*** an industrial society. In the future, it ***will become*** more and more a service society. It ***will depend*** on other countries for industrial production. Its agricultural production ***will continue*** to be very high but ***will be based*** on huge agribusiness operations.

Present Perfect
Present perfect is used for indefinite past time meanings, especially in introductory statements. Then, predictions are made about the future.

*I **have visited** Mexico on vacation many times. I **will return** there next year to study Spanish at a school in Mexico City. I **will live** in Mexico for at least one year.*

General Truth
General truth statements can also be used as background for predictions about the future.

*This university **does not have** a strong computer science department. However, the future **should be** bright. Next year, a local industry **will provide** $1,000,000 to build a new computer lab. The university **will match** that money with another $1,000,000 to hire new faculty who are experts in computer science. In two years, the university **will begin** to attract outstanding students to study in the expanded department.*

Future Time Adverbs and Adverbial Modifiers

In addition to verb choices, you have many ways to indicate future time by using various adverbs and other modifiers with future time meaning. Working with a partner, add as many future time words as you can think of to the chart on the next page. Take five minutes to think of words and phrases; then, put the chart aside for at least 30 minutes. When you look at the chart again, see how many more words you can add to the list. Then, compare your list to those of other students, and add any words from their lists that you want to have on your list.

tomorrow	_after class_			

Speaking about the Future

• •

We often talk with other people about the future. We make plans with family members, friends, and colleagues. We make promises, discuss opportunities, and share daydreams. Basically, we have the same grammatical choices in talking about the future as we do in writing about the future. However, our conversational English is usually more informal than written English. Information on punctuation and spelling of contractions is given on page 305 in Chapter Twelve.

Contractions
In speaking about the future, Americans often use contractions.

"**I'll see** you in the library after lunch."

"I **can't go** to the library this afternoon."

"He **won't eat** lunch today because he has to study."

Be Going To

In speaking about the future, the less formal *be going to* is used more than it is in written English. The written form *going to* has a contracted pronunciation that is spelled *gonna* in cartoons, comics, and dialect writing. That spelling is not used in other kinds of writing.

pronunciation "gonna eat"

*"I'm **going to eat** lunch in the cafeteria after class."*

Have To

In speaking, you can also expect to hear and to use other less formal verbs. For example, *have to* is used to mean *must*. If you listen carefully to Americans as they speak, you will realize that the pronunciation of *have to* is something like "hafta."

pronunciation "hafta run"

*"I **have to run** by the library after class to turn in these books that are due today."*

Practice Speaking about the Future

To find out more about the ways that people from the United States talk informally about the future, plan a survey on one of the topics suggested below. Work with two other students to interview at least three U.S. students who are native speakers of English. Ask permission to make a taperecording of the interview. Then, make a transcript of the exact words that are said. With the rest of your class, first analyze the content of the interviews. What are the ideas of the U.S. students? Do they seem to agree with each other about the future? Then, analyze their grammar. What verbs and adverbs do the U.S. students use? How do they pronounce the verbs? What contractions do they use? On a sheet of paper, make a list of the verbs, adverbs, and contractions that were discovered by the whole class in the interviews. After checking the spelling of those words, keep the list in your Grammar Notebook for future reference.

Possible Topics: the future of this city, the future of this university, the future of the United States, the future of the environment, or any other future-oriented topic.

Writing about the Future

We seldom write complete essays or whole papers that communicate only about the future. Writing about the future occurs frequently at the end of a composition when the writer makes a prediction about the future. In addition, writing about the future is often mixed with writing about general truth.

More Formal

Written English is usually more formal than spoken English. Generally, academic writers use the full form rather than the contracted form (*will* rather than *'ll* and *cannot* rather than *can't*).

formal written version
*The new leader **will make** many changes.*

usually not used in formal written English
*The new leader'll make many changes.

More Variety

In addition to *will*, you have many other possibilities for future time meanings, including the various meanings of the modal auxiliaries. You can add variety to your writing by using some of these other choices.

*The new leader **is going to make** many changes. The economic system **will** certainly **be modernized**. The agricultural system **might be modified**. New officials **will be appointed** in every department. Stagnation **is** our present; change **is** our future.*

Practice with the Future Time Frame

A. Write a sentence to answer each of the following ten questions about your plans for the future. Follow the verb pattern in each question as you practice the different verb choices for future time. Compare your answers to those of another student in your class. After making any needed corrections, put your list of answers in your Grammar Notebook to use as examples.

1. What are you going to do tonight?
2. What are you planning to do next weekend?
3. What will you do tomorrow morning?
4. When will you take your next exam?
5. What television show are you going to watch tonight?
6. In what year will you be 50 years old?
7. What will you be doing in five years?
8. What are you going to do at this time tomorrow?
9. What food are you having for dinner tonight?
10. What time does your first class begin tomorrow?

B. As in the example, indicate the time meant by each sentence. Your choices include future time, general truth, and present time.

I am taking four courses this semester.   <u>Present time</u> _____

1. Students usually take 15 hours each quarter. _____

2. When I finish ESL, I am going to move to Miami. _____

3. I am walking to the library after class. _____

4. I am taking accounting next quarter. _____

5. When students graduate from high school, they often go to college. _____

6. This has been a difficult week; I am going to rest all weekend. _____

7. We are studying future time today. _____

8. I am taking a midterm exam tomorrow. _____

C. As in the example, each of the following sentences has a mistake in its verb form. Edit each sentence by (1) finding the error and (2) making the correction as in the example.

Fahid ^is ^*going to a football game tonight.*

Plans

1. Carlos and Juanita is not going to the football game.

2. They are go to a movie instead.

3. Adel will studies at the library tonight.

4. He is plan to finish his research paper.

5. He is going go to another football game next weekend.

D. Complete the following sentences with correct forms of the verb in parentheses. There is more than one correct answer to some of the sentences.

1. The meeting <u>*begins / will begin*</u> at 9:00 tonight.   (begin)

2. Dr. Anderson _____ to the students next Monday.   (lecture)

3. All of the students in the class _____   (be)
   ready at 11:00 tomorrow morning.

4. Our teacher _____ the assignment   (explain)
   tomorrow.

5. I _____ for the test with my friends   (study)
   tonight.

6. There _____ an important test next   (be)
   Friday.

7. Many students _____ the play on   (attend)
   Saturday.

8. The math tutor _____ us with the new   (help)
   lesson.

9. Koji _____ the library books tomorrow   (return)
   evening.

10. I _____ a different ESL class next   (take)
    quarter.

E. Each of the following sentences refers to a past time event. Use the same information to make sentences about the future. First, change the verbs in each sentence to a future time verb form. You will also want to make some changes in the time expressions. Write your future time sentences on a sheet of paper. After editing the sentences carefully, put them in your Grammar Notebook to use as examples.

1. Everyone ate lunch at the student cafeteria yesterday.

   Everyone is going to eat lunch at the student cafeteria today.

2. Juan spoke to his professor about the assignment after class.
3. The students wrote a description of their favorite holiday yesterday.
4. The class members read *Moby Dick* three weeks ago.
5. Carol got to class on time this morning.
6. We went to a lecture last night.
7. The students read the assignment carefully yesterday.
8. I saw the dean two days ago.
9. Mansoo sold his calculator and bought a new one last week.
10. Rudy learned how to use the spellcheck on his computer the day before yesterday.

F. Complete the following sentences using information about yourself and using future time verb forms. Your sentences should be meaningful, and the verb forms should be correct. After editing your sentences carefully, compare your future to that of other students in your class: what answers do they give to complete sentences 2 and 5?

1. _____ in 20 years.

2. _____ after I finish ESL.

3. _____ in a few minutes.

4. _____ one year from now.

5. _____ when I graduate.

G. Discussion Assignment: What do you think life will be like in 50 years? Do you want to travel to another planet on a space shuttle? What can computers do today? What do translators do? Do you think it is possible to design a computer that will translate one language into another instantaneously?

Grammar Assignment: Read the title of the following paragraph. What time frame do you expect to find in this paragraph? As you read, place double lines under each verb; what verb forms are used? Why are they used?

Life in the Twenty-First Century

[1]Life in the twenty-first century will be very different from life in the twentieth century. [2]People will probably live longer than we do today because scientists will have developed cures for AIDS, cancer, and diabetes, the major killers of the twentieth century. [3]People will likely power their cars and airplanes with inexpensive solar power, and nuclear generators will produce electricity for homes and offices. [4]The deserts of the world will probably be irrigated and transformed into

fertile land to feed the increased population. [5]In addition, some people in the twenty-first century might be living on the moon, and trips to the moon on space shuttles may be as easy as flying from New York to London today. [6]Machines will surely be developed to translate languages, and people will be able to understand each other as they speak their own languages. [7]Some telephones in the future will probably have video screens, and instant translation from one language to another will be available. [8]Technology will make life in the twenty-first century easier than life in the twentieth century.

H. Discussion Assignment: Would you like to travel in space? What do you think about governments spending so much money on space flight when so many people here on earth live in poverty?

Grammar Assignment: Complete the following paragraph with appropriate forms of the verbs in parentheses, and circle the time expressions that go along with the time meanings of the verbs.

Space Voyages

Scientists have made great progress in space exploration. Since 1957, several men _____ in spaceships far above the surface of
    [1](live and work)
the earth and _____ on the moon. Unmanned spacecraft
    [2](walk)
_____ to our exploration of space. In 1977, scientists
[3](also, contribute)
_____ Voyager 2 into deep space. Cameras on the craft
[4](launch)
_____ us the first close-up pictures of Saturn, Jupiter,
[5](give)
Uranus, and Neptune. In 1989, the United States _____
                                                      [6](launch)
Magellan to take close-up pictures of Venus, one of the planets between the sun and the earth. Partly sponsored by the German Ministry of Technology, Galileo _____ Jupiter in the mid-1990s.
                          [7](explore)
Galileo _____ in space for six years before it reaches
        [8](travel)
Jupiter, and then it _____ ten orbits around the giant
                         [9](make)
planet. During the orbits, it _____ information back to
                                 [10](send)
earth. The Mars observer, a space voyage to explore Mars for one martian year or 637 earth days, _____ one of the first
                                                      [11](be)

View of Venus

joint Soviet-American trips into outer space. Scientists

_____ a man to other planets until they have used robots
^{12}(not, send)

and unmanned space vehicles to test the conditions on these other

planets. With the information from the various space flights, scientists

_____ determine if a man can survive on another planet.
^{13}(be able to)

Someday a man or a woman from the United States, Russia, Japan,

France, England, or some other country _____ the first
^{14}(be)

human being to step on another planet.

Adapted from Cook, William J., with Joannie Schrof. "The Edge of Infinity." *U.S. News and World Report* (May 15, 1989): 58–59.

I. In American academic writing, predictions are often used in the conclusions of compositions. These predictions come at the end of some compositions as small as a paragraph or as long as a chapter in a book. This technique has been used by the writers of several passages in this textbook. Read the following passages, and find the predictions that have been made. What verbs are used to make the predictions? Do you agree with the predictions? If you do not agree, how would you change them?

1. "Crossword Puzzles" on page 117 in Chapter Three
2. "The Greenhouse Effect" on page 110 in Chapter Three
3. "Suggestions for Keeping Your Body Healthy" on page 145 in Chapter Five
4. "Space Voyages" on page 177 in Chapter Six
5. "Communication" on page 380 in Chapter Sixteen
6. "The Laser" on page 295 in Chapter Eleven

J. Write a prediction about the events of the next year in a paragraph of 10–12 sentences. After you have revised the paragraph to have the meaning that you want, underline each verb twice. Then, edit the verbs for form and spelling. Share your predictions with other students in your class. Is there any general agreement about the future?

K. Write a paragraph about what you plan to do for your next vacation or holiday. After you are satisfied with the organization and meaning of the paragraph, edit it carefully for verb choices and form.

L. Write a paragraph about what you expect your life will be like in ten years. You might consider where you will live, what your job will be, what your family will be, what you will enjoy as a hobby, and so forth. After you are satisfied with the organization and meaning of the paragraph, edit it carefully for verb choices and form.

SECTION

THREE

Additional Grammar Topics of Importance

CHAPTER

7

Questions and Commands

CHAPTER ORGANIZATION

Importance of Questions

In your work at a U.S. university, you will ask and answer many questions every day. Questions are an important part of your work as a student, and you ask questions of your instructors and answer their questions in class and on tests. This chapter works with the grammar and use of information questions, yes-no questions, and tag questions. It also explains the use that instructors and textbooks make of commands in the formation of test "questions" and assignments.

Purposes of Questions

Questions are used for many different purposes.

Information
A question can seek information.

Student to another student: *"When are you going to the library?"*

Command
A question can be used to make a polite command.

Teacher to student: *"Will you close the door, please?"*

Request
A question can be used to make a request or an invitation.

Student to a friend: *"Can you go to the movie at the Student Center tonight?"*

Conversation
A question can be used to begin a conversation. One purpose of such questions is to get information. However, another important purpose is to begin a conversation.

Student to another student at their first meeting: *"What is your major?"*

Student to another student waiting for class to begin: *"Did you get all of the homework done for today?"*

Comment
A question can be used to make a comment. The teacher really means *"You have too many spelling errors in this paper."*

Teacher to student: *"Do you have a dictionary?"*

Check Knowledge
Teachers often use questions to check student knowledge. The teacher knows the answer and wants to find out if the student knows the answer.

Teacher to student: *"What is the past participle of 'write?'"*

Review of the Basic Grammar of Yes-No Questions

The following are yes-no questions that U.S. students frequently ask their instructors.

> *Will the test include Chapter One?*
> *Can we use our dictionaries during the test?*
> *Is class attendance required?*
> *Do we have to type the research paper?*

The basic grammar for a yes-no question has these features: a basic sentence is changed to form a question. The questioner changes (1) the word order and (2) the intonation of the basic sentence to turn it into a question. (3) In writing, the final period is changed to a question mark.

basic sentence
*The test **will include** Chapter One.*
yes-no question
***Will** the test include Chapter One?*

basic sentence
*We **can use** our dictionaries during the test.*
yes-no question
***Can** we use our dictionaries during the test?*

Move First Auxiliary or *Be*
In these three examples, the first auxiliary word or the form of *be* moves in front of the subject.

basic sentence
*Class attendance **is** required.*
yes-no question
***Is** class attendance required?*

A problem occurs if there is no auxiliary verb or form of *be*, for example, when you use simple present or past tense verbs.

Add *Do*

In this example, there is no word to move in front of the subject. To substitute for the auxiliary, add a form of the word *do*.

Juan took calculus last year.

***Did** Juan **take** calculus last year?*

Check Agreement

Remember that subject-verb agreement must be followed for singular subjects with present tense verbs, so *do* changes to *does*, and the verb loses its *-s*.

*The bookstore and the cafeteria **require** a picture ID to cash a check.*

***Do** the bookstore and the cafeteria **require** a picture ID to cash a check?*

*The library **requires** a picture ID to check out a book.*

***Does** the library **require** a picture ID to check out a book?*

In American English, *have* is treated like other verbs in the formation of questions.

*The library **has** books about the United Nations.*

***Does** the library **have** books about the United Nations?*

*The International Student Association **had** a meeting last night.*

***Did** the International Student Association **have** a meeting last night?*

. . . .

Practice with the Grammar of Yes-No Questions

A. Work with another student in your class to show how to change these sentences into questions to demonstrate that you both understand the grammar of **yes-no questions.** Draw a circle around the word that moves to the beginning of the sentence to form the question. Then, draw an arrow to show where the word should be placed.

✓ *The research paper (Will) be due on the last day of class?*

1. The university has planned to expand the computer laboratory.

2. The library is going to close at 9:00 P.M. during the summer.

3. Dr. Jones has been president of the university for 10 years.

4. Students who complete the ESL sequence will receive 10 hours of credit toward graduation.

5. Students who can speak Spanish as well as English will have many opportunities in the business world of the twenty-first century.

B. Working alone, change these sentences into yes-no questions; write your questions on a sheet of paper. Then, compare your answers to those of other students in your class. After you have edited for grammar and spelling, put your corrected questions in your Grammar Notebook to use as examples.

1. The university offers a degree in biophysics.
2. The computer laboratories give free lessons for students.
3. The library has a computerized catalog.
4. The textbook for chemistry cost $50.
5. The university's swimming pool opens at 8:30 A.M.
6. New students attended an orientation session on the first day of class.
7. The president gave a reception for new students.
8. Most universities require medical insurance for their students.
9. The soccer team lost its first five games.
10. A student has to have a current ID to check out a book.

Purposes of Yes-No Questions

A yes-no question is often used to get more than just a simple *yes* or *no* for the answer. Discuss the following examples with the other students in your class.

Example One

....

A student is in class. He knows there will be a test and wants more details about the kinds of questions. Specifically, he wants to know if he will have to write an essay or if all the test will be made up of short-answer or multiple-choice questions. So he asks, *"Will we have to write an essay?"* What kind of answer will satisfy him? Probably he will expect more than just *yes* or *no*. The teacher will probably explain the kinds of questions to be expected on the test.

"No, you will not have an essay question on this test, but you will on the final exam. This test is really a quiz; it will have all multiple-choice questions."

Example Two

....

In another situation, a *yes* or *no* may be all that is wanted. A student has entered class 10 minutes late (because his bus was late). He wants to know if the teacher has already called the roll so that he knows if he has already been counted absent. He whispers quietly to his neighbor, "Did he call the roll at the beginning of class?" He probably just hopes for a very quick, very quiet *yes* or *no*.

Examples One and Two show that yes-no questions can be used for two very different purposes.

Often yes-no questions are used to introduce a topic with the expectation that the person who answers will say more than just *yes* or *no*.

After a test a friend says to you: *"Was question number 20 confusing to you?"* What answer do you give?

Sometimes they are used just to get *yes* or *no*.

You are driving around the parking lot looking for a place to park. You see a man standing by his car, and you want to know if he is leaving. You say: *"Are you leaving?"* What answer do you hope to get?

. . . .

Practice with the Formation of Yes-No Questions

A. To check your own knowledge of the grammar of yes-no questions, turn each of the following sentences into a yes-no question. After writing your questions on a sheet of paper, check your answers with another student, and make any necessary changes.

1. Juan can speak French.
2. You will go to the library after class.
3. Maritza has lived in Mexico City.
4. You have done all the homework.
5. Marcus is living with his family.
6. We are having a test tomorrow.
7. Today is Monday.
8. Ali is from Egypt.
9. Irregular verbs are important to learn.
10. Irregular verbs take a long time to learn.
11. When you lived in Mexico City, you studied Spanish.

12. After you left the library, you went to the bookstore.
13. You have trouble with mathematics.
14. The university has many international students.
15. Peter lives with his brother.
16. Peter has a car.
17. Irregular verbs will be on the test.
18. You speak Spanish.
19. You made an "A" on the midterm.
20. You live close to campus.
21. You live with your family.

B. If you made any errors in exercise A, analyze the types of problems that you have. Put your answers on page 456 of the Grammar Journal.

Review of the Basic Grammar of Information Questions

• •

Information questions are questions using the words *who, what, when, where, why, how, how much, how many,* and a few others. These questions are used when you know part of the information but not all of it.

For example, you might know that something will happen but not know who will do it as in this example. You do not know the subject of the sentence.	***Someone*** *will teach my grammar class this term.*
To ask the question, you substitute *who* for the unknown subject. In writing, you change the period to a question mark.	***Who*** *will teach my grammar class this term?*

Each of the question words replaces a particular part of the sentence.

Who	subject
For human beings, *who* refers to the subject or the object of a sentence.	***Who*** *owns that book?*
	direct object/informal
	Who *did you see in the library?*

Thomas Edison in his
laboratory

Whom
Whom is used only to refer to an
object. It is required immediately
after a preposition.

object of preposition/formal
*From **whom** did Edison receive
funding for his research?*

What
What refers to either subject or
object for everything not human.

subject/not human
***What** caused the explosion?*
object/not human
***What** did you say for question 2
on the quiz?*

When
When refers to adverbials of time.

***When** does class start?*

Where
Where refers to adverbials of
place.

***Where** is the computer lab?*

Why
Why refers to adverbials of
reason.

***Why** was the test so difficult?*

How
How refers to adverbials of
manner.

***How** do you turn this computer
on?*

How Much and *How Many*
Both of these are used to refer to quantities. *How much* must always be used to refer to noncount nouns. *How many* refers to plural-count nouns.

How much information do you need?

How much did this computer cost?

How many dictionaries do you own?

How many student assistants work in the computer lab?

Structure of Information Questions

Information questions can be divided into two types based on their grammar.

Questions about Subjects
The first type questions the subject of a sentence using either *who* or *what*. The word order of the sentence does not change.

subject
Who knows the answer to this question?
subject
What happened at the lecture?

Questions about Objects and Adverbials
The second type asks about the other parts of the sentence such as objects and adverbials. The first auxiliary moves in front of the subject.

direct object
What will you study for the test?
adverbial modifier of time
When did you leave the library?

Asking Questions about Subjects of Sentences

When asking a question about a subject, just substitute *who* or *what* for the unknown subject. No other changes are necessary except to use a question mark in the written question.

Something will be included on the test.
What will be included on the test?

Someone bought your car.
Who bought your car?

Asking Questions about Objects and Adverbials

When asking a question about an object or an adverbial, the sentence grammar changes. Compare this sentence and the two possible questions. Then, write a list of the differences that you can see. Notice that *who* is used in an informal question while *whom* is used for the formal version.

Both questions are grammatically correct, but the version with *who* is much more common in spoken English. Compare your analysis to that of other students in your class.

1. *The university will hire* **someone** *as the international student advisor.*
2. **Who** *will the university hire as the international student advisor?*
3. **Whom** *will the university hire as the international student advisor?*

You should follow these steps to change a statement into an information question:

Add and Move

Add the correct question word at the beginning of the question, and move the first auxiliary or form of *be* in front of the subject. When writing questions, be sure to use a question mark rather than a period.

subject   direct object
You are reading something.
direct object
What are you reading?

Practice with the Formation of Information Questions

A. Work with another student in your class to change these sentences into questions to demonstrate that you both understand how this rule works. Notice that the examples use all of the verb forms except the simple present and the simple past. After editing your examples for grammar and spelling, write them on a sheet of paper to keep in your Grammar Notebook for future reference.

1. You can talk to **someone** about your problem. (2 possible questions)
2. You will have **something** for dinner.
3. You will go **somewhere** after class.
4. You have studied in the library **sometime**.
5. You are taking English grammar this term **for some reason**.
6. Your apartment is **somewhere**.
7. Your rent is **some amount**.

B. An additional step must be taken when the verb is in the simple present tense or the simple past tense. What is the problem when you try to follow the rule for this sentence? Write the changed forms after each step.

Example: *You saw* **someone** *at the library.*

Substitute the correct question word for the object, and put that question word at the beginning of the sentence. Move the auxiliary in front of the subject.

Obviously, the problem is that there is no auxiliary to move. Therefore, you must substitute the correct form of *do* and change the sentence's verb to its simple form. Write the correct question in this space.

Revised Rule for Asking Questions about Objects and Adverbials

Follow these steps in forming these questions. For example, make an information question to find out what courses Juan will take or the quarter when he will graduate.

*Juan will take **something** next quarter.*
*Juan plans to graduate **sometime**.*

Add Question Word
Add the correct question word and put it at the beginning of the question.

What   *When*

Move First Auxiliary
At the same time, move the first auxiliary or the form of *be* in front of the subject.

will Juan take

Add *Do*
If there is no auxiliary in the verb, use the correct form of *do* and change the sentence's verb to its simple form. (This step is used only for simple present tense or simple past tense forms of *be*).

does Juan plan

Add Question Mark
When writing the question, finish the sentence, and change the period to a question mark.

next quarter?   *to graduate?*

Complete Questions
These are the complete written questions.

What will Juan take next quarter?

When does Juan plan to graduate?

Practice with Information Questions

Work with another student to write the correct questions for the following sentences. After editing them for grammar and spelling, put the corrected questions on a sheet of paper to keep in your Grammar Notebook to use as references when you are editing your written questions.

Discuss with your class how each of these sentences illustrates a different problem with these questions. For example, how is #2 different from #3?

If you make any errors in writing these questions, analyze the types of problems that you have, and put your answers on page 456 of the Grammar Journal.

1. You gave **something** to your sister for her birthday.
2. Your sister works **somewhere.**
3. Your brother and your sister work **somewhere.**
4. You study in the library **sometime.**
5. You study in the library with **someone.**
6. You met **someone** in the cafeteria.
7. You went to the library **for some reason.**

Tag Questions

Tag questions are formed by adding a "tag" to a statement. The form of the tag is controlled by the form of the verb in the statement.

Formation

A positive sentence has a negative tag.

positive sentence: negative tag
You will graduate this quarter, won't you?

A negative sentence has a positive tag.

negative sentence: positive tag
Juan will not graduate this quarter, will he?

The tag is formed with the first auxiliary and with a pronoun based on the subject of the sentence.

Gloria can speak French, can't she?

Gloria cannot speak Arabic, can she?

Sentences with simple present and simple past tense verbs form their tags using *do, does,* or *did.*

Gloria speaks Spanish, doesn't she?

Gloria does not speak Greek, does she?

Gloria studied English in high school, didn't she?

Notice that negative tags are always contracted even in formal written English. However, tag questions are rare in written English.

Gloria did not study Dutch in high school, did she?

Use

Primarily, tag questions are used to seek confirmation or agreement. The speaker thinks that the sentence is true and asks another person to confirm the statement. The student asks the teacher to confirm the statement: *We have a test.*

TEACHER: *"Study Chapter Five for our next class."*

STUDENT: *"We have a test, don't we?"*

TEACHER: *"Yes. We'll talk about Chapter Five after you take the test."*

. . . .

Practice with Tag Questions

To check your ability to form tag questions, change the following statements into tag questions. After writing your questions on a sheet of paper, compare your answers with those of another student. Keep your corrected questions in your Grammar Notebook for future reference.

1. We will have a final examination.
2. We can use dictionaries during the test.
3. We cannot compare answers during the test.
4. We will not have a test on irregular verbs this week.
5. You speak Spanish.
6. You cannot speak Russian.
7. We have a quiz on verbs tomorrow.
8. English seems hard to many students.
9. English is easy for some students.
10. Juan is from Mexico.
11. Juan is not from Chile.
12. You are leaving for a trip tomorrow.
13. You are taking physics this quarter.
14. You are not going to the lecture tonight.
15. Maria lost her dictionary.
16. Maria's dictionary was stolen.
17. Maria's dictionary was not stolen.
18. We are not having a test tomorrow.

Questions Inside of Statements

A question can be used as part of another sentence. For example, a question can be used as the subject or the object of a sentence. Grammarians often call this **an embedded question.** This combination happens frequently in conversations for two reasons: (1) to report on a previous conversation or (2) to repeat something that another person did not hear or did not understand.

Conversation #1

MARIA: "What should I take next quarter?"
JOSE: "I'm sorry. I couldn't hear what you said. It is too noisy in here."
MARIA: "I asked what I should take next quarter."

Conversation #2

JOSE: "I talked with Maria earlier today. She had a question about next quarter."
TUAN: "What did she want to know?"
JOSE: She asked what she should take next quarter."

Word Order Change

When the question is put into a sentence, the form changes. The auxiliary goes back to its original place with the rest of the verb phrase.

MARIA: *"What should I take next quarter?"*

I asked what I should take next quarter.

She asked what she should take next quarter.

No Auxiliary *Do*

If the verb in the sentence is in the simple present tense or the simple past tense, the embedded question does not use the auxiliary *do.*

"Where does Marcus live?"

I asked where Marcus lives.

"What did Maria take last quarter?"

I asked what Maria took last quarter.

Pronoun Change

Note how the pronoun of the question had to be changed.

JUAN: *"Where can I buy used textbooks?"*

Juan asked where he can buy used textbooks.

Verb Choices for Formal Version

The most formal version of these embedded questions will require changes in the verb. If the main verb is in past tense, then the verb of the question changes to a past form, too.

formal version
He asked where he could buy used textbooks.

informal version
He asked where he can buy used textbooks.

Embedded Yes-No Questions

This example shows how to change a **yes-no question.** Use *if* or *whether or not*. Change the word order, and combine.

MARIA: *"Should I sell my used textbook?"*

She asked if she should sell her used textbook.

She asked whether or not she should sell her used textbook.

Verb Changes in Formal English

In formal written English, the following changes are usually made for embedded sentences.

Basic Verb Changes

Simple present tense becomes simple past tense.

When does class start?

The student asked when class started.

Simple past tense becomes past perfect.

Why did you move to Chicago?

He asked why I had moved to Chicago.

Present perfect becomes past perfect.

How long have you lived here?

He asked how long I had lived here.

Past perfect does not change.

Had you studied English before coming to the U.S.?

She asked if I had studied English before coming to the U.S.

Modal Changes

Will becomes *would.*

When will you take physics?

They asked when I would take physics.

Can becomes *could.*

Can you speak French?

She asked if I could speak French.

Practice with Embedded Questions

A. Change the question in parentheses to make it part of the statement. When two answers are possible, give both. After writing your sentences on a sheet of paper, compare your answers to those of the other students in your class. Make any necessary corrections, and put your answers in your Grammar Notebook to use for future reference.

1. I asked (What should Maria study next quarter?)
2. He asked (Why should we take biology?)
3. He asked (Why should I study in the library?)
4. Maria asked (Should we study Chapter One for the test?)
5. We asked (When will the final examination be given?)
6. I asked (Where does Juan live?)
7. He told me (Where does Juan live?)
8. Juan asked (Has the teacher called roll yet?)

B. Working with another student, write a list of five questions that students frequently ask in class. Compare your list with the lists of the other students in your class, and select the best five questions to use in this exercise. After editing them for grammar and spelling, write the questions on a sheet of paper.

C. Change each of the questions you wrote for exercise B to be part of a statement. Be careful to make any necessary adjustments in the pronouns, the word order, and the form of the verb. After editing them for grammar and spelling, write them on a sheet of paper to keep in your Grammar Notebook for future reference. Example: *We asked how long the test would be.*

Commands

The term ***command*** is used for sentences that have the following grammatical form: no subject is used, and the verb is the simple form. The verb does not change for time or for subject-verb agreement.

Give Orders

Commands can be used to tell someone to do something.

Put down your pencils, and turn in your papers.

Give Instructions

Commands are also used to give instructions, in recipes and other directions on how to make things.

Add salt before serving.

Commands are used in textbooks to give instructions for exercises and activities.

Write five examples.

Give Warnings

Commands can be used to give warnings.

Open the container carefully because it was packed under pressure.

Ask Questions

Commands are often used on quizzes and examinations. While Americans call these "questions," they have the grammar of commands.

Explain the term "negative balance."

Give Advice

Commands are used to give advice. The meaning is similar to that of *should*.

Do your homework every day.

You should do your homework every day.

Practice with Commands

A. Commands are often used to give advice. Study the following two pieces of advice. Do you agree with them? What do you agree with and what do you think is wrong?

Never study with another student. You will waste your time and learn another person's mistakes.

Always study with other students. They can give you emotional support and will encourage you to do your best work.

Avoid discussions on politics and religion. These topics can easily cause anger and confusion. You can make enemies rather than friends by talking about such topics.

Find out about other people's ideas on politics and religion. These topics are so interesting that everyone has something to say about them.

B. The advice given in exercise A combines commands with comments about the command. Use a highlighter to mark each command. Put brackets around the comments.

C. Discuss with your class topics that you know enough about to give advice to other people: how to be a good student, how to find an apartment, how to live well, how to be a good child to your parents. Select one of those topics for this exercise. Then, work with another student to write two pieces of advice in the same style as that used in Exercise A: combine a command with a comment. Share your advice with the class. Revise the sentences if you want to change the meaning based on the discussion. Edit the grammar, especially the form and spelling of the verbs. Then, write your advice on a sheet of paper to keep in your Grammar Notebook. You might want to add good advice from other students to your list.

Practice with Questions and Commands

A. Watch a videotaped segment of a television interview show during which members of the audience ask questions of the host and the guests. Write down the exact words of the questions. You can use the replay features of the VCR to make this task easier since you cannot expect to write as quickly as native speakers can talk. What kinds of questions are asked? Is the complete grammatical form used for yes-no or information questions? Is a short answer ever given to a yes-no question? Why?

B. With a team of two or three students go to various places at your school to listen and record questions and answers. Work together to write down exactly what is said; write both the question and the answer. Do people ever misunderstand each other? What caused the misunderstanding? In most situations, it will be polite to explain to the person in charge of the area what you are doing and to ask permission to carry out the project. Be very careful not to interfere with the work going on in the situation. Spend a total of 60 minutes in your assigned situation. Because it is difficult to concentrate for long periods of time, you should divide the time into 15-minute segments. But you should try to stay in the area for at least 15 minutes each time. Write a report about the conversations that you listen to. In your report, include (1) place, (2) number of people you listened to and their relationships (for example, "15 customers, 1 sandwich maker in the snack bar"), (3) exact wording of all questions, (4) answers to any special questions about your situation, and (5) an analysis of the types of questions that were asked.

1. Go to the snack bar at your school. Write down the exact questions the person who works there asks of each customer. Are any yes-no questions used? Are short or long answers given?
2. Go to the reference desk in your library. What kinds of questions do the librarians ask? What kinds of questions do the students ask?
3. Sit with the receptionist in your department. Listen to the questions that she or he is asked. What kinds of questions are asked? What kinds of questions does she or he ask? What kinds of answers are expected?
4. Go to an undergraduate laboratory class in physics, chemistry, or biology. What kinds of questions does the teacher ask? What kinds of questions do the students ask? What kinds of answers are given/expected?
5. Go to the information desk in the admissions office. What kinds of questions do potential students ask? What kinds of questions does the receptionist ask of the potential students? Be sure to write the exact wording of the questions.

C. After doing exercise B, each group will report to the whole class. What kinds of questions were asked? Were there any differences in different situations? Were grammatically complete questions ever asked? Where? When? By whom?

D. You and the other students in your class could conduct interviews with people in your community to find out more about life there. Discuss together some of the things that you would like to know about the community.

1. To prepare for the interview, discuss with your class the characteristics of interviews in the U.S. For example, the interviewer always begins with introductions and a short statement about the purpose of the interview; then, she or he asks the questions. The interview closes with a short statement of thanks to the person for sharing his or her time and information.
2. Work with another student to prepare a script for your interview. Write down what you will say in your introduction, questions you will ask, and your final statement of thanks. Go over what you have written with your instructor and the other students in the class to check your script to see if you have prepared useful and interesting questions—and to be sure that your introductions and thanks are culturally appropriate. Since this interview will be more formal than many other situations in which you ask questions, you should plan to use the complete grammatical forms of the questions that you ask.
3. In the interview, you can use notes to remind you of the questions, but you must not read the questions. To prepare for the interview, rehearse it with your instructor and other students in the class. It

might be useful to videotape the rehearsal so that you can also practice the appropriate body language and can observe changes that you make in your interviewing style. Rehearse the interview several times until you are very familiar with the content of the materials and are comfortable with your presentation.

4. Conduct the interview. Immediately after the interview, make notes on the answers that you received and also on the general characteristics of the interview. What kind of person did you meet— talkative, quiet? What was the place like that you were in—an office (big, little, messy desk), a home (hot, cold, clean, dirty)? What did the person look like? How did you feel? Did you get all the questions answered? Did any interruptions occur?

5. Write a description of the interview. Begin with a description of the purposes and circumstances of the interview. Then, give the material that you received in a question-answer format: first give the question that you asked, and then give the answer that you received. (Use quotation marks to indicate any exact words that you are using from the remarks of the person that you interviewed.) Share your interview with the other students in your class.

E. Skit is the name for a type of short dramatic presentation often used in the U.S. both for entertainment and for presentation of educational materials. People write their own skits for presentation at special events or parties. Students write and present skits that give humorous interpretations of events at their school. Trainers for businesses write and present skits to illustrate points that they want to make about management techniques: for example, how to interview new employees correctly.

1. At the end of this exercise, you will find a skit that was written for educational purposes to illustrate the frustrations that newcomers to the U.S. have with everyday activities. Your instructor will ask two students to volunteer to play the parts of Juan and the server. As they rehearse in front of the class, you will all help them to improve their presentation. In this skit, tone of voice and stress are important.

2. Analyze with another student the content of the skit. Have you had the experience of ordering a meal in a U.S. restaurant (not a fast-food restaurant but a place with a menu and servers)? Notice the order in which the food is selected. Is that the order you would have expected in your home country? Do you order everything at once from drink through dessert? Who asks most of the questions?

3. Analyze the grammar of the questions that are used in the skit. Which are complete questions? Which are reduced questions? Working with another student, make a list of all the reduced questions asked in the skit. Compare your list to those of other students to be sure that it is complete. Then, write the complete question for each

reduced question. Compare that list to those of the other students in your class.

Juan Orders Dinner

Scene: Juan has just arrived in the U.S. He has never ordered a meal in English. He is very hungry, but he does not speak much English. He goes into the restaurant at his hotel and sits down. A server comes over to his table. Juan's plan is to order the simplest thing he can think of—steak and potatoes.

SERVER: Good evening, sir. Would you care for a drink before dinner?

JUAN: I don't speak much English. I want steak and potatoes.

S: What was that, sir? What do you want?

J: Steak. Potatoes. I want steak and potatoes

S: What kind of steak? We have New York strip and sirloin steaks.

J: What is the difference?

S: The New York strip costs more.

J: Well, I want the other kind.

S: Oh. Okay. One sirloin steak. How do you want it cooked?

J: What? Cooked? Yes, I want it cooked.

S: How do you want it cooked? Rare, medium, well-done?

J: What is rare?

S: Not cooked very much.

J: No, no. I want it cooked very much.

S: Okay, well-done. What kind of potatoes do you want?

J: Potatoes? Yes, I want potatoes.

S: French fries, baked, mashed. How do you want the potatoes cooked?

J: Baked. I want a baked potato.

S: With butter? sour cream?

J: What is sour cream?

S: I don't know what it is. It's for baked potatoes.

J: No, no sour cream.

S: Okay, one baked potato with butter. The steak comes with a salad or cole slaw. Which would you prefer?

J: Cole slaw? What is that?

S: A kind of cabbage salad.

J: Cabbage? What is cabbage?

S: A vegetable. It's green. It's used in cole slaw.

J: Just a regular salad, please. Something simple and easy to order.

S: Okay, a green salad. What kind of dressing do you want?

J: I just want a simple steak and potato dinner. What is dressing?

S: For the salad. Bleu cheese, thousand island, house, Italian. What do you want on the salad?

J: You pick one. Anything is okay.

S: A well-done sirloin steak with a baked potato with butter. A green salad with thousand island dressing. What would you like to drink?

J: Drink? Coffee, I think. Yes, some coffee.

S: Regular or decaf?

J: What, another choice! I just want some hot coffee.

S: Yes, sir! Would you care for any dessert?

J: No, no, just my steak and potatoes. After I know more English, I'll order dessert.

F. With the rest of your class, brainstorm a list of situations in which a lot of questions are asked, for example, at an information counter in an airport. Work with a small group of students to write a skit that takes place in one of the settings. Share the skit in written form with the whole class. Discuss any changes that might need to be made to make the English more authentic.

Work with volunteers who will play the roles in your group's skit to help them give the best possible presentation. You and they might benefit from having the rehearsal videotaped so that you can make improvements in body language as well as in presentation of the words of the script.

Present either the final videotaped production or a live presentation of your skit to your whole class. If appropriate, you might like to invite other students and instructors to attend this final presentation.

CHAPTER

8

Prepositions

CHAPTER ORGANIZATION

"Preposition" Defined

Prepositions are words like *in, on, at,* and many others. These words are used to connect nouns and noun phrases to a sentence.

Prepositions are often used to create adverbial modifiers to give information about place or time as in the first examples.

place
*He put the book **on** the table.*

time
*They got here **at** 8:15 P.M.*

Prepositions are sometimes used to explain the relationship of a noun to the rest of the sentence. *With* means that a *hammer* is the **instrument** used to break the bottle. *By* means that a *car* is the **method** used to go home.

instrument
*He broke the bottle **with** a hammer.*

method
*She goes home **by** car.*

Practice Remembering Prepositions

Make a list of all the prepositions that you can remember. If you are not sure if a word is a preposition, look it up in your dictionary to check its classification. After you have made your list, compare it to the list of a classmate. After making any necessary corrections, put the list in your Grammar Notebook for future reference.

What can you do to improve your ability to use prepositions accurately? Use the information on learning styles and strategies in First Steps to give you ideas about ways to study and to learn.

Appendix E contains lists of common prepositions and of combinations of prepositions with other words.

Nine Most Common Prepositions

Grammarians tell us that the following are the nine most common prepositions. Thus, they are the most important ones to be learned.

at	*from*	*on*
by	*in*	*to*
for	*of*	*with*

Practice with the Nine Most Common Prepositions

A. Each of the nine most common prepositions can be used for several different meanings. Look in your dictionary to see what meanings are possible for the preposition *at*. Two are given here. Working with the rest of the students in your class, add examples to illustrate the other possible uses of *at*. Keep your examples in your Grammar Notebook for future reference.

At	(place)	*I live at 3835 NW 17th Street.*
	(time)	*I usually get up at 5:45 a.m.*

B. Divide your class into eight small groups. Each group should look up one of the other eight prepositions in the list of the nine most common prepositions: *by, for, from, in, of, on, to,* and *with*. Then, each group should write examples to illustrate the meanings of its preposition to share with the rest of the class. Keep a complete list of these examples in your Grammar Notebook.

In, On, At for Time and Space

Three of the most frequently used prepositions are *in, on,* and *at*. They can be used to communicate about time or about spatial relationships. For both meanings, they seem to have a systematic relationship for most of their uses. (See page 335 in Chapter Fourteen for information on the ordering of adverbial phrases.)

Examples of *In*, *On*, and *At* for Time Meanings	
In is the most general.	*I was born in 1953.*
On is more specific than *in*.	*I was born on March 14.* *I was born on March 14, 1953.* *The baby was born on Monday.*
At is the most specific.	*I was born at 7:32 a.m. I was born at 7:32 a.m. on March 14, 1953.*

Examples of *In*, *On*, and *At* for Space Meanings	
In is the most general.	*I live **in** Dallas.*
On is more specific than *in*.	*I live **on** 17th Street.*
At is the most specific.	*I live **at** 3892 17th Street.*
Usually the order is from more specific to more general. However, the name of the town or city can be given first. The number and name of the street remain together.	*I live **at** 3892 17th Street **in** Dallas* *I live **in** Dallas **at** 3892 17th Street.*

Practice with the Meanings of *In, On,* and *At*

Working alone, write examples for the meanings of *in*, *on*, and *at* for time and space. Try to write sentences that tell true or interesting facts. After you have revised and edited the sentences, share your examples with the other students in your class. Then, make any necessary corrections, and write the sentences on a sheet of paper to keep in your Grammar Notebook to have as examples for future reference.

Relationship Meanings for Prepositions

Grammarians have observed the following meanings for some commonly used prepositions.

Agent
by in passive sentences: who or what did this?

*The computer was damaged **by** the electrical storm.*

Means or Method
by: how was this done?

*He comes to school **by** bus.*

Source
from: where did it come from?

*He got the information **from** his cousin.*

Together
with

*She studies **with** her friends.*

Tool or Instrument
with

*He cut the hamburger **with** his knife.*

To Help Someone
for

*He took notes in class **for** his sick friend.*

To Replace Someone
for

*The chairman taught the class **for** the sick teacher.*

Use of Prepositions

Prepositions are seldom found alone. They are usually found in combination with nouns and with noun phrases.

The combination of a preposition with its object is called a **prepositional phrase** or a **preposition phrase.** In this sentence, the three prepositional phrases are *on the table, under the window,* and *beside the door.*

The student put his books on the table under the window beside the door.

Practice Recognizing Prepositional Phrases

A problem for some ESL students in reading and in writing is to recognize when a prepositional phrase begins and when it ends. To practice recognition of prepositional phrases, mark the phrases in this passage by putting parentheses around each prepositional phrase.

The student put his books (on the table) (under the window) (beside the door).

The Flight of the Columbia

[1]After years of research, the United States made its first test flight of a space shuttle on April 12, 1981. [2]The name of the first shuttle was Columbia, and this vehicle was launched into space from the Kennedy Space Center at Cape Canaveral, Florida. [3]After a successful flight in

The Space Shuttle Columbia rises off the pad at Kennedy Space Center, Florida, on April 12, 1981.

space, the spacecraft made a deep descent toward land, and the pilots glided the craft to a landing. [4]Astronauts John Young and Robert Crippen emerged from the new space vehicle at Edwards Air Force Base in California on April 14, 1981, 54 hours after lift-off.

Adapted from *Encyclopedia Americana*, 1983 ed., s.v. "space shuttle."

To as a Preposition

The word *to* has two important grammatical functions.

Infinitive
To is used to make infinitives.   *He likes **to read** about computers.*

Preposition
To is used as a preposition.   *He went **to the library**.*

To is used as a preposition with certain frequently used phrases such as the following:

be accustomed to	*be used to*	*look forward to*
be opposed to	*get used to*	*object to*

The first two examples are correct, but the third example is wrong because *to* is used as a preposition and must be followed by a noun or a gerund.

correct
I am looking forward to the party.
correct
*I am looking forward to **going** to the party.*
incorrect
I am looking forward to **go to the party.*

Look forward to is very frequently used in formal letters. Notice that the object is often a gerund, but nouns such as *arrival* can be used.

We look forward to hearing from you on this matter.

I am looking forward to your arrival in St. Louis.

Meanings of the Possessive

Grammarians have explained that the word *possessive* covers many different meanings. It might help you use *of* and *'s* more confidently if you think about the different meanings these forms can have.

Practice with the Meaning of Possessives

With the other students in your class, analyze the meanings in these phrases. Use one of the following terms to label each phrase: ownership, relationship, time, location, amount-value, body part, measurement, and agent/source. ("Agent" means the person who did something.)

1. the teacher's lecture   *agent/source*

2. two dollars' worth of candy   *amount/value*

3. John's foot   *body part*

4. the top of the car   *location*

5. an ounce of perfume   *measurement*

6. Mary's book   *ownership*

7. the musician's daughter   *relationship*

8. last year's budget   *time*

9. the first of the week _____

10. Roberto's apartment _____

11. Mary's sister's child _____

12. Bell's telephone _____

13. Elisa's question _____

14. the end of the year _____

15. my brother's arm _____

16. a dollar's worth of gasoline _____

17. a pound of tea _____

Making Choices between *Of* and the Apostrophe for Possessives

The difficult questions that many students ask include: when do I use *of* and when do I use *'s*? Grammarians have given the following answers.

Ownership or Relationship
With proper nouns, *'s* must be used to refer to ownership or relationship.

ownership
Maria's house
relationship
Maria's mother

Of cannot be used to express ownership, possession, or relationship involving proper names.

incorrect	correct
the arm of Jose	*Jose's arm*

incorrect	correct
the book of Ali	*Ali's book*

incorrect	correct
the aunt of Esther	*Esther's aunt*

Body Parts
English uses the possessive when talking about an individual's body, but the articles are used to talk about bodies in general or in scientific communication.

*The fall broke **Mike's** arm.*
personal use
***His arm** will be in a cast for six weeks.*
technical or scientific use
*Dr. Smith's research is about **the human arm.***

Human Beings

's is preferred when the noun refers to human beings or to the higher animals.

the student's question

the leopard's spots

Inanimate Nouns

Of is preferred for inanimate nouns.

the top of the car

the sound of music

Practice with Prepositions

A. As a review, turn to the Diagnostic Test on page 14 of First Steps, and look closely at items 56–60. Compare your answers today with your answers from the first week of this course.

B. Mark with a highlighter all of the prepositions that you used in the Diagnostic Paragraph in First Steps; notice especially any errors that you made with prepositions in that writing sample. Answer the questions on page 457 of the Grammar Journal.

C. Discussion Assignment: Share any information that you have about volcanoes with your class. For example: What is the name of a famous volcano? Would you want to live near a volcano?

Grammar Assignment: Add appropriate prepositions in the spaces provided, and then put parentheses ( ) around all of the prepositional phrases in the passage. There are more prepositional phrases to identify than there are exercise blanks.

Volcanoes

[1]Volcanoes have always fascinated people; however, the damage (from five famous volcanoes) illustrates their danger. [2]____ A.D. 69, there was a violent earthquake near Pompeii, and ____ the next ten years, there were many small quakes. [3]Then, ____ August 24, the eruption of Mount Vesuvius began and continued ____ eight days. [4]The city ____ Pompeii was buried ____ volcanic ash, and many ____ its inhabitants died. [5]____ 1783, after a week of numerous earthquakes, the Laki fissure in Iceland opened ____ June 8. [6]A strong lava flow

continued _____ mid-August, and weak explosive activity continued _____ several months. [7]The ash from the volcano destroyed crops and caused a severe famine. [8]_____ 1815, the eruption _____ the Tambora Volcano on the island of Sumbawa may have been the greatest ever witnessed _____ man. [9]The first warning came _____ 1812 when people observed a cloud of fumes at the summit. [10]Three years later, _____ April 5, violent explosions began; these explosions could be heard 1,000 miles away and continued _____ April 12. [11]There was complete darkness _____ three days. [12]The eruption killed 10,000 people directly, and 82,000 others died _____ starvation or disease. [13]_____ another major volcanic explosion, Mt. Katmai _____ Alaska erupted _____ 1912 after a week of numerous earthquakes. [14]_____ the afternoon _____ June 6, 2½ days of intense explosions began. [15]Ash was thrown many miles _____ the air; _____ Kodiak, 100 miles away, the ash was nearly a foot thick. [16]Volcanoes sometimes surprise us. [17]The Helgafell volcano on the island of Heimaey had been dormant _____ thousands of years when it erupted without warning _____ 1:00 A.M. _____ January 23, 1973, and rained hot ashes and lava on the town _____ Vestmannaeyar, Iceland. [18]The town was evacuated, and the eruption continued _____ four weeks. [19]Many houses were destroyed _____ the fire or buried under tons of lava and ash. [20]Today, scientists attempt to predict volcanic eruptions in order to save lives and property.

Adapted from *Collier's Encyclopedia*, 1987 ed., s.v. "volcanoes."

D. Analyze the writing that you have done this term, and make a list of any errors with prepositions that were marked by your instructor. What kinds of mistakes did you make? Word choice? Spelling? Did you find the same mistake more than one time? Write the analysis on a sheet of paper to keep in your Grammar Notebook. What will you do about this problem?

E. With the other students in your class, look over the front page of today's newspaper. Make a list of all the prepositional phrases that you find in the headlines. What prepositions were used most often? Which of the two meanings were used: time/space or relationship?

F. What are the prepositions that can be used to talk or write about time and time relationships? In the text, you reviewed *in, on,* and *at.* However, there are several other time prepositions. Work with the students in your class to make as complete a list as you can. For each preposition in your list, write a sentence to illustrate the use of the word. Share your examples with the rest of the class. Then, write the list of words and the example sentences on a sheet of paper to keep in your Grammar Notebook.

G. A good English-English dictionary can help you expand your knowledge of English grammar. But, you must be careful to use the dictionary in an effective way. For example, look up the meaning of *of* in your dictionary. Talk with the members of your class about ways in which you can use that information. How can you get the information out of the dictionary and into your own English?

1. Many students learn new information through listening. If you are such a learner, perhaps you would benefit from making a tape of the information in the dictionary. First, read the definition aloud, then add examples and illustrations for each possible meaning, and then listen to the tape.
2. Other students learn from writing and looking at what they have written. The physical act of writing helps get the information into their memories. If you are such a learner, perhaps you would benefit from writing the definition in your Grammar Notebook with an example to illustrate each possible meaning. Then, read through the information you have written. Does it help to read the material at frequent intervals?
3. What other ways are useful for learning new information? Use the information on learning styles and strategies in First Steps to guide your discussion of ways to learn new materials.

H. Wherever English is used, prepositions will be used. Working with another student, analyze the advertisements from a current magazine for one of these products: cars, medicine, food, computers. Find at least three different advertisements for the product. What prepositions did you find? Which ones are most frequently used? What meanings are used: time/space, relationships, possession?

I. To practice editing someone else's written English, turn to Section Four. Study the information about editing on page 404, and then do the editing exercises on page 419.

J. For additional writing topics, turn to Section Four, page 428.

C H A P T E R

9

Nouns, Articles, and Determiners

CHAPTER ORGANIZATION

Articles and Other Determiners

Determiners are words like *this, some,* and several others that are used to "determine" the meaning of nouns. *A/an* and *the* are probably the most important members of this group of words. *A/an* and *the* are also called **articles.**

Determiners

a/an	*any*	*this/that*	*my*	noun + 's
the	*some*	*these/those*	*his*	noun + s'
	each		*her*	
	every		*its*	
	no		*your*	
			our	
			their	
a book	*each book*	*this book*	*my book*	*Mary's books*
the book	*some books*	*these books*		*the students' books*

	Articles			
	Singular	**Plural**	**Noncount**	**Proper**
a/an	*a book*	—	—	—
the	*the book*	*the books*	*the money*	*the Smiths*
no article	—	*books*	*money*	*John Smith*

Note: — means that no such form exists.

Selection of articles (*a/an* or *the*) is one of the most difficult areas of English grammar for many ESL students. In order to make the correct selection, you must know (1) the grammatical type of the noun and (2) the meaning of the noun.

Types of Nouns

214

Noun Meaning

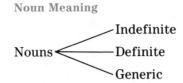

Selection of the correct article is one of the ways that you give a noun the exact meaning that you want it to have. In this chapter, you will first study nouns as preparation for selection of *a/an* and *the*.

Proper and Common Nouns

Proper nouns are the names of specific people, places, and things such as *Bill, Michigan State University, Seattle, Sears,* and so forth. **Common nouns** are all of the rest; common nouns include words such as *book* and *intelligence.* Usually, articles are not used with proper nouns. However, some important exceptions are listed below.

Articles with Proper Nouns

Use *The*	Do Not Use *The*
1. Use *the* with these countries. *the Netherlands* *the Soviet Union* *the Sudan* *the United Arab Emirates* *the United States*	1. Do not use *the* with other countries. *Brazil* *India* *Italy* *Nigeria*
2. Use *the* with geographical locations: canals, deserts, forests, oceans, rivers, seas. *the Atlantic Ocean* *the Black Forest* *the Mediterranean Sea* *the Nile River* *the Panama Canal* *the Sahara Desert*	
3. Use *the* with plural islands, lakes, and mountains. *the Great Lakes* *the Hawaiian Islands* *the Rocky Mountains*	3. Do not use *the* with singular islands, lakes, and mountains. *Mount Hood* *Lake Michigan* *Maui*

Use **The**	Do Not Use **The**
4. Use *the* in *the University of _____* . *the University of Wyoming*	4. Do not use *the* when a proper name comes first. *Idaho State University*
5. Use *the* when referring to people. *the Italians*	5. Do not use *the* with names of languages. *Italian* But use *the* if the word *language* is included. *the Italian language*

Practice with Articles Used with Proper Names

A. Working with the other students in your class, make a list of the colleges and universities in the state where you are now studying. You can get the information in several ways. First, compile a list based on the names known by the students in your class. Second, show the list to students who have lived in the area for a long time. Then, talk with a reference librarian about ways to make the list more complete. Write the complete names of each institution on a sheet of paper. After writing the names, draw a circle around any name that must include the article *the*. Then, compare your list to those of other students in your class. Make any necessary corrections, and put your corrected list in your Grammar Notebook.

B. Select a state in the United States that you would like to visit. Then, seek information in the reference section of the library about the physical geography of that state. Make a list of the names of canals, deserts, forests, rivers, lakes, and mountains in the state. Share this information with other students in your class by showing them a map of the state and the locations of each of these physical features.

C. Add *the* where necessary with the following proper nouns. Compare your answers to those of other students in your class. Make any necessary changes, and follow the directions in exercise D.

1. _____ University of Alabama
2. _____ Japan
3. _____ United States
4. _____ Hong Kong
5. _____ Alabama

6. _____ Asia
7. _____ Philippine Islands
8. _____ French language
9. _____ Arabic
10. _____ Finger Lakes

11. _____ Amazon River   20. _____ Kansas State University

12. _____ Suez Canal   21. _____ Rocky Mountains

13. _____ Hawaii   22. _____ Africa

14. _____ Duke University   23. _____ Arctic Ocean

15. _____ China Sea   24. _____ Lake Michigan

16. _____ University of Nevada 25. _____ Wichita State University

17. _____ Soviet Union   26. _____ Mount Ararat

18. _____ Mojave Desert   27. _____ United Arab Emirates

19. _____ Saudi Arabia   28. _____ Turkey

   D. Analyze the answers that you gave in exercise C by filling in the
following blanks.

1. How many articles did you add?   _____

2. Write the proper nouns and their articles from the list above in the
   following spaces.
   a. Use *the* with specific countries.

   the United States   _____   _____

   b. Use *the* with canals, deserts, forests, oceans, rivers, seas.

   _____   _____   _____

   _____   _____

   c. Use *the* with plural islands, lakes, mountains.

   _____   _____   _____

   d. Use *the* in the *University of* ____ .

   _____   _____

   e. Use *the* in the ____ *language.*

   _____

Count Nouns

· ·

Count nouns are those that have singular and plural form, for example, *book/books.*

Regular plural nouns are spelled by adding -*s* or -*es* to the singular.	*car/cars* *bus/buses*
Irregular plural nouns are formed in other ways. Your dictionary gives the spelling of plural forms of these irregular nouns.	*man/men* *radius/radii*

Noncount Nouns

· ·

A **noncount noun** is a word such as *furniture* or *sugar* that does not have either a singular or a plural form. Here are some categories for analysis of noncount nouns. Add other words that you and your fellow students know belong to each group.

1. Things that come in very small pieces: *rice, salt, sand*

   _____   _____   _____

2. Wholes made up of similar parts (the parts are often count nouns): *food, furniture, luggage*

   _____   _____   _____

3. Names of subjects of study: *ESL, biology, mathematics*

   _____   _____   _____

4. Abstractions: *happiness, justice, luck*

   _____   _____   _____

5. Liquids/fluids: *blood, milk, water*

   _____   _____   _____

6. Gases: *carbon monoxide, hydrogen, oxygen*

   _____   _____   _____

7. Solids/minerals: *gold, ice, mercury*

    _____   _____   _____

8. Sports/types of recreation: *chess, tennis, soccer*

    _____   _____   _____

9. Natural phenomena: *dew, rain, snow*

    _____   _____   _____

10. Diseases: *measles, mumps, smallpox*

    _____   _____   _____

. . . .

Practice with Identifying Count and Noncount Nouns

A. Complete the following list with a classmate. Classify the following nouns into two groups: count nouns (singular and plural forms) and noncount nouns. Then, add the plural forms of each count noun. Check the plural forms in your dictionary.

advice	*essay*	*library*	*pollution*
air	*experiment*	*man*	*rain*
book	*foot*	*mathematics*	*report*
calculator	*gold*	*money*	*rice*
coffee	*happiness*	*news*	*storm*
computer	*homework*	*novel*	*student*
desk	*honesty*	*occupation*	*suggestion*
equipment	*information*	*paragraph*	*weather*

Count Nouns	Plural Form	Noncount Nouns
1. _____	_____	1. _____
2. _____	_____	2. _____
3. _____	_____	3. _____
4. _____	_____	4. _____
5. _____	_____	5. _____

6. _____   _____   6. _____

7. _____   _____   7. _____

8. _____   _____   8. _____

9. _____   _____   9. _____

10. _____   _____   10. _____

11. _____   _____   11. _____

12. _____   _____   12. _____

13. _____   _____   13. _____

14. _____   _____   14. _____

15. _____   _____   15. _____

16. _____   _____   16. _____

B. Working with another student, make a list of 20 nouns that are often used in the classroom: for example, *pencil* and *homework*. Then, divide the nouns into two lists; make one list of count nouns and a second list of noncount nouns. Add the plural forms of each count noun as is done in exercise A. Use your dictionary to check the spelling of the plural form of each noun.

Count Nouns	Plural Form	Noncount Nouns
1. _____	_____	1. _____
2. _____	_____	2. _____
3. _____	_____	3. _____
4. _____	_____	4. _____
5. _____	_____	5. _____
6. _____	_____	6. _____
7. _____	_____	7. _____
8. _____	_____	8. _____

9. _____ _____   9. _____

10. _____ _____   10. _____

11. _____ _____   11. _____

12. _____ _____   12. _____

After you have finished, compare your answers to those of other students in the class. Correct any errors that you find on the charts. Add to your chart any words that you like and think are important to know.

Counting Noncount Nouns

Noncount nouns are not countable in English except by adding another phrase.

You cannot say *a furniture or *two furnitures.

incorrect
*I need a furniture for my apartment.

correct
I need some furniture for my apartment.

incorrect
*I bought two furnitures for my apartment.

correct
I bought two pieces of furniture for my apartment.

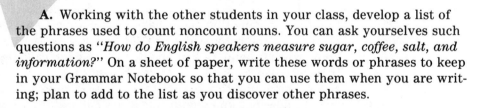

Practice with Counting Noncount Nouns

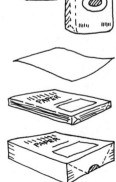

A. Working with the other students in your class, develop a list of the phrases used to count noncount nouns. You can ask yourselves such questions as *"How do English speakers measure sugar, coffee, salt, and information?"* On a sheet of paper, write these words or phrases to keep in your Grammar Notebook so that you can use them when you are writing; plan to add to the list as you discover other phrases.

**Words Used by English Speakers to Measure
Sugar, Coffee, Salt, and Other Noncount Nouns**

a teaspoon of sugar   a sheet of paper
a package of sugar   a package of paper
a pound of sugar   a box of paper

B. Add to your list by interviewing U.S. students to get them to tell you possible phrases to use in counting noncount nouns. Ask them to tell you the words they would use in the blank space in the following sentence. Then, compare your answers to those of other students in your class. Add new words and phrases to the list you made in exercise A.

In the supermarket, I can buy _____ *of butter.*

_____ *of cereal.*

_____ *of coffee.*

_____ *of salt.*

Meanings of Nouns

· ·

When English speakers use common nouns to communicate, the nouns are always definite, indefinite, or generic. Grammarians tell us that these are fundamental ideas in English communication.

Definite means that the speaker thinks that the listener knows what is being talked about. When a person says *"The book is on the table,"* the speaker thinks that the listener knows exactly what book is being talked about. The meaning of *the book* is **definite** and **specific.**

definite/specific
The book *is on the table.*

Indefinite means that the speaker thinks that the listener does NOT know what is being talked about. If the speaker says *"A car hit my sister,"* he or she thinks that the listener does not know anything about that particular car. After mentioning the car, the speaker changes to *the* because the listener knows about the car. *Old man* is **indefinite** because the speaker thinks that the listener does not know about the old man yet. However, a **specific** old man is meant.

indefinite/specific
A car *hit my sister.*

definite/specific   indefinite/specific
The car *was driven by **an old man.***

definite/specific   indefinite/specific
The old man *had taken **some strong medicine.***

definite/specific
The medicine *made him sleepy.*

Generic means that the speaker is talking about a whole class of people or things. This use of the noun *doctors* has generic meaning because the word is referring to doctors as a class of people. The sentence is NOT about **specific** doctors; the meaning is **nonspecific** and **generic.**

generic/nonspecific
Doctors *work many hours each day.*

How English Speakers Make Situations Definite

When is a noun definite? A noun is definite if you think your reader or listener knows the same information that you do. Also, the meaning is about something specific rather than about something generic or general.

When can I be sure that the reader knows the same things I do? Grammarians have suggested a number of different situations in which a speaker or writer can assume that a reader or listener would understand a noun as definite. This list is not complete, but it can help you understand the concept of **definite** more clearly.

Situations That Are Definite

Unique
The noun refers to something that is unique for everyone in the world.

the *sun,* ***the*** *moon,* ***the*** *universe,* ***the*** *stars*

Setting
The noun is made specific by its setting. For example, everyone in the classroom will understand the same meaning for these nouns.

the *blackboard,* ***the*** *instructor,* ***the*** *students*

The nouns refer to the parts of some whole that is being talked about. If you are describing a house, then you can write *the windows, the doors.* If you are describing a computer, you can write *the disk drive, the monitor.*

Last weekend, we painted our house. Painting ***the*** *doors and* ***the*** *windows was especially hard work.*

I do not have much room on my desk for my computer, so I set ***the*** *monitor on top of* ***the*** *disk drive unit.*

223

Second Mention

A writer can mention something one time, using *a* or *an* because the reader does not share the same information. But after that first use, the writer changes to *the* because the information is now shared with the reader. Grammar texts usually illustrate this use with the beginning sentences of a story.

*Long ago, **an** old woman lived in **a** village. **The** old woman had two grandchildren who came to **the** village to visit her every Sunday.*

This use is not, however, restricted to folktales.

*To carry out this procedure, **a** new computer program had to be written. **The** program was extremely expensive.*

Phrases/Clauses

A writer can make a noun definite by adding a phrase or a clause to define it.

***the** president of our organization*

***the** house next door to mine*

***the** car that I hit in the parking lot*

Superlatives/Numbers

The parts of sets are considered definite. This group includes the superlative adjective form because it marks a definite member of a set.

***the** first page*

***the** slowest walker*

***the** most difficult assignment*

Known to Particular Group

Members of a particular group share meanings. For example, if you say *"the president,"* Americans will assume that you mean the president of the U.S.

***The** president went to Europe yesterday.*

Pointing

A speaker can point (with a finger, a nod of the head) at something and use *the* because he or she assumes that the listener then understands the particular object being talked about. This is almost impossible for a writer.

*She pointed to the desk and said, "Give me **the** book over there."*

Practice with Definite Meaning

A. Write two sentences to illustrate the first and second categories of definite meaning for nouns. Share your four sentences with the other students in your class. Select your favorite examples, and write them on a sheet of paper to keep in your Grammar Notebook.

B. Circle every definite article in the following sentences, and identify which of the seven situations described above applies to each article. Discuss your choices with the rest of your class.

1. **The** library is **the** tallest building on campus.

   Reason: _the library = SETTING_

   Reason: _the tallest building = SUPERLATIVE_

2. The study areas in the library are on the second floor.

   Reason: _____

   Reason: _____

   Reason: _____

3. Every student needs a library card to check out books. The library card must be validated each semester in the business office.

   Reason: _____

   Reason: _____

4. Students who want to check out books must go to the circulation desk with their library cards.

   Reason: _____

5. Students who need help in finding a particular book should go to a reference librarian. The reference librarian will help them find the book.

   Reason: _____

   Reason: _____

Specific Meaning Compared to Generic Meaning

Both **definite** nouns and **indefinite** nouns refer to **specific** people, objects, and ideas. In contrast, **generic** nouns are used to communicate about classes or groups of people, objects, and ideas. That is, **generic** is **nonspecific** and **general.**

Sometimes a noun refers to a particular individual, as in the first example.

definite/specific
*You know **the teacher** of this class.*

In other instances, the noun can be used to refer to a kind of person rather than to a specific individual. This sentence is about teachers as a group or as a profession rather than about specific teachers.

generic/nonspecific
***Teachers** usually have many years of training.*

The generic is also often used to place people in categories; it identifies them by their job or some other group.

generic/nonspecific
*My brother is **a teacher.***

Generic is different from indefinite. In this example, the indefinite noun refers to a specific teacher, but the speaker does not think that the listener shares the information. The philosophy teacher from Greece is a specific person, but the speaker does not think you know who is being talked about, so the indefinite is used to introduce the topic. In contrast, the speaker in the last example has the ambition to be one of this type of teacher.

indefinite/specific
*I met **a philosophy teacher** from Greece at the reception.*

generic/nonspecific
*I want to be **a philosophy teacher.***

Practice with Indefinite, Definite, and Generic Meanings of Nouns

A. Identify the meaning of the italicized nouns in the following sentences: indefinite or definite or generic.

definite   1. I saw the **dean** in the administration building yesterday.

_____   2. **Students** take many tests during their years at school.

_____   3. A **counselor** called you yesterday.

_____   4. I made a serious **mistake** on my last history exam. It lowered my grade to a "B."

_____   5. I want to give my roommate a **book** for her birthday.

_____   6. I saw a **book** on the Middle East in the bookstore. It cost $35.

_____   7. The **book** for my world history course is out of date.

_____   8. I usually eat in the **cafeteria.**

_____   9. When I study, I listen to **music.**

_____   10. I wrote an **essay** last night.

_____   11. **Essays** are common in English classes.

B. Construct sentences with the following nouns: the first sentence should show generic meaning, and the second sentence should show specific meaning.

1. *book*
   Generic: *Books are tools for learning.*
   Specific: *I brought a book to class. The book on the table is mine.*

2. *computer*

   Generic: _____

   Specific: _____

3. *homework*

   Generic: _____

   Specific: _____

4. *student*

   Generic: _____

   Specific: _____

227

5. *university*

Generic: _____

Specific: _____

Four Types of Generic Nouns

The generic meaning can be formed in four different ways. Singular, plural, noncount, and proper nouns can be used for generic meaning.

Generic-1
This first type has the pattern of "*a/an* + singular noun." In this example, a singular noun with the article *a* is used for generic meaning; the category "teacher" is being discussed.

generic-1
A teacher must have years of training.
generic-1
My father is a teacher.

Generic-2
The second pattern is "*the* + singular noun." In the example, a singular noun with the article *the* is used for generic meaning; the category "teacher" is being discussed.

generic-2
The teacher has many responsibilities to society.

This is the formal way that writers indicate generic meaning. Research has shown that this generic type is the one preferred in technical or informative writing on plants, animals, inventions, and other technical topics.

generic-2
The tiger is greatly feared by rural Indians.

Generic-3
The third pattern uses plural nouns with no article for generic meaning. Generic-3 is used in less formal situations, especially in conversations, to give generalities about a type of thing or group of people.

generic-3
Teachers are seldom paid as much as lawyers.
generic-3
Teachers should be patient with students.

This generic type is a less formal version of the Generic-2 type. It can be used anywhere that Generic-2 is used.

generic-3
Books *are basic for a student's life.*

generic-3
Computers *have altered the ways in which business is conducted.*

generic-3
Tigers *are greatly feared by rural Indians.*

Note: Generic-4 has limited use and is not discussed in this text. Examples can be found in P. Byrd and B. Benson, *Improving the Grammar of Written English: The Handbook.*

Generic-5

Remember that noncount nouns form their generic without any article at all.

generic-5
Sugar *is Cuba's most important agricultural product.*

A common problem for ESL students is to use *the* for this meaning.

incorrect
***The** *water is necessary for* **the** *human life.*

correct
Water *is necessary for* **human life.**

incorrect
All human cultures have developed* **the *music.*

correct
All human cultures have developed **music.**

The is used with noncount nouns only when a phrase or clause is added to make the meaning **definite.**

definite
The water that I drank before class *tasted strange.*

definite
The water in my glass *was cloudy.*

. . . .

Practice with Generic Meaning for Noncount Nouns

A. In the following sentences, noncount nouns are used for generic meaning. Use a highlighter to mark all of these noncount nouns.

1. People must have food, water, and shelter to live.
2. "Street people" are poor people who do not have shelter.
3. They cannot find food easily.
4. Our city government needs information about these poor people.

B. Use a highlighter to mark the noncount nouns in these sentences, and then edit the grammatical errors in each sentence.

1. I do not have much food in my kitchen: only salt, the vinegar, the sugar, and coffee.
2. The admissions office provides the information about the university.
3. Human life should include more than the shelter, the food, and water. We also need the happiness and the love.
4. My brother is studying the mathematics, but I prefer physics.

Summary of the Use of Articles

Two Important Facts to Notice about Articles

1. Singular-count nouns must always have either an article or a determiner.
2. For generic meaning, noncount nouns never have an article or a determiner.

Using *The*

The is used for these four meanings:

Some Proper Nouns
With some proper nouns — ***the*** *United States*

Singular- or Plural-Count Nouns/Definite
With singular- or plural-count nouns to mean **definite**

*I bought **the** required textbook for this class yesterday.*

*I bought **the** required textbooks for this class yesterday.*

Noncount Nouns/Definite
With noncount nouns to mean **definite**

*I found **the** information for my research project.*

Singular-Count Nouns/Generic
With singular-count nouns to mean **generic**

*Modern life has been changed by **the** computer.*

Using *A/An*

Use *a/an* for these two meanings:

Singular-Count Nouns/Indefinite
With singular-count nouns to mean **indefinite**

*I met **a** musician at the concert; his daughter studies at our university.*

Singular-Count Nouns/Generic
With singular-count nouns to mean **generic**

*My mother is **a** teacher.*

Note: Remember that *a* is used before consonant sounds and *an* before vowel sounds. The pronunciation of *university* begins with a consonant sound.

an apple
a book
a university

Using No Article or Determiner

For the following meanings, a noun is used without an article or determiner. In most uses without an article or determiner, a noun has the generic meaning. Remember that a singular-count noun must have an article or determiner.

Proper Nouns/Definite
With most proper nouns (which are **definite** in meaning)

definite place
*He lives in **Alaska**.*

Plural Nouns/Generic
With plural-count nouns to mean **generic**

general type of animal
***Tigers** are both beautiful and dangerous.*

Noncount Nouns/Generic
With noncount nouns to mean **generic**

general type of substance
*People need **water** to live.*

. . . .

Practice with Nouns and Articles

A. Add *a* or *an* to the singular-count nouns in the following list. Not all of the following nouns are count nouns. Then, answer the questions at the end of the list.

an exam	____ laboratory	____ assignment
____ school	____ problem	____ classroom

_____ homework	_____ test	_____ tutor
_____ essay	_____ advice	_____ library
_____ book	_____ grade	_____ football field
_____ gymnasium	_____ cafeteria	_____ computer
_____ bookstore	_____ information	_____ auditorium
_____ calculator	_____ equipment	_____ lecture

1. How many times did you add *a*?   _____

2. How many times did you add *an*?   _____

3. How many noncount nouns did you find?   _____

B. Add *a* or *an* in the appropriate places to the following sentences.

1. There is dictionary on the desk.
2. The students worked for hour on the test.
3. This is very difficult chapter.
4. Yesterday, I met friend at the city library.
5. Tuan has college degree.
6. Mathematics is difficult subject.
7. Political science is interesting subject.
8. Spanish is important language.

C. Use a highlighter to mark each of the singular nouns in the following sentences. It is important to be able to identify singular-count nouns because these nouns must always have an article or a determiner.

1. For this class, all students need a notebook, a pen, a dictionary, and the two required textbooks.
2. The notebook will be used to take notes, to keep copies of each test, and to record the daily assignment.
3. The dictionary will be used in each class and on all tests.
4. The textbooks can be bought at the bookstore.
5. Each student must have his or her own copies of the texts.

D. Use a highlighter to mark each of the singular nouns in the following sentences. Edit the sentences by adding articles or determiners where they are needed. These sentences are about a classroom situation: a student named John needs information about one question that he missed on a test.

1. John raised arm to ask question.

2. Teacher answered John's question carefully.

3. John did not understand answer.

4. He raised arm again and asked same question again.

5. Teacher asked John to use different words to ask question.

6. John's classmates all tried to help teacher understand question.

7. Finally, teacher understood and answered question.

Determiners and Quantifiers with Count and Noncount Nouns

Determiners are words such as *a/an, the, some,* and *my.* (See page 214 for a more complete list of these words.) In addition to determiners, nouns can be modified by words that grammarians call **quantifiers.** These are words such as *many, little,* and *few.*

Determiners and Quantifiers **with Count and Noncount Nouns**		
Singular	**Plural**	**Noncount**
a book	*some books*	*some water*
one book	*two books* *several books*	
	many books *a lot of books* *few books* *a few books*	*much water* *a lot of water* *little water* *a little water*
my book	*my books*	*my water*

Two determiners cannot be used with the same noun. However, a determiner can be combined with a quantifier.

incorrect
***The my** book*

correct
***My many** grammar books*

Some as the Plural for *A/An*

The articles *a* and *an* can only be used with singular-count nouns. *Some* is used for indefinite meaning with plural nouns and with noncount nouns.

Singular/Indefinite
These examples illustrate the use of *a* and *an* for indefinite meaning. The speaker is thinking about a specific dictionary and a specific orange but thinks that you do not know which one he is talking about.

indefinite/specific/singular
*I bought **a** new dictionary.*

indefinite/specific/singular
*I bought **an** orange for lunch.*

Plural/Indefinite
This example illustrates the use of *some* for a plural noun with indefinite meaning.

indefinite/specific/plural
*I bought **some** new books*

Noncount/Indefinite
Some can be used with noncount nouns for indefinite meaning.

indefinite/specific/noncount
*I bought **some** coffee for breakfast.*

Some and *Any*

Some and *any* are similar in meaning but are used in different sentences. Study the examples given in the chart, and then answer the questions in exercise A.

Some	*Any*
*I need **some** time for this project.*	*I do not have **any** time to work on this project.*
*He borrowed **some** money for his tuition.*	*He did not borrow **any** money.*
*We saw **some** friends in the library.*	*We did not see **any** friends in the library.*

Much, Many, and *A Lot Of*

Much, many, and *a lot of* are similar in their meanings but are used in different kinds of sentences. Look carefully at the sentences in the chart, and then with the other students in your class, answer the questions in exercise B.

	a lot of	many	much
Noncount Nouns	*He has **a lot of** paper.*	—	—
	*Did you buy **a lot of** paper?*	—	*Did you buy **much** paper?*
	*I don't have **a lot of** paper.*	—	*I don't have **much** paper.*
Plural-Count Nouns	*I have **a lot of** books.*	*I have **many** books.*	—
	*Do you have **a lot of** books?*	*Do you have **many** books?*	—
	*I don't have **a lot of** books.*	*I don't have **many** books.*	—

Note: — means that no such form exists or that the combination is not generally used.

Practice with *Some, Any, Much, Many,* and *A Lot Of*

A. Working with the other students in your class, answer the following questions about the examples in the chart on *some* and *any*.

1. *Some* is used with what kind(s) of nouns?
2. *Any* is used with what kind(s) of nouns?
3. How are *some* and *any* different in the kinds of nouns they can go with?
4. How are the sentences different for *any* as compared to *some*?

B. Working with the other students in your class, answer the following questions about the examples given in the chart on *much, many,* and *a lot of.*

1. What kinds of nouns are used with *a lot of*?

2. What kinds of nouns are used with *much*?
3. What kinds of nouns are used with *many*?
4. Which word(s) are used in questions?
5. Which word(s) are used with negative verbs?
6. Which word(s) are used in statements?
7. How is *a lot of* different from *much* and *many*?

C. Write five sentences about things that you do not have. For example, *I do not have much time to study.* Use *much, many, a lot of,* or *any* as appropriate. Then, compare your sentences to those of the other students in your class. What similarities do you find? What differences?

D. Write five questions to ask another student. Use *many, much, a lot of, some,* or *any* as appropriate. For example, *Do you have any brothers or sisters?* Then, join other students to write at least 20 of these questions on the board. First, check the grammar to be sure that all of the questions are accurate. Then, talk about the meaning of the questions: it is important to discuss your own sense of the politeness of the questions by your personal and cultural standards. What kinds of questions can you ask another person about his or her possessions? about his or her family?

E. *Some* has an indefinite meaning with plural or noncount nouns. Often it is used to introduce a topic and is followed by a more definite statement.

Seing: *I really need some money.*
Pom: *How much?*
Seing: *$512.55. To pay for repairs on my car.*

Work with another student to write a similar scene between two friends. The first friend needs something—some money, some time, some help, etc. The second friend asks a question to find out more details. The first friend answers with exactly what he or she needs. Share your scene with the rest of your class. You might write it on the board, or you might perform it for the class.

F. Analyze the following pairs of sentences, and write the rule for choosing between *much* and *many.*

How **much money** do you want for the computer?
How **many computers** do you have?

Rule: *Much is used with* _____

Many is used with _____

Circle the correct words in the following sentences.

1. There are (much) (many) buildings on campus.

2. There is (much) (many) snow on campus in January.

3. We did not receive (much) (many) information about student aid at the orientation session.

4. My roommates studied at the library for (much) (many) hours last night.

5. Last quarter, I wrote (much) (many) paragraphs.

6. I read (much) (many) pages of history last night.

7. I do not spend (much) (many) time watching television.

8. I do not have (much) (many) plans for next quarter break.

G. Use *many* with the plural form of the following count nouns and *much* with the noncount nouns.

1. book	*many books*	12. assignment	_____
2. air	*much air*	13. appointment	_____
3. pen	*many pens*	14. news	_____
4. advisor	_____	15. mistake	_____
5. idea	_____	16. test	_____
6. food	_____	17. information	_____
7. computer	_____	18. experiment	_____
8. rain	_____	19. intelligence	_____
9. student	_____	20. essay	_____
10. courage	_____	21. advice	_____
11. water	_____	22. report	_____

H. Add *much, many,* or *a lot of* to the following sentences.

1. Hirut did not make ＿＿＿＿＿＿ mistakes on her last exam.

2. She studied ＿＿＿＿＿＿ hours for the exam.

3. She did not have ＿＿＿＿＿＿ difficulty with the information in Chapter Ten.

4. She wrote ＿＿＿＿＿＿ exercises last week to improve her handwriting.

5. She still has ＿＿＿＿＿＿ trouble with spelling.

6. To improve her spelling, she writes every word she misspells

   ＿＿＿＿＿＿ times.

7. She also works on vocabulary and carefully does ＿＿＿＿＿＿ homework every night.

8. She tries to learn ＿＿＿＿＿＿ new English words every week.

9. English class is difficult because she does not speak ＿＿＿＿＿＿ English at home.

10. Like Hirut, ＿＿＿＿＿＿ people all over the world are learning to understand, speak, read, and write English.

Little and *Few*

Small amounts are often described using the words *little* and *few*. They have similar meanings and can both be paraphrased as "not much" or "not many." However, they are used with different types of nouns. To discover more about using these words, do the following exercise.

. . . .

Practice with *Little* and *Few*

Analyze the following pairs of sentences, and write the rule for choosing between *little* and *few*.

> *I have **little time** for play.*
> *I own **few books** in English.*
>
> *I lost **little weight** on the new diet.*
> *I found **few mistakes** in grammar on my essay.*

Rule: *Little* is used with _____

Rule: *Few* is used with _____

Circle the correct words in the following sentences.

1. I made (little) (few) mistakes on my last paragraph.
2. (Little) (Few) students think that writing paragraphs is easy.
3. I have been to the library (little) (few) times.
4. I have (little) (few) time to study, so I usually find a quiet place in the student center.
5. I speak (little) (few) English outside the classroom.
6. (Little) (Few) people learn a foreign language quickly.

A Little and *A Few*

The difference between *few* and *a few* and between *little* and *a little* is one of emphasis.

Few and *little* emphasize a small number or quantity and have a negative feeling. They mean "not many" or "not much."

few = not many
*He has **few** friends;
he is not a popular person.*

little = not much
*She has **little** money;
she has many problems about money.*

In contrast, *a few* and *a little* have a positive feeling. Their meaning is similar to that of *some*.

a few = some
*We have invited **a few** friends to a party.*

a little = some
*Because I have **a little** time before class begins, I can help you with your homework.*

. . . .

Practice with *A Little* and *A Few*

A. Discuss the differences in meaning between the following pairs of sentences:

1. I drank **a little** water a few minutes ago, so I am not thirsty.
2. I have drunk **little** water in the last few hours, so I am very thirsty.
3. I have **few** friends here in this city, so I am very lonely.
4. I have **a few** new friends and hope to be less lonely.

239

B. Working with another student, decide on appropriate ways to complete the following sentences. Compare your ideas with those of other students in your class. Discuss whether the situation is good or bad. Why?

1. I have few friends, so _____

2. I have few grammar problems, so _____

3. I have a few financial problems, so _____

4. I have few financial problems, so _____

5. I have little unhappiness in my life, so _____

6. I get little rest, so _____

C. Write 10 sentences about things that you have *little of* or *few of*. Mix together good and bad statements. Compare your answers to those of other students in your class. How are your and their lives alike and different? After editing the sentences, write them on a sheet of paper to keep in your Grammar Notebook. Example: *I have few enemies. I have little time for my family and friends.*

. . . .

Practice with Articles and Determiners

A. Write the general rule to explain the determiners and quantifiers used with the following sets of words.

1. *some books   some students   some tests*

   Some is used with _____

2. *a student   a calculator   a desk*

   A is used with _____

3. *some equipment   some advice   some information*

   Some is used with _____

4. *an essay   an assignment   an outline*

   An is used with _____

5. *the computer*   *the equipment*   *the assignment*
   the computers   *the assignments*

The is used with _____

6. *a little money*   *a little time*   *a little advice*

A little is used with _____

7. *a few minutes*   *a few meetings*   *a few paragraphs*

A few is used with _____

B. Discussion Assignment: Why have some places become famous outside their own countries? What are some historical places that you have studied or visited?

Grammar Assignment: Notice how the writer uses different times to tie together a coherent description. Why does the writer use simple present tense in sentences 1 and 2? Why does the writer shift to simple past tense for sentences 3, 4, and 5? Why does the writer go back to simple present tense for the remainder of the paragraph?

Put a check mark above all the nouns in the following sentences. Then, complete the chart that follows with the nouns and their articles. (Ignore the words in italics and quotation marks as you complete the chart.)

The Acropolis

Athens, Greece:
The Acropolis

[1]Americans usually visualize the Acropolis in Athens, Greece, when they hear the word *acropolis.* [2]The word comes from *akro* which means "high" and *polis* which means "city." [3]The word originally meant a natural fortification, typically a hill, which would be a place of safety from enemy attacks. [4]Residents frequently lived at the base of the hill, and the location became the site of the city. [5]If enemies arrived, residents moved to the acropolis for safety. [6]Today, there are many acropolises in Greece, but the Acropolis in Athens is the most famous acropolis for Americans. [7]It sits on a limestone hill and dominates the city. [8]Visitors can see the finest examples of classical architecture in the three buildings that sit on the top: the Parthenon, the Erechtheum, and the Temple to Athena. [9]The Propylaea is the fourth famous part of the Athens Acropolis; it is a monumental marble entryway. [10]These structures remind visitors of the fame of ancient Greece.

Adapted from *World Book Encyclopedia*, 1988 ed., s.v. "Athens."

Sentence	Singular-Count	Plural-Count	Noncount	Proper	Nouns Used as Adjectives
1	the word			Americans Athens Greece the Acropolis	
2					
3		attacks	safety		enemy
4					

Sentence	Singular-Count	Plural-Count	Noncount	Proper	Nouns Used as Adjectives
5					
6					
7					
8					
9					
10					

C. Discussion Assignment: How many different languages have you studied? How many different languages can you speak? How many different languages can you understand? Some dictionaries provide a chart of language families. Does your dictionary give a listing of languages and language families?

Grammar Assignment: Working with a partner, decide on the time relationship between the sentences. Subdivide the paragraph into different parts according to the different times. Then, put a check mark above all the nouns in the following sentences. Only the singular nouns have errors. Decide if a particular singular noun needs an article or determiner. Put ∧ where the article should be added, and write in the appropriate article.

Languages

[1]Scholars have classified languages into families since early

twentieth century. [2]These language families are groups of languages with similar characteristics. [3]Languages in family often developed from single earlier language or parent language. [4]For example, when speakers of parent language moved apart from each other, language of each new group changed. [5]After several generations, individual groups spoke differently and sometimes could not understand each other any longer. [6]However, these languages belong to same language family because they came from same parent family. [7]Today, Indo-European is important language family because many people speak languages in this family. [8]Languages in Indo-European family have clearly defined parts of speech like nouns, verbs, adjectives, and pronouns. [9]In addition, many basic words—*mother* in English, *meter* in Greek, *mater* in Latin, *mat* in Russian, *mata* in Sanskrit, and *madre* in Spanish—are similar in Indo-European languages. [10]Although English, Greek, Latin, Russian, Sanskrit, and Spanish come from same language family, speakers of these languages cannot understand each other.

Adapted from *World Book Encyclopedia*, 1988 ed., s.v. "language."

D. Discussion Assignment: Most cultures have traditions of handicraft making, such as the origami discussed in the following passage. What other types of handicraft do you know about? Can you or any of your relatives do any of them?

Grammar Assignment: Complete the paragraph by adding *a*, *an*, *the* or X (meaning no article is needed). First, decide on the type of noun (count or noncount) and on the meaning (indefinite, definite, or generic).

Then, analyze the changes of time used by this writer. The paragraph can be divided into four sections as the writer moves from a general introduction, to a definition, to one personal example, and to a second personal example. Work with another student to mark the division of the paragraph into these four parts.

Origami: An Important Part of My Life

[1]In my country, people have been folding pieces of _____ paper into special designs for many centuries. [2]They enjoy making _____ animals, _____ flowers, and other interesting objects from a piece of _____ paper. [3]This art is famous around the world by its Japanese name *origami*. [4]*Ori* means "folding," and *gami* means "paper." [5]I first learned to fold

_____ paper from my sister when I was three years old. ⁶When I entered the first grade, my teacher taught me new designs. ⁷I still like to fold _____ paper and make _____ animals to give away to my friends. ⁸I can make _____ beautiful object in a few minutes, and people of all ages enjoy my designs. ⁹I have taught several American friends to have fun in this way. ¹⁰They enjoy learning _____ new hobby, and I like teaching them.

E. Working with other students in your class, carry out the following steps.

1. Circle the nouns in the following paragraph.
2. Label each noun as singular-count, plural-count, noncount, or proper.
3. Decide if any of the proper nouns should have articles. When are articles ever used with proper nouns?
4. Decide if any of the noncount nouns should have articles. When are articles ever used with noncount nouns?
5. For each singular-count noun, add an appropriate article (_a_, _an_, or _the_).

Origami: A Japanese Craft

¹For people around the world, paper provides opportunities for writing and for designing. ²Paper was invented in China in A.D. 105, spread to Japan in 7th century and was introduced in Europe in 12th century. ³Today, paper is inexpensive, easily acquired, and easy to work with. ⁴Since invention of paper, many people have used it to create beautiful objects. ⁵Origami is craft of paper folding. ⁶In Japanese language, _ori_ means "folding," and _gami_ means "paper." ⁷In origami, paper is folded into designs and shapes. ⁸Most designs are made without cutting or pasting. ⁹Sometimes there are moveable parts to imitate movement of people, animals, or plants that are illustrated. ¹⁰To make origami figure, artists frequently use square piece of brightly colored paper. ¹¹Although origami was originally pastime for Japanese children, it is now popular craft for adults and children around world, especially in Germany, Spain, and United States.

Adapted from *Encyclopedia Americana,* 1983 ed., s.v. "paper crafts."

F. To practice editing your writing for articles, select a short passage that you have written recently with 10–12 sentences. Circle all of the singular-count nouns and the noncount nouns. Ignore the plural nouns for this exercise. Then, review the rules for the meaning of these nouns with the different articles. Review the information on pages 230–231 of this chapter. What choices do you have for articles with singular nouns? with noncount nouns?

Write each of the singular or noncount nouns in your composition on a sheet of paper in a row leaving space in front for an article or determiner. In front of each noun, write the article or determiner that you used in your composition.

Work with another student to decide if you need to (1) change any of the articles or determiners that you used or (2) add articles or determiners where you did not use them. Finally analyze the changes that you made. Did you remove any articles from noncount nouns used for generic meaning? Did you change from *a/an* to *the*? Did you change from *the* to *a/an*? Did you add any articles to singular-count nouns? Write a description of your use of articles to keep in your Grammar Notebook.

G. Do exercise F again later in the term on a different piece of your own writing. Make notes about your work and any changes you notice to keep in your Grammar Notebook.

H. As a review, turn to the Diagnostic Test on page 13 in First Steps, and look closely at items 61–65. Compare your answers today with your answers from the first week of this course. Space is provided on page 458 in the Grammar Journal for you to analyze your use of articles and determiners.

I. To practice editing someone else's written English, turn to Section Four. Study the information about editing on page 404, and then do the editing exercises on pages 417–418.

CHAPTER

10

Adverbial, Relative, and Noun Clauses

CHAPTER ORGANIZATION

Examples of Clause Types
Traditional Definitions
Recognizing Different Types of Clauses
    Adverbial Clauses
    Relative (Adjective) Clauses
    Noun Clauses
Recognizing Common Sentence Problems
Correcting Common Sentence Problems
Sentence-Combining Practice
    Adverbial Clauses
    Relative Clauses
Sentence Combining
    Making Decisions about Combining Sentences

Examples of Clause Types

Adverbial Clauses

CONTRAST

\#

Although he prefers history, Pom is studying calculus.

TIME

\#

Pom took notes when his instructor explained the requirements to pass the course.

REASON

\#

Because he arrived early, Pom reviewed his homework.

Relative Clauses

RESTRICTIVE

\#

The students who attended the lecture asked many questions.

RESTRICTIVE

\#

The lecture that they heard was required for all new students at the university.

NONRESTRICTIVE

\#

Ms. Strickland, who teaches the course, is a dynamic lecturer.

Noun Clauses

\#

The dean stated that there would be no late registration.

\#

Dr. Hardin announced that he would postpone the midterm exam.

Traditional Definitions

You will need to be able to use these words when you talk about sentence types and sentence combining. See Chapter One for a review of sentence types.

Clause
A clause is a group of words with a subject-verb combination. There are two types of clauses:

1. **independent** or **main**
2. **dependent** or **subordinate**

Independent or Main
An independent or main clause is complete by itself.

1. A **simple sentence** is an independent clause. Each independent clause has one subject-verb combination.
2. A **compound sentence** combines two independent clauses using special joining words and punctuation.

Dependent or Subordinate
A subordinate or dependent clause must be attached to an independent clause. Each subordinate clause has one subject-verb combination. There are three types of subordinate clauses.

1. **Adverbial clauses** Adverbial clauses give manner, place, reason, time, and other adverbial meanings.
2. **Relative (adjective) clauses** Relative clauses influence the meanings of nouns.
3. **Noun clauses** Noun clauses take the place of nouns.

    A complex sentence adds a subordinate clause to an independent clause.

Note: Subordinate (dependent) clauses cannot stand alone as sentences. They must be connected to independent (main) clauses. If a subordinate clause is written alone, it is called a **fragment**. A fragment is an incomplete sentence and should be avoided in formal written English.

Recognizing Different Types of Clauses

Adverbial Clauses

A subordinate clause is introduced by a subordinating word, a word that relates the meaning of the subordinate clause to the meaning of the independent clause. Writers can choose among several subordinating

249

words to find the best word to express the relationship between adverbial clauses and independent clauses.

Definition
The words *after, although, because, if, since,* and *when* are called **subordinating words** or **subordinating conjunctions.** The clauses created with these subordinating words are called **adverbial clauses.** Adverbial clauses are types of **subordinate** or **dependent clauses.** (See Appendix B for information on joining words to use to make compound and complex sentences.)

After the test was over, *we went to the cafeteria for lunch.*

*We went to the cafeteria for lunch **after the test was over.***

Purpose
Adverbial clauses provide information like that provided by single-verb adverbs. Adverbial clauses and simple adverbs answer questions such as when? where? why? how?

adverbial clause of time
When class was over, *we went to the computer lab.*

adverb of time
*We went to the lab **immediately.***

Formation
Adverbial clauses frequently precede independent clauses, but they can appear at the end of independent clauses. Varying the positions of subordinate clauses in a paragraph can control the emphasis and provide sentence variety.

adverbial clause after independent clause
*Juan studied in the library **before he went to class.***

adverbial clause before independent clause
Before he went to class, *Juan studied in the library.*

When an adverbial clause precedes an independent clause, a comma is used after the adverbial clause.

After I graduated from college, *I went to work as a sales manager.*

No comma is needed when an adverbial clause follows an independent clause.

*I went to work as a sales manager **after I graduated from college.***

Two Patterns for Location of an Adverbial Clause

Pattern #1

Subordinating Word	Subordinate Clause	Independent Clause
After Although Because Before If Since When	subject + verb,	subject + verb.

subordinate adverbial clause   independent clause
When we finished the project, we had a party to celebrate.

Pattern #2

Independent Clause	Subordinating Word	Subordinate Clause
Subject + verb	after although because before if since when	subject + verb.

Independent clause   subordinate adverbial clause
We had a party to celebrate when we finished the project.

Adverbial Clauses That Show Time Relationships

After

The past perfect is used to refer to an action or event that came before another event in the past. The past perfect verb form is used in the subordinate clause. Note the comma when the subordinate clause comes before the independent clause.

*She took the driving test **after** she (had) learned to drive.*

***After** she (had) learned to drive, she took the driving test.*

251

Simple present tense or the present perfect verb form can be used in the subordinate clause.

After she learns to drive, she will take the driving test.

Before
The past perfect is used in the independent clause.

She had passed the test **before** she bought a car.

The simple present tense or the present perfect verb form can be used in the subordinate clause.

She will pass the test **before** she buys a car.

Since
Since means "from that past time until now." Use the present perfect verb form in the independent clause with this meaning of *since*. -

She has driven every day **since** she passed the driving test.

Until
Until means "to a particular time and then no longer."

She saved her money **until** she had enough to buy a car.

When
When means "at the same time."

When the traffic signal turned red, she stopped the car.

Notice how these four examples of *when* are used for different meanings. What is the time relationship between the two clauses for each example?

When the traffic signal turned red, she was looking at the dashboard.

When the traffic signal turned red, she had already stopped.

When the traffic signal turns red, she always stops.

Whenever
Whenever means "every time."

She remembered the accident **whenever** she stopped at a red light.

She remembers the accident **whenever** she stops at a red light.

While
While means "during that time." Use *while* with two actions that happen at the same time.

While she was waiting, she relaxed and closed her eyes.

While is often used with progressive verb forms.

While she was driving, she was listening to the radio.

Practice with Adverbial Clauses of Time

Complete the following sentences by supplying an appropriate time subordinating word. Analyze the verb forms used.

1. Last night Yoshi went to the library _____ he had eaten dinner. (He ate dinner first.)

2. In contrast, he plans to eat dinner _____ he goes to the library tonight.

3. He usually watches television _____ he is eating dinner. (He does both at the same time.)

4. Yoshi has not seen the 10:00 news _____ he started going to the library every night.

5. _____ he studies at the library, he usually leaves at 11:00.

6. He studies there _____ he hears the closing bell.

7. Then, he and his friends meet at Wendy's at midnight. Last week,

   they stayed at Wendy's _____ the restaurant closed at 1:00.

8. _____ Yoshi woke up the next morning, he wished that he had gone to bed earlier.

9. _____ he was sitting in class, he fell asleep.

Adverbial Clauses That Show Reason Relationships

As, Because, Since
As, because, and *since* have the same meaning in these sentences.

Because *the temperature is only 20 degrees Fahrenheit, everyone needs to wear warm clothing.*

Everyone needs to wear warm clothing **because** *the temperature is only 20 degrees Fahrenheit.*

Notice the comma when the subordinate clause comes before the independent clause.

Since Monday is Martin Luther King, Jr.'s birthday, schools and government offices will be closed.

As the streets are slippery from the rain, drivers should proceed carefully.

Practice with Adverbial Clauses for Reasons

On a sheet of paper, write sentences that combine the following sets of sentences. Use one of the subordinating words that show reason. Before you can combine the sentences, you must decide which sentence causes the action in the other sentence.

1. Yoko was absent from class yesterday.
   She missed the lesson on adverb clauses.

2. Kazeem has to get up at 6 a.m.
   He has an 8 a.m. class.

3. The five-page project is due tomorrow.
   Mansoo cannot watch television tonight.

4. Mona is taking English classes at night.
   Morning English classes were not available.

5. The library is a good place to work.
   It is quiet.

Adverbial Clauses That Show Contrast Relationships

Although and *Even Though*
In these examples, *although* and *even though* have the same meaning.

Although calculus is my favorite subject, I enjoy economics.

I enjoy economics even though calculus is my favorite subject.

Practice with Adverbial Clauses That Show Contrasts

As in the example, rewrite the following sentences to include adverb clauses that begin with *although, because, even though,* or *since.* The first one is done as an example.

1. People have always polluted their surroundings, but pollution was not a major problem until recently.

   Although people have always polluted their surroundings, pollution was not a major problem until recently.

2. People have used the world's natural resources to make their lives more comfortable; however, these resources are not always used wisely.

3. Millions of people have recently become alarmed by the dangers of pollution, so many people are now working to reduce pollution.

4. Technological advances in agriculture, industry, and transportation have improved our way of life, but many advances harm the environment.

5. The automobile engine is an example of a very useful technological development, but the pollution that it creates harms the environment.

6. All parts of the environment are closely related to one another, so one kind of pollution that chiefly harms one part of the environment may also affect other parts.

7. There are about 3,000 spoken languages today, but only 12 are widely used.

8. England, France, Portugal, and Spain established colonies in various parts of the world; therefore, English, French, Portuguese, and Spanish are now spoken in many nations outside their countries of origin.

Adapted from *World Book Encyclopedia*, 1988 ed., s.v. "environmental pollution" and "world."

Adverbial Clauses That Show Conditional Relationships

If

In the first example, *if* is used for future time conditional meaning. Notice the modal in the independent clause. The verb in the *if*-clause is in the simple present tense.

future time

Jose will watch the soccer game on television tonight if he finishes his homework.

The second example shows general truth meaning for a habitual action.

general truth/habit

Jose watches television every night if he finishes his homework.

The third example shows a past time hypothetical meaning. Jose did not finish his homework; he did not watch television.

past time/hypothetical

Jose would have watched television last night if he had finished his homework.

Unless
Unless means "if not."

*Jose does not watch television **unless** he finishes his homework.*

Practice with Adverbial Clauses

A. Discussion Assignment: Do you know how to use a computer? Do you have one at home? Do you use one at school? Do you know anyone who uses one at work?

Grammar Assignment: Mark each of the subordinate adverbial clauses with [ ], and put a # above the subordinating words. Compare your answers with those of other students, and make any necessary corrections.

Computer Use by Adults

[1]In 1984, 21% of the people in the United States used a computer at home, school, or work, and computer ownership was most likely in households with incomes of $50,000 or more. [2]Although direct use ("hands-on" experience) of a computer at work was reported by 25% of the employed adult population, this use was highest among white males. [3]Although fifteen million adults had a computer at home, persons age 65 and over probably did not have one. [4]Persons age 35 to 55 were the most likely to own a home computer because they were the most likely to have children at home. [5]The probability of having a computer at home increased with both family income and the education of the individual. [6]However, if an adult lived in the South, that person probably did not have a home computer in 1984.

Adapted from U.S. Bureau of the Census. "Computer Use in the United States." *Family Economics Review*, vol. 1, no. 4. Pages 19–20.

B. Write five sentences on one topic using adverbial clauses. Place some of the adverbial clauses at the beginning of the sentences and some at the end. After you are satisfied with the meaning of the sentences, edit them carefully, especially for punctuation. Then, share your ideas and information with other students in your class.

C. To practice editing for clauses, select a newspaper passage that contains 10–12 sentences. Use a highlighter to mark all of the adverbial clauses. Ask yourself the three questions listed below. Share the information that you find with the other students in your class.

1. What verb forms were used?
2. What subordinating words were used?
3. What punctuation was used?

D. To practice editing for clauses, select a passage that you have written recently that contains 10–12 sentences. Use a highlighter to mark all of the adverbial clauses. Ask yourself the three questions listed below, and make any necessary changes in the passage.

1. Did I use the correct verb forms?
2. Did I spell the subordinating words correctly?
3. Did I use the correct punctuation?

Relative (Adjective) Clauses

Definition
In sentences like these examples, the words *who, whom, whose, which,* and *that* (and also *where* and *when*) are called **relative pronouns.** The subordinate clauses created with these relative pronouns are called **relative clauses.**

*I met a student **who speaks seven different languages.***

*He has a new computer **that cost only $500.***

*We live in an apartment building **where all the tenants are university students.***

relative
(adjective) clause

Another name for a relative clause is an **adjective clause** because the relative clause functions like a single-word adjective. Both modify the meaning of nouns. In these two examples, the relative clause and the adjective both modify the meaning of the noun *dictionary.*

*She has a dictionary **that cost over $50.***

adjective
*She has an **expensive** dictionary.*

257

Formation

Relative clauses can be added to almost any noun. Relative clauses occur after nouns used as the subject, the direct object, and the object of prepositions.

subject + relative clause

The dictionary that I bought last year does not list irregular verbs.

direct object + relative clause

*I bought **a dictionary that defines 100,000 words.***

preposition + noun + relative clause

*I look up new words **in the dictionary that I bought for my ESL class.***

A relative pronoun replaces a noun that has already appeared earlier. Note how the two sentences are combined. Sentence one and sentence two contain the same noun. The relative pronoun *that* replaces the words *her dictionary* to make the relative clause.

sentence 1

*She has **a dictionary.***

sentence 2

*Her **dictionary** cost over $50.*

relative clause

that cost over $50

combined sentence

*She has a dictionary **that cost over $50.***

Relative clauses usually come immediately after the words they describe.

I know a person who . . . .

She has a dictionary that . . . .

Relative Pronouns

The relative pronouns *who* and *whom* replace nouns that refer to people. In spoken English, *that* is sometimes used to refer to people.

*I know a **student who** owns an expensive dictionary.*

The relative pronouns *that* and *which* replace nouns that refer to things and animals.

*She has a **dictionary that** is very expensive.*

*Her grandfather owns a small **bird which** sings beautiful songs.*

Whose primarily refers to people but can refer to things and animals.

*The **professor whose** name I have forgotten teaches economics.*

Whom is used only to replace objects. *Who* is often used in place of *whom*, especially in spoken English. This sentence combines two shorter sentences. Here are the two sentences that were combined to make the example with *whom*.

*I have had one outstanding teacher from **whom I** learned many important lessons about life.*

sentence 1

I have had one outstanding teacher.

sentence 2
I learned many important lessons about life from that teacher.

relative clause
from whom I learned many important lessons about life

Relative Clauses with Proper Nouns

When the noun being described is a proper noun, the name of someone or something, you use commas to separate the relative clause from the rest of the sentence.

nonrestrictive relative clause inside a sentence
*Professor Jones, **who has taught here for 10 years,** speaks three languages.*

nonrestrictive relative clause at the end of a sentence
*Yesterday Maria met Professor Jones, **who has taught here for 10 years.***

The commas indicate that extra information has been added; this information is not necessary to identify the person or thing being discussed. Grammarians call this type of relative clause a **nonrestrictive relative clause.**

*The University of Georgia, **which was founded in 1789,** is one of the oldest universities in the U.S.*

That cannot be used in these nonrestrictive relative clauses.

incorrect
*Miami, that is the biggest city in Florida, has a very international population.

correct
Miami, which is the biggest city in Florida, has a very international population.

Problems

In English, the relative pronoun replaces some part of the second sentence. This grammar is different from that of some languages that use the relative pronoun like a conjunction or linking word. In the incorrect sentence, *that* and *it* are both the direct object of the second sentence.

*incorrect
*The book **that** I bought **it** for this class has six sections.*

sentence 1
The book has six sections.

sentence 2: direct object
*I bought **the book** for this class.*

relative clause: direct object
***that** I bought for this class*

correct combined sentence
*The book **that I bought for this class** has six sections.*

Relative Clause Pattern I: Subject Pronouns *(who, which, that)*

Relative clauses can be formed when the subjects of two sentences are the same: *who, which,* or *that* can replace the subject of a sentence. The second sentence becomes part of the first sentence.

The second sentence is changed to become a relative clause in the first sentence.

sentence 1: subject
The man *helps students with their problems.*

The relative pronoun *who* substitutes for the subject in the second sentence.

sentence 2: subject
The man *runs the computer laboratory.*

relative clause
who *runs the computer laboratory*

combined sentence: subject
The man who runs the computer laboratory *helps students with their problems.*

sentence 1: subject
The textbook *has 600 pages.*

The relative pronoun *that* substitutes for the subject in the second sentence.

sentence 2: subject
The textbook *is required for our computer class.*

relative clause
that *is required for our computer class*

combined sentence: subject
The textbook that is required for our computer class *has 600 pages.*

Relative clauses can also be formed when the last noun in a sentence is the same as the subject of the second sentence. The second sentence becomes part of the first sentence. This pattern is often used with proper nouns, so nonrestrictive relative clauses are used. Notice the comma to separate the clause from the rest of the sentence.

Information about Brazil is added to the end of the sentence.

sentence 1: ends with proper noun
Roy comes from **Brazil.**

The relative pronoun *which* substitutes for the subject of the second sentence.

sentence 2: subject
Brazil *is the largest country in South America.*

relative clause
which *is the largest country in South America*

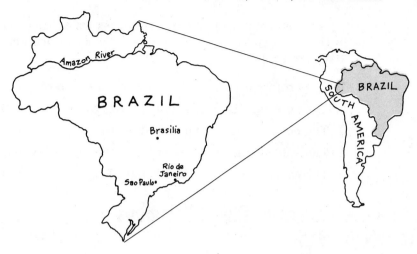

combined sentence
*Roy comes from **Brazil, which is the largest country in South America.***

Information about Dr. Green is added to the end of the sentence.

sentence 1: ends with proper noun
*Roy's economics professor is **Dr. Green.***

sentence 2: subject
***Dr. Green** has taught for twenty years.*

The relative pronoun *who* substitutes for the subject of the second sentence.

relative clause
***who** has taught for twenty years*

combined sentence
*Roy's economics professor is **Dr. Green, who has taught for twenty years.***

Practice with Relative Pronouns

A. Write sentences that combine the following pairs of sentences by using *who, which,* or *that.* Then, put brackets around each relative clause.

1. The tutor is in the computer lab every morning. She helped me yesterday.
2. The pencil is mine. The pencil is lying on the floor.
3. The test is next week. The test covers adjective clauses.
4. The student sits next to me in grammar class. The student speaks five languages.

B. Complete the following sentences by writing *who, which,* or *that* in the blank space in each sentence. Then, put brackets around each relative clause.

1. The professor [_____who_____ was here yesterday] is ill.

2. The person _____ is sitting next to me is from Taiwan.

3. The pen _____ I borrowed is red.

4. The student _____ sat next to me yesterday is absent.

5. The calculator _____ I bought last weekend is missing.

Relative Clause Pattern II: Object Pronouns
(who[m], which, that)

· ·

Relative clauses can be formed when relative pronouns replace the direct object in a sentence. The second sentence becomes part of the first sentence. In this set of examples, the relative clause modifies the subject of the first sentence.

Example One
The relative pronoun *that* substitutes for the direct object of the second sentence. The relative pronoun must be at the beginning of the relative clause.

sentence 1: subject
The textbook *has the most recent information on the AIDS epidemic.*

sentence 2: direct object
Dr. Hardin will require **the textbook** *next quarter.*

Notice the grammar of the relative clause: *that* is the direct object; *Dr. Hardin* is the subject.

relative clause
that *Dr. Hardin will require next quarter*

combined sentence: subject
The textbook that Dr. Hardin will require next quarter *has the most recent information on the AIDS epidemic.*

Example Two
The relative pronoun *whom* is used as the direct object of the second sentence in the more formal example. *Who* is used in the less formal version of the sentence.

sentence 1: subject
The student *sits next to me in my economics class.*

sentence 2: direct object
I met **this student** *at the reception for new international students.*

relative clause: formal
whom *I met at the reception for new international students*

relative clause: informal
who I met at the reception for new international students

combined sentence: formal
The student whom I met at the reception for new international students *sits next to me in my economics class.*

combined sentence: informal
The student who I met at the reception for new international students *sits next to me in my economics class.*

Example Three
A relative clause can be added to a noun used as the direct object in a sentence.

sentence 1: direct object
*Yesterday Roy bought **the book**.*

sentence 2: direct object
*Dr. Green requires **the book** for Economics 310.*

The relative pronoun *that* is substituted for the direct object in the second sentence.

relative clause
***that** Dr. Green requires for Economics 310.*

Then, the relative clause is added to the direct object of the first sentence.

combined sentence: direct object
*Yesterday Roy bought **the book that Dr. Green requires for Economics 310.***

Example Four
The relative pronouns *whom* or *who* can be used for the direct object of the second sentence. *Whom* is used for the formal version.

direct object
*Yesterday Roy met **a friend** to have lunch.*

direct object
*He likes **this friend** very much.*

relative clause: formal
***whom** he likes very much*

relative clause: informal
***who** he likes very much*

combined sentence: formal
*Yesterday Roy met **a friend whom he likes very much** to have lunch.*

combined sentence: informal
*Yesterday Roy met **a friend who he likes very much** to have lunch.*

. . . .

Practice with Relative Clauses

A. Combine the following pairs of sentences by using *who(m)*, *which*, or *that*. Then, put brackets around each relative clause.

1. The midterm exam was easy. I took the midterm exam yesterday.

2. The calculator is expensive. Emanuella wants to buy it.

3. The lesson was not difficult. We did the lesson yesterday.

4. The student is majoring in music. I met the student at a party last night.

5. The teacher gives difficult tests. The students respect the teacher very much.

6. Yesterday Pepe saw the teacher in the library. Pepe had the teacher for algebra last quarter.

B. On another sheet of paper, write complete sentences by adding a relative clause to make each sentence correct.

1. The answer that _____ is correct.

2. The lecturer whom _____ was brilliant.

3. The apartment that _____ is five blocks from campus.

4. Waleed has lost the book that _____ .

5. The lesson that _____ seems rather easy.

C. Complete the following sentences by writing *that*, *which*, *who*, or *whom* in the blank space in each sentence. Then, put brackets around each relative clause.

1. One assignment [_____ I did last night] took two hours.

2. Tam is the friend _____ I met at the library last night.

3. I learned many things _____ I do not want to forget.

4. I enjoyed the article _____ Dr. Swofford assigned for homework.

5. The sentence-combining exercise _____ we did for homework was easy.

Relative Clause Pattern III:
Objects of Prepositions

• •

Relative clauses can be added to nouns that are the objects of prepositions. In these examples, the second sentence becomes part of the first sentence.

Example One
The relative clause is added to a prepositional phrase.

sentence 1: object of preposition
*I bought my books from **a friend.***

sentence 2
***My friend** took this course last quarter.*

relative clause
***who** took this course last quarter*

combined sentence: relative clause in object of preposition
*I bought my books from **a friend who took this course last quarter.***

Example Two
This combination is more complicated. The relative clause is formed from a sentence with a prepositional phrase.

sentence 1
*Jose is the name of **the friend.***

sentence 2
*I bought this dictionary from **the friend.***

The relative pronoun replaces the noun that is the object of the preposition. If the preposition is moved to the beginning of the relative clause, *whom* must be used. In informal English, *who* replaces the noun, and the preposition is left at the end of the relative clause.

relative clause: formal
***from whom** I bought this dictionary*

relative clause: informal
***who** I bought this dictionary from*

combined sentence: formal
*Jose is the name of **the friend from whom I bought this dictionary.***

combined sentence: informal
*Jose is the name of **the friend who I bought this dictionary from.***

Example Three
That cannot be used immediately after a preposition.

incorrect
The tuition increase is a problem **about that all students are very concerned.*

sentence 1
*The tuition increase is **a problem.***

sentence 2
All students are concerned about a problem.

relative clause: formal
about which all students are concerned

That can be used if the preposition is left at the end of the relative clause.

relative clause: informal
that all students are concerned about

correct combined sentence: formal
The tuition increase is a problem about which all students are concerned.

correct combined sentence: informal
The tuition increase is a problem that all students are concerned about.

· ·

Practice with Relative Clauses Involving Prepositions

Combine the following sentences by turning the second sentence into a relative clause to use in the first sentence. If two different forms are possible, write both combinations. After editing your combined sentences, put the corrected sentences in your Grammar Notebook to use as examples.

1. Kim learned about this school from a friend.
   The friend now lives in another state.

2. Every week, Kim talks on the telephone with a friend.
   The friend gives him advice about his problems.

3. Alexis is the student.
   Maria bought her books from that student.

4. Alexis is the person.
   Maria bought a birthday present for that person.

5. Atmospheric pollution is a problem.
   There are no easy solutions for that problem.

6. The scientists offer conflicting solutions.
   People get their information from these scientists.

Relative Clause Pattern IV: Possessive Pronoun *(whose)*

The relative pronoun *whose* substitutes for the possessive noun phrase in the subject of the second sentence.

sentence 1
*At the reception for new students, Pepe met an **Indian student**.*

sentence 2
***The student's** family lives in London.*

relative clause
***whose** family lives in London*

combined sentence
*At the reception for new students, Pepe met an Indian **student whose family lives in London**.*

The relative pronoun *whose* substitutes for the possessive noun phrase in the second sentence.

sentence 1
*Pepe has economics class with **Dr. Green**.*

sentence 2
***Dr. Green's** class is demanding because of the required research project.*

relative clause
***whose** class is demanding because of the required research project*

The relative clause is set off with a comma because it modifies a proper noun.

combined sentence
*Pepe has economics class with **Dr. Green, whose class is demanding because of the required research project**.*

Practice with Relative Clauses Using *Whose*

Combine the following sentences by turning the second sentence into a relative clause to use in the first sentence. After editing your combined sentences, put the corrected sentences in your Grammar Notebook to use as examples.

1. Maria knows a student. The student's backpack was stolen in the library.
2. The student was very angry because her textbooks were in the backpack. The student's backpack was stolen in the library.

3. Alexis bought a book. The book's author lives in Mexico City.
4. The book won an international award. The book's author lives in Mexico City.
5. Pepe wants to be like the soccer player. The soccer player's skill led him to fame and wealth.
6. The soccer player gave a scholarship for poor children to attend school. The soccer player's fame is known all over the world.
7. Many scientists are working on the problem. The problem's solution will increase the world's food supply.
8. The problem involves making seeds more disease-resistant. The problem's solution will increase the world's food supply.

Practice with Relative Clauses

A. Combine the following pairs of sentences by using *who, whom,* or *whose*. Then, put brackets around each relative clause. Notice that all of these sentences involve nonrestrictive relative clauses that modify proper nouns. Edit the punctuation of each sentence carefully.

1. Abraham Lincoln was the 16th U.S. president. He died before the end of the Civil War.
2. John F. Kennedy was the 35th U.S. president. His death saddened millions.
3. Martin Luther King, Jr., was an important U.S. civil rights leader. His birthday is celebrated on January 16.
4. George Washington Carver was a famous U.S. scientist. He improved methods of agriculture.
5. Geronimo was a famous Indian leader. His name spread panic in the frontier settlements of the southwestern United States.

B. Select five famous or important people living or dead from your country. Write sentences about them like those in exercise A. Use a nonrestrictive relative clause in each sentence. After you have revised and edited the sentences, share them with the other students in your class.

C. Put square brackets [ ] around each relative clause, and add the appropriate joining word to each sentence.

1. The lecture [_____ I went to last night] was very informative.

2. The lecturer, _____ came from Canada, spoke about multicultural education.

3. The students _____ attended the lecture enjoyed it.

4. After the lecture, several students went to the reception _____ was sponsored by the International Student Club.

5. The International Student Club at my school has over 50 members _____ come from 22 different countries.

6. Dr. Bill Peters, _____ is the faculty advisor for the International Student Club, spoke briefly to the visitors.

7. He invited everyone to the International Student Festival, _____ will be held in two weeks.

8. The International Student Festival is an annual event for all students _____ want to learn more about other cultures.

9. The lecture last night introduced the idea of multicultural education to several students _____ knowledge of this topic was limited.

10. The International Student Festival is the next place _____ this topic will be discussed.

D. Discussion Assignment: What kinds of foods can be bought at a supermarket? Name the different departments that you expect to find in a large supermarket.

Grammar Assignment: Use a pencil to put brackets around all relative clauses in this passage. After you have marked the relative clauses, use a pen to put brackets around the adverbial clauses.

Supermarket Salad Bars

[1]Salad bars, which are relatively new additions to supermarkets, are now available in 45% of the supermarkets in this country. [2]Some ingredients that are purchased from salad bars can reduce home preparation time and can save money for consumers. [3]Items that cost more at salad bars are basic salad ingredients; items that cost less include salad toppings, meats, and cheeses. [4]Customers might also want to consider other cost-related issues.

[5]Even though nationwide figures on the impact of salad bar sales are not available, the number of salad bars is increasing. [6]According to recent data from USDA's Economic Research Service, total per capita consumption of fresh produce, including selections that are available in most salad bars, has risen in the past few years. [7]Salad bars offer a variety of fresh fruits and vegetables which are good sources of fiber and several vitamins and minerals. [8]Fruits and vegetables are also low in calories, fat, and sodium, and they contain no cholesterol. [9]Therefore, fruits and vegetables are an important part of a healthful diet. [10]Salad bars also offer items that are high in fat, sugar, and/or sodium such as salad dressings, cheese, ham, and bacon bits. [11]From a nutritional perspective, which foods are the "best" choice will depend on the amounts to be consumed and the consumer's choices of food for the rest of the day. [12]Both cost and nutritional concerns are important in making salad bar selections.

Note: The USDA is the United States Department of Agriculture.

Newman, Eileen Patz and Dianne D. Odland. "Supermarket Salad Bars—Cost vs. Convenience." *Family Economics Review*, vol. 1, no. 4. Washington: GPO, 1988, 8–10.

Salad bar in a U.S. supermarket

E. Mark each relative clause in "Oral Cancer" on page 116 with square brackets [ ]. Put a # above the relative pronoun, and circle the noun that each clause describes. Compare your answers to those of other students in your class, and make any necessary changes.

F. To practice editing for clauses, select a short passage that you have written recently. Use a highlighter to mark all of the relative clauses. Make sure that the relative clauses are placed immediately after the words they describe. Did you use commas appropriately? Did each clause contain a subject and a verb in the correct form?

Noun Clauses

Definition
In sentences like these, the word *that* is a **subordinating word** used to create a **noun clause.**

*I think **that economics is required for business majors.***

Formation and Use
Noun clauses are most often used as objects or complements of sentences.

*He feels **that his education will help his family.***

that omitted
*He feels **his education will help his family.***

The word *that* is frequently omitted in conversational English when it introduces a noun clause used as a direct object or complement.

Noun clauses used as direct objects frequently follow these verbs:

ask	*say*
believe	*state*
hope	*tell*
know	*think*
report	*wish*

Practice with Noun Clauses

Discussion Assignment: What jobs use computers? Do you think adults or children use computers more? Do you think men or women use computers more?
Grammar Assignment: Mark each of the subordinate noun clauses with [ ], and put a # above the subordinating words.

Computer Use at Work and Home

[1]In October 1984, less than 20% of the adult population said that they used a computer at home, work, school, or in more than one of these places. [2]Of the employed adult population, 25% reported that they used computers at work. [3]Over 50% of the adults with a computer in their homes stated that they actually used their computers. [4]However, overall use of computers by adults was less than the use by children even though the rates by persons age 25 to 34 were the highest of any age group in the report. [5]In the working place, women reported that they used a computer more than the men in their offices. [6]Across occupational categories, persons with managerial or professional positions were most likely to have a computer at home; however, this report from the Bureau of the Census also thought that the rate for home use declined for low-level administrative support positions.

Adapted from U.S. Bureau of the Census. "Computer Use in the United States." *Family Economics Review*, vol. 1, no. 4. Pages 19–20.

Recognizing Common Sentence Problems

There are three common sentence problems in writing. They frequently involve subordinate clauses.

Fragment

A **fragment** is a subordinate phrase or clause that is written alone rather than as part of an independent clause.

A **fragment** is an incomplete sentence.

Fragments are common in spoken English, but they should be avoided in academic written English.

incorrect in written English
***After the test was over.** I went home.*

incorrect in written English
***Because I forgot to study chapter four.** I failed the quiz.*

"Why are you late?"

acceptable in spoken English
"Because my car had a flat tire."

Comma Splice

A **comma splice** occurs when two independent clauses are joined by a comma and no joining word.

incorrect
**I forgot to study chapter four, I failed the quiz.*

Run-On Sentences

A **run-on sentence** occurs when two independent clauses are written as one sentence without any punctuation.

incorrect

I forgot to study chapter **four I failed the quiz.*

Correcting Common Sentence Problems

. . . .

The following examples show ways to correct three common problems with sentences: fragments, comma splices, and run-on sentences. Compare the correct sentences with the incorrect sentences given above.

Fragment Correction

A **fragment** can be corrected by joining the subordinate phrase or clause to an independent clause.

After the test was over, I went home.

Because I forgot to study chapter four, I failed the quiz.

Comma Splice and Run-on Sentence Correction

Comma splices and run-on sentences can be corrected in five ways.

1. Use a period.

   1. *I forgot to study chapter four. I failed the test.*

2. Use a semicolon.

   2. *I forgot to study chapter four; I failed the test.*

3. Use a semicolon and a transition word.

   3. *I forgot to study chapter four; **therefore**, I failed the test.*

4. Use a comma and a coordinating conjunction.

   4. *I forgot to study chapter four, **so** I failed the test.*

5. Use a subordinating word, and attach the new clause to an independent clause.

   5. ***Because** I forgot to study chapter four, I failed the test.*

. . . .

Practice Identifying Fragments, Comma Splices, and Run-On Sentences

Identify the mistakes in the following sentences as fragments (FR), comma splices (CS), or run-on sentences (RO). Then, use the editing symbols on page 407 to correct the sentences. Compare your answers to those of other students in your class, and make any necessary corrections.

Example: _RO_   *I forgot to study chapter four. So, I failed the test.*

Computer Owners

1. _____ Although direct use ("hands-on" experience) of a computer at work was reported by 25% of the employed adult population. This use was highest among white males.

2. _____ There were 13 million adults. Who were in school or college in the fall of 1984.

3. _____ Children in the Midwest showed high levels of school use children in the South showed low levels.

4. _____ Computer use was high for full-time students, part-time students also used computers.

5. _____ Persons age 35 to 44 often lived in households with computers, persons age 65 and over rarely lived in households with computers.

6. _____ A high rate of computer use was reported by women. Because they often held jobs in sales and administrative support.

7. _____ Home use of computers increased with the education of the individual people in managerial and professional positions frequently used home computers.

8. _____ Fifteen million adults age 18 and over had a computer at home persons living in married-couple households frequently had computers at home.

Adapted from U.S. Bureau of the Census. "Computer Use in the United States." *Family Economics Review*, vol. 1, no. 4. Pages 19–20.

Sentence-Combining Practice

. . . .

Adverbial Clauses

A. Combine the following sentences to form complex sentences with adverbial clauses. Add the subordinating words given for each sentence as well as any needed punctuation. Try to vary the positions of the adverbial clauses. The example shows the use of *although*.

sentence #1
Computer use in school was more likely for full-time students.

sentence #2
Part-time students experienced greater combined rates of use at home, school, and work.

combined sentence
Although computer use in school was more likely for full-time students, part-time students experienced greater combined rates of use at home, school, and work.

Computer Use

1. (if)
   Computer use by children was common.
   Their parents had a high income (over $50,000) or a college degree.

2. (although)
   Persons age 35 to 44 often lived in households with a computer.
   Persons age 65 and over rarely lived in households with a computer.

3. (because)
   Persons age 35 to 44 may have been the most likely to own a home
      computer.
   They were the most likely to have children at home.

4. (since)
   A higher rate of computer use at work was reported by women.
   Women often held jobs in sales and administrative support (including
      such occupations as sales clerks, secretaries, and administrative
      clerical workers).

5. (when)
   In 1984, computers were usually found in homes.
   The income levels and educational levels of the wage earners were
      high.

Adapted from U.S. Bureau of the Census. "Computer Use in the United States." *Family
Economics Review*, vol. 1, no. 4. Pages 19–20.

Relative Clauses

   A. Combine the following sentences to form complex sentences with
relative clauses. Add relative pronouns and punctuation as needed.

   sentence #1
   In the fall of 1984, there were 13 million adults.

   sentence #2
   These 13 million adults were enrolled in college.

   combined sentence
   *In the fall of 1984, there were 13 million adults who were enrolled in
   college.*

1. Computer use was popular for students.
   The students were enrolled in college full-time.

2. Part-time students used computers.
   The computers were most often found at work.

3. Only 4% of the children had a home computer.
   The children's parents had only high school degrees.

4. In contrast, 30% of the children had a home computer.
   The children's parents had college degrees.

5. Adults most frequently used computers in 1984.
   The adults were age 25 to 44, white, male, and single.

Adapted from U.S. Bureau of the Census. "Computer Use in the United States." *Family Economics Review*, vol. 1, no. 4. Pages 19–20.

B. Discussion Assignment: Read the following sentences, and be ready to discuss their meaning with the rest of your class. Does any of the information surprise you? How are these words (like *paleolithic*) spelled in your language? Are the American pronunciations similar to or different from the pronunciations used in your language?

Grammar Assignment: After you are sure that you understand the meaning of the sentences, work with another student to find ways to improve the style of the paragraph by combining the sentences. Use relative clauses only where appropriate; other types of combinations are also possible in this exercise. Combine the sentences below into one paragraph with 10 sentences. Add the appropriate punctuation. After you have completed the paragraph, be ready to discuss your combinations with the rest of the class. What types of sentences did you write for the paragraph (simple, compound, complex, or compound-complex)?

The Stone Age

1. The people of the Stone Age used tools and weapons.   (that)
   The tools and weapons were made of stone.

2. That period of time began about 2 million years ago.   (and)
   That period of time ended about 3000 B.C.

3. Scientists have divided the Stone Age into three periods.   (that)
   The periods are based on the tools of the period.

4. During the Paleolithic Age, the use of fire was developed.   (which)
   The Paleolithic Age lasted until 8000 B.C.

5. During the Ice Age, people lived in caves.   (which)
   During the Ice Age, people developed new tools.
   The Ice Age was part of the Paleolithic Age.

6. The people made pottery.   (who)
   The people developed the bow and arrow.
   The people used bone for knives.
   The people lived during the Mesolithic Age.

7. The Neolithic Age brought drastic changes to people.   (who)
   People lived during this time.

8. Neolithic man learned to produce food.   (and)
   Neolithic man learned to domesticate animals.
   Neolithic man learned to weave textiles.

9. During this period, there was a rapid increase in
      population.   (which)
   This period ended when people learned to form bronze from a
      combination of tin and copper.

10. The Stone Age is an important period of time.   (no combining word
                                                       needed)
    The Stone Age was important in the civilization of man.

Adapted from *Encyclopedia Americana*, 1983 ed., s.v. "Stone Age."

Sentence Combining

. . . .

The rest of this chapter is composed of several sentence-combining exercises that will provide you with some controlled writing practice.

Any sentence can become a subordinate clause as long as you link its meaning in some logical way to the meaning of another sentence. Since any sentence can be subordinated, which sentence you choose to subordinate depends on which idea you believe is more important. The more important idea(s) should be placed in the main clause, and the less important idea(s) should be placed in the subordinate clause. You will improve your writing ability as you learn to recognize your writing options and then begin to choose the option that is the most appropriate for your writing assignment.

The exercises that follow ask you to combine several short sentences into compound sentences, complex sentences, compound-complex sentences, and even into longer simple sentences. In some exercises, the joining words to be used are found in parentheses; in other exercises, you will need to choose your own joining words. Always remember that sentence combining is a matter of making choices. See Appendix B for information on ways to use joining words to make compound and complex sentences.

You may want to read your sentences aloud to help you choose the one you like best, and you may want to compare your sentences with those of other students in the class. Working with a partner also provides the opportunity for additional suggestions and combinations.

Your ability to recognize and create correct compound, complex, and compound-complex sentences from several short, simple sentences indicates that you already know a great deal about writing English sentences. You also know that the English language allows writers to express the same information in different ways. Your writing will improve as you become more aware of your options.

Each of the sentence-combining exercises should be written as one paragraph, and each group of sentences should be combined to form one effective sentence. The spaces between groups of sentences indicate where one sentence ends and the next sentence begins. You may want to look at the explanation of punctuation in Chapter One and Chapter Twelve, and you may choose to add such transitional expressions as *for example, however, in addition, in fact, next,* and *therefore* to produce better paragraphs. Consider meaning, word order, joining words, and punctuation as you work on these sentence-combining exercises. The first exercise is a review of compound sentences. In addition to working with compound sentences, you will practice creating complex sentences using adverbial and relative clauses in other exercises. These exercises encourage you to combine sentences in different ways and ask you to try new sentence-combining possibilities. They invite you to experiment with words and phrases and to explore new ways to express your ideas.

Making Decisions about Combining Sentences

As a writer, you have several decisions to make before combining these three short, simple sentences:

sentence #1
The student studies in the library.

sentence #2
The student works in the computer center.

sentence #3
The student sits next to Pepe in grammar class.

Simple Sentence with Parallel Verbs
1. *The student studies in the library, works in the computer center, and sits next to Pepe in grammar class.*

Complex Sentence with Relative Clause
2. *The student who sits next to Pepe in grammar class studies in the library and works in the computer center.*

Complex Sentence with Relative Clause
3. *The student who works in the computer center sits next to Pepe in grammar class and studies in the library.*

Compound Sentence with *And*
4. *The student sits next to Pepe in grammar class, and she studies in the library and works in the computer center.*

Compound-Complex Sentence with Semicolon

5. *The student who sits next to Pepe in grammar class studies in the library; she also works in the computer center.*

Which option do you prefer? Why?

To combine these three sentences, you have the same choices illustrated above. However, since a proper noun is used, the relative clause must be set off with commas.

sentence #1
Pepe comes from Peru.

sentence #2
Pepe speaks three languages.

sentence #3
Pepe wants to be a translator at the United Nations.

Simple Sentence with Parallel Verbs

1. *Pepe comes from Peru, speaks three languages, and wants to be a translator at the United Nations.*

Complex Sentence with a Nonrestrictive Relative Clause

2. *Pepe, who comes from Peru, speaks three languages and wants to be a translator at the United Nations.*

Complex Sentence with a Nonrestrictive Relative Clause

3. *Pepe, who speaks three languages, comes from Peru and wants to be a translator at the United Nations.*

Compound Sentence with *And*

4. *Pepe comes from Peru, and in addition, he speaks three languages and wants to be a translator at the United Nations.*

Compound-Complex Sentence with Semicolon

5. *Pepe, who comes from Peru, speaks three languages; he wants to be a translator at the United Nations.*

Which option do you prefer? Why?

Practice with Combining Sentences

Think about the meanings of all of the sentences in each of the following exercises before starting to combine the sentences. Then, work with another student to find ways to improve the style of the paragraphs by combining the sentences in each pair into one sentence.

Add the appropriate joining words and punctuation. After you have completed the paragraph, discuss your combinations with the rest of the class. What types of sentences did you write: simple, compound, complex, or compound-complex?

Arabic

1. Approximately 100 million people speak Arabic as their first language.
   A much larger number of people understand it.

2. No one knows when Arabic originally developed.
   The people of the Arabian Peninsula spoke it first.

3. There are two very different forms of Arabic.
   One form is spoken.
   The other form is written.

4. Spoken Arabic consists of several dialects.
   There is only one form of the written language.
   It is called the classical form.

5. The classical form is the religious language of all Muslims.
   The classical form was standardized by the Koran.

6. Because of the Koran, written Arabic has not changed in centuries.
   Because of the Koran, the spoken dialects have not become different languages.

Arabic

7. The Arabic alphabet has 28 symbols.
   Arabic letters are all consonants.
   The vowels are signs inserted above or below the letters.

8. The language is written from right to left.
   The language is written from the top of the page to the bottom of the page.

9. The spread of the Arabic language was the result of the spread of Islam.
   Many of the speakers of Arabic are not Arabic in their ethnic background.

10. Today, many Arab countries are involved in world affairs.
    Arabic has become a major language in international politics.
    Arabic has become a major language in international business.

Adapted from *World Book Encyclopedia*, 1988 ed., s.v. "Arabic language."

Korean

1. The Korean language is spoken by more than 50 million people.   (which)
   The Korean language is the official language of South Korea.
   The Korean language is the official language of North Korea.

2. The grammatical structure of Korean resembles that of the Japanese language.   (although)
   Approximately half of all Korean words come from Chinese.

3. For over a thousand years, most of the writing was in Chinese characters.   (which)
   Chinese characters are still used to write words of Chinese origin.

진달래꽃

나 보기가 역겨워.
가실 때에는
말없이 고히 보내 드리우리다

영변(寧邊)에 약산(藥山)
진달래꽃
아름따다 가실 길에 뿌리우리다.

가시는 걸음걸음
놓인 그 꽃을
사뿐히 즈려 밟고 가시옵소서。

나 보기가 역겨워
가실 때에는
죽어도 아니 눈물 흘리우리다

Korean

4. There are six major dialects of the Korean language.   (even though)
   Most Koreans can understand all the dialects.

5. Today, the Korean language uses a unique alphabet.   (that)
   The Korean alphabet is called *Hangul*.

6. *Hangul* was invented.   (before)
   Koreans used the Chinese language for written communication.

7. *Hangul* has 24 letters.   (and)
   There are 14 consonants.
   There are 10 vowels.

8. This special alphabet was created 500 years ago.
   It was created by a group of scholar-officials.

9. The symbols are simple.   (although)
   The spelling rules are complicated.   (because)
   The system of word structure is complex.

10. Many *Hangul* texts appeared in the last half of the 15th
    century.   (although)
    Hangul was not accepted until the 20th century.

Adapted from *Collier's Encyclopedia*, 1987 ed., and *World Book Encyclopedia*, 1988 ed.,
s.v. "Korea."

African Languages

1. The people of Africa belong to hundreds of ethnic groups.
   Each group consists of people who are similar in their religion,
      history, language, and way of life.

2. Most African ethnic groups have their own language or dialect.
   In most cases, language helps to identify members of a particular
      group.

3. More than 800 languages are spoken in Africa.
   Communication is sometimes difficult.

4. Certain languages are spoken widely.
   Arabic, Swahili, and Hausa are spoken widely.

5. Millions of Africans speak more than one language.
   They use their languages when traveling or conducting business.

6. The languages spoken in Africa can be classified into three groups.
   One group is the Black African languages.
   A second group is the Afro-Asian languages.
   A third group is the Indo-European languages.

7. Black African languages are spoken by 290 million people.
   These people usually live south of the Sahara and west of southern
      Sudan.

8. Afro-Asian languages are spoken in the northern half of Africa.
   Approximately 120 million Africans speak these languages.

9. Two Indo-European languages are spoken by 6 million people.
   These are Afrikaans and English.

10. Many Africans speak English, French, or Portuguese.
   The European languages are used for communication in international
      business.
   The European languages are used for communication in government
      affairs.

Adapted from *World Book Encyclopedia*, 1988 ed., s.v. "Africa."

Swahili

Mtego wanaotega, ninaswe nianguke,
Sifa yangu kuvuruga, jina liaibike,
Mungu mwema mfuga, nilinde lisitendeke,
Na wawekao kiaga, kudhuru watakasike.

Kwa wingi natangaziwa, maovu nisiyotenda,
Na habari nasikia, kila ninapokwenda,
Lakini Allah mwelewa, atalifanya kuwanda,
Jina wanalochukia, badala ya kukonda.

Badala ya kukonda, jina litanenepa,
Ugenini litakwenda, lisipopendeza hapa,
Kutafuta kibanda, ambako halitatupwa,
Huko wataolipenda, fadhili litawalipa.

CHAPTER

11

Passive Sentences

"Passive" Defined

In English, we usually make sentences that begin with the person or thing that does the action.

The subject of the sentence is the person who does something. In the first example, the writer focused on "John" and the action that John did.

active sentence
***John** damaged the computer yesterday afternoon.*

However, writers sometimes want to change the focus of a sentence to communicate about the action and not about the person who did the action. In these passive examples, the writer focused on "the computer."

passive sentence
***The computer** was damaged by John yesterday afternoon.*

passive sentence
***The computer** was damaged yesterday afternoon.*

Comparing Active and Passive Sentences

Look carefully at the two example sentences given here. Make a list of all the differences that you can see between them. You should begin by marking the parts of the sentence.

1. *John damaged the computer yesterday afternoon.*

2. *The computer was damaged by John yesterday afternoon.*

The second example used above is called a **passive sentence.** Another way to talk about such sentences is to say that the verb is in the **passive voice.** To use passive sentences correctly and effectively, you have to learn two quite different things: the correct form and the correct use of passive sentences.

Here are two common errors made with the verb in passive sentences.

incorrect
The computer was **damage by John.*

incorrect
The computer was **damaging by John.*

correct
*The computer was **damaged** by John.*

When to Use Passive Sentences

English speakers use passive sentences when they want to change the focus from the subject to the direct object. We might want to make that change for several reasons.

Actor Unknown
We do not know the person who did the action.

The wheel was invented early in the history of human civilization.

Actor Unimportant
The person who did the action is not important. Or, the action is more important than the "actor." This is often true in scientific and technical writing. In a scientific report, the scientist does not say "I did this. I did that." The focus of the report is on the actions rather than the scientist.

This report was prepared with a grant from the Ford Foundation.

Actor Hidden
We have a reason to hide the name of the person who did the action. This can be politeness, or it can be done to deceive.

When Maria talked with her boss, she did not want to cause problems for John. Therefore, she said, "The computer was damaged, but I fixed it. Everything is fine now."

Actor Hidden to Deceive
Advertisers can use the passive to deceive buyers. The maker of a medicine claims that the medicine is effective because of tests. A careful buyer thinks, "But, who tested it?"

"This new medicine has been tested around the world."

Practice Analyzing the Grammar of Passive Sentences

Analyze the following set of sentences. In all of these sentences, the focus is on the subject doing something. Underline the complete subject with one line; underline the complete verb with two lines; and put a circle around the direct object.

Version One: The Active Voice Version

1. *John damaged the computer.*

2. *Maria repaired the computer.*

3. *Maria moved the computer to a safer location.*

Version Two: The Passive Voice Version

In the first version of the story, the writer focused on the actions of John and Maria. However, it is possible to tell the story in another way with the focus on the computer rather than the people. Underline the complete subject with one line; underline the complete verb with two lines; and put / / around adverbial modifiers. Notice that passive sentences cannot have direct objects because the direct object has become the subject.

To make a passive sentence, you use as the subject the words that would usually be the direct object. In this second version, you write about the computer rather than about John and Maria.

The computer was damaged.

The computer was repaired.

The computer was moved to a safer location.

Making Passive Verbs

The passive verb is a combination of **be** + past participle of a verb. The form of *be* can be any of the various forms of the verb from simple past to the most complicated combination.

Note the verbs in these example sentences. What changes? What stays the same?

*The computer **is** broken.*

*The computer **was** broken.*

*The computer **has been** broken.*

*The computer **had been** broken.*

*The computer **is being** repaired.*

*The computer **was being** repaired.*

*The computer **will be** repaired.*

*The computer **will have been** repaired.*

Practice with the Formation of the Passive Verb

A. Before continuing with this chapter, you should try writing different forms of the passive verb. First, work with a partner to write two passive sentences that have the verb in the simple past tense. Perhaps you can write sentences about something that happened in your class or your school. Then, write the sentences in the space provided below. Underneath that sentence write the passive verb in the following forms in this order.

Model sentence #1: _____

Changed Verb

1. simple present tense   _____

2. *will* + verb   _____

3. present perfect   _____

Model sentence #2: _____

Changed Verb

1. simple present tense   _____

2. *will* + verb   _____

3. present perfect   _____

B. Answer the questions; then, change the following information to make the sentence focus on the event rather than on the people doing the action. Write the answers to the questions and the passive sentence in the space provided.

1. *Mark Jones opened a new restaurant yesterday.*

    a. What is the subject of the active sentence? _____

    b. What happens to the subject to make a passive sentence? _____

    c. What is the direct object of the active sentence? _____

    d. What happens to the direct object to make a passive sentence? _____

    e. What is the verb of the active sentence? _____

f. How is the verb changed to make the passive
sentence?   _____

Passive version: _____

2. *He advertised the opening in the local newspaper.*

a. What is the subject of the active sentence?   _____
b. What happens to the subject to make a passive
sentence?   _____

c. What is the direct object of the active sentence?   _____
d. What happens to the direct object to make a
passive sentence?   _____

e. What is the verb of the active sentence?   _____
f. What happens to the verb to make the passive
sentence?   _____

Passive version: _____

3. *Many people attended the opening.*

a. What is the subject of the active sentence?   _____
b. How is the subject changed to make a passive
sentence?   _____

c. What is the direct object of the active sentence?   _____
d. What happens to the direct object to make a
passive sentence?   _____

e. What is the verb of the active sentence?   _____
f. How is the verb changed to make the passive
sentence?   _____

Passive version: _____

4. *The local newspaper took many pictures.*

a. What is the subject of the active sentence?   _____
b. What happens to the subject to make a passive
sentence?   _____

c. What is the direct object of the active sentence?   _____
d. What happens to the direct object to make a
passive sentence?   _____

e. What is the verb of the active sentence? _____

f. How is the verb changed to make the passive
   sentence? _____

Passive version: _____

Using the *By*-Phrase

· ·

Usually the active subject is just dropped and not used at all. However, sometimes the person who did the action is important (just not the focus of the communication).

By-Phrase Not Important

Do not use the **by-phrase** unless the information is important to the meaning of your communication. In the first example, the **by-phrase** is a waste of words because only a thief would steal. In the second example, the **by-phrase** adds useful and interesting information.

unnecessary **by-phrase**

My car was stolen last weekend **by a thief.**

My car was stolen last weekend.

My car was stolen last weekend **by a teenager who did not know how to drive;** *he wrecked it.*

By-Phrase Important

If you are writing about a book, the focus would be on the book. However, the name of the author would probably be important to include.

This book on boxing was written **by Muhammad Ali's former manager.**

Muhammad Ali

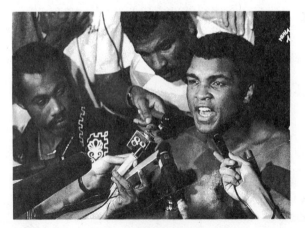

By-Phrase Not Known

Sometimes you cannot include the **by**-phrase because you do not know the information. In this example, your grammar would be technically correct if you added "by someone," but the information is not very meaningful. In this example, the **by**-phrase would weaken the style of the sentence.

unnecessary **by**-phrase

*The wheel was invented **by someone** early in the history of civilization.*

The wheel was invented early in the history of civilization.

By-Phrase Hidden

Sometimes you do not include the **by**-phrase because you are being polite or deceptive. Remember the example about John, Maria, and the computer. In this new version, Maria wanted her boss to know that John was responsible for damaging the computer, but she *still* wanted to focus on the computer rather than John. Remember that to protect John she would need to leave off the **by**-phrase.

The computer was damaged by John, but it is working now.

The computer was damaged, but it is working now.

Practice with the *By*-Phrase

Decide whether each **by**-phrase is necessary to the meaning of the following sentences. Be ready to explain why each one should or should not be omitted.

1. According to tradition, the Taj Mahal, located in northern India, was designed by a Turkish architect in 1630.
2. Pretzels were first made by monks as a reward for students who had learned their prayers. The crossed sections of a pretzel represent praying hands.
3. The Great Wall of China was built by the Chinese to keep out invaders from the North.
4. Nobel prizes are awarded annually by the Nobel Committee for the most important inventions or discoveries in the fields of chemistry, economics, literature, physics, and physiology.

5. The Mediterranean Sea has been considered by many people as one of the world's chief trade routes since ancient times.

6. Microfilm, which reduces printed material, is widely used in libraries and businesses by students and employees; when needed, a paper copy can be quickly produced by a microfilm copier.

7. The earliest civilization in the region of Greece was developed in Crete by people about 6100 B.C. Today, the settlement of Knossos is dated by a carbon 14 analysis.

8. Leif Ericson was a Norwegian explorer who may have led the first European expedition to the mainland of North America; Leif Ericsson Day is observed by some people in the United States on October 9.

9. The first European expedition to reach the Mississippi River was led by Hernando De Soto.

10. Oxygen was discovered by two chemists working independently; their discoveries were published by the men in 1777.

Adapted from *World Book Encyclopedia,* 1988 ed., s.v. "exploration," "food," and "Taj Mahal." *Encyclopedia Americana,* 1983 ed., s.v. "Crete," "Great Wall of China," "oxygen," and "Nobel prizes."

Passive Look-Alikes

• •

The correct forms of some phrases look like passives but technically are not. For ESL students, the most difficult problem seems to be to remember to use the past participle. These phrases are often used in descriptions of places and locations for events.

be found beside/in/on/near and other location prepositions	*The book that you need **is found** **on** the fourth floor of the library.*
	incorrect **The university is **locate** at the corner of Decatur and Piedmont.* correct *The university **is located at** the corner of Decatur and Piedmont.*
be made of/from	*This book **is made of** paper, glue, ink, and plastic.*
be situated in/near/beside/between	*My hometown **is situated between** two large rivers.*

be surrounded by

incorrect
*Their home is **surrounding** by trees and shrubs.

correct
Their home **is surrounded by** trees and shrubs.

Practice with Passive Look-Alikes

A. Write five sentences using passive look-alikes to describe a place that you know well: for example, your home, your apartment house, your city, or your school. After you are sure that your information is accurate, edit the sentences for grammar and spelling, paying special attention to the past participles in the verbs. Then, share your information with the other students in your class. Write the corrected sentences on a sheet of paper to keep in your Grammar Notebook for future reference. Example: *The University is located in Washington. The library is surrounded by grass and tall trees.*

B. Select an object that you carry with you to school every day: for example, a book, a pen, or a calculator. Write a sentence in which you describe the materials used to make the object. Share your example with the other students in your class to get their help to be sure that your description is accurate. After you are sure that your information is correct, edit the sentence for grammar and spelling. Then, write the example on a sheet of paper to keep in your Grammar Notebook for future reference.

Practice with Passive Sentences

A. As a review, turn to the Diagnostic Test on page 14 in First Steps, and look closely at items 31–35. Compare your answers today with your answers from the first week of this course.

B. Discussion Assignment: As a result of political, economic, or military conquests, countries have often added treasures to their national museums. For example, Native American artifacts are in the Smithsonian Museum in Washington, D.C. Or, Greek statues are in the British Museum. Do you know of any other similar situations? What do you think should be done about these situations?

Grammar Assignment: Fill in each blank with the correct form of the verb in parentheses. Some verbs are active; some are passive. What is the general time frame? What different verb forms are used?

The British Museum

The British Museum _____ in 1753, and
                    [1](establish)
visitors can view three famous treasures there. The Elgin

Marbles _____ under the supervision of the
        [2](create)
great sculptor Phidias almost 2,500 years ago. At one time,

they _____ the exterior of the Parthenon in
     [3](decorate)
Athens, Greece. However, the Parthenon

_____ by an earthquake in the nineteenth
[4](destroy, partially)
century, and the Elgin Marbles _____ by Lord
                                [5](remove)
Elgin, the British ambassador. The British Museum also has

a superb collection of Egyptian relics. The most prized

Egyptian piece is the Rosetta Stone, which

_____ near Rashid, Egypt, in July 1799. This
[6](discover)
stone _____ the key for deciphering ancient
      [7](provide)
Egyptian hieroglyphic writing. The third treasure in the

British Museum is one of the original copies of the Magna

Carta; this famous document _____ by King
                            [8](sign)
John more than seven hundred years ago. It

_____ the rights of the common man. These
[9](guarantee)
three archeological treasures are among thousands of items

on display at the British Museum.

Adapted from *Encyclopedia Americana*, 1983 ed., s.v. "British Museum."

Partial view of
The Rosetta Stone

C. Discussion Assignment: What are the purposes of art museums? Is there such a museum in the place where you are now living or at your school?

Grammar Assignment: Fill in each blank with the correct form of the verb in parentheses. Some verbs are active; some are passive. What is the general time frame? What different verb forms are used?

The Louvre

The Louvre, one of the most famous museums of art in the world,

_____ on the Right Bank of the Seine River in Paris,
¹(locate)

France. This museum, which _____ originally a royal
²(be)

palace, _____ into a museum in the late 18th century.
³(make)

Today the Louvre _____ for its elaborate rooms and
⁴(know)

galleries and magnificently painted ceilings. Over 125 of the museum's

3,000 paintings _____ as great masterpieces. The most
⁵(classify)

famous painting in the museum _____ Leonardo da Vinci's
⁶(be)

famous "Mona Lisa." This portrait _____ famous for the
⁷(be)

inscrutable expression of the woman in the painting. Art pieces by

Rembrandt, Goya, Titian, and Raphael _____ also on
⁸(be)

display. Two famous sculptures in the museum _____
⁹(be)

"Venus of Milo," a statue of the Roman goddess that

_____ in 1826, and the "Winged Victory," an eight-foot
¹⁰(purchase)

marble sculpture that _____ on the Greek island of
¹¹(find)

Samothrace. The "Winged Victory" _____ by today's art
¹²(consider)

critics as a masterpiece of Hellenistic sculpture. Because of its famous

collection, the Louvre _____ as one of the greatest
¹³(regard)

museums in the world.

Adapted from *Collier's Encyclopedia*, 1987 ed., s.v. "Louvre."

D. Discussion Assignment: Lasers, computers, and other forms of technology are changing human life. Some changes are good; some are harmful. Discuss the benefits and dangers of high technology.

Grammar Assignment: Fill in each blank with the correct form of the verb in parentheses. Some verbs are active; some are passive. What is the general time frame? What different verb forms are used?

The Laser

The laser _____ in 1960 by Dr. Theodore Maiman at
¹(create)

the Hughes Research Laboratories in Malibu, California. The word *laser*

is an acronym for Light Amplification by Stimulated Emission of

Radiation. Today, lasers _____ in industry to cut, drill,
²(use)

weld, and engrave on steel, glass, plastic, and ceramic. They are popular because they are fast, accurate, and do not wear out.

Lasers contain concentrated waves that have the same frequency and wavelength. The power of a laser beam _____ on the ³(base) amount of energy that _____ on a target. For example, a ⁴(focus) laser can focus a beam on a spot the size of the period at the end of this sentence. Space uses of lasers are common. The Apollo 11 astronauts _____ lasers to measure the distance between the earth ⁵(use) and the moon. Lasers _____ with fiber optic telephone ⁶(use, also) lines to allow people across the country to hear the person on the other end of the telephone line.

Perhaps the most important contribution that lasers have made is their use in the medical profession. Today, surgeons _____ ⁷(use) lasers to weld detached retinas back to eyeballs, treat blocked arteries, and cut away diseased growths. In the future, most family dentists _____ away tooth decay using lasers. It is difficult to ⁸(burn) remember that the laser _____ only thirty years ago. ⁹(discover)

Adapted from *World Book Encyclopedia*, 1988 ed., s.v. "laser."

Laser technology

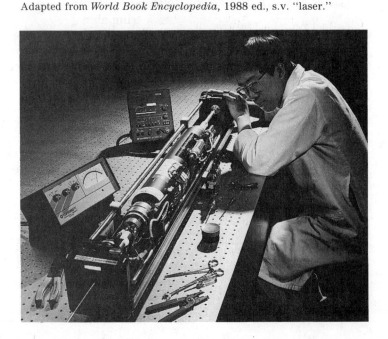

E. Discussion Assignment: What is a backache? What other types of problems have similar names in English; what other aches can people have? Do you have problems with your back? Do you know anyone who does?

Grammar Assignment: As you read this passage, look at the diagram of the vertebrae system. When you find vocabulary in the passage that is the same as on the diagram, circle the words in the passage. Use the correct form of the verb in parentheses to complete each sentence. Some verbs are passive; others are active.

Anatomy of a Backache

Knowing a little about the spine and its parts _____ it

1(make)

easier to understand backaches. Human beings _____ born

2(be)

with 33 separate vertebrae—the bones that _____ the

3(form)

spine. However, by adulthood, most people _____ only 24

4(have)

because the nine vertebrae at the base of the spine _____

5(grow)

together. Five of these vertebrae _____ a triangular bone

6(form)

that _____ the sacrum—those two dimples in most

7(call)

everyone's back _____ the point where the sacrum

8(be)

_____ the hipbones (the sacroiliac joint). The lowest four

9(join)

_____ the tailbone, or coccyx. Frequently, the coccyx

10(form)

_____ with the sacrum above.

11(unite)

Physicians _____ a code to identify the vertebrae.

12(use)

The seven in the neck _____ the cervical vertebrae; these

13(call)

_____ and _____ movement for the head.

14(support)   15(provide)

These cervical vertebrae _____ C1 to C7. The thoracic

16(call)

vertebrae _____ with and _____ by the

17(join)   18(support)

ribs; they _____ T1 to T12. Because they

19(number)

_____ fairly rigid, thoracic vertebrae

20(be)

_____ much movement. As a result, they

21(not permit)

_____ as often as the other vertebrae. The lumbar

22(not injure)

vertebrae _____ below the thoracic vertebrae and above

23(be)

the sacrum; they _____ most frequently involved in back

24(be)

pain. They _____ as L1 to L2.

25(know)

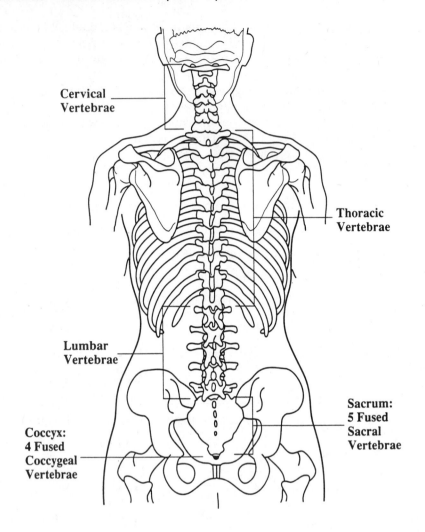

Cervical Vertebrae

Thoracic Vertebrae

Lumbar Vertebrae

Sacrum: 5 Fused Sacral Vertebrae

Coccyx: 4 Fused Coccygeal Vertebrae

The vertebrae ＿＿＿＿＿＿＿＿＿＿ one on top of the other
26(be not)
in a straight line; each ＿＿＿＿＿＿＿＿＿＿ on the one below at an
27(rest)
angle, forming an S-curve when they ＿＿＿＿＿＿＿＿＿＿ from the side.
28(view)
Tough ligaments ＿＿＿＿＿＿＿＿＿＿ the vertebrae to each other;
29(secure)
strong muscles and tendons ＿＿＿＿＿＿＿＿＿＿ the spinal column
30(keep)
upright.

Between each pair of adjacent vertebrae ＿＿＿＿＿＿＿＿＿＿ a
31(be)
spinal disc—23 discs in all. Discs ＿＿＿＿＿＿＿＿＿＿ flat, round
32(be)
structures of tough outer tissue that ＿＿＿＿＿＿＿＿＿＿ a soft, white
33(contain)

jelly-like center. Each disc _____ to the vertebrae above
_{34(connect)}
and below it by cartilage. The discs _____ the vertebrae
_{35(keep)}
apart and _____ as shock absorbers. They
_{36(act)}

_____ when weight _____ on them; they
_{37(compress)} _{38(put)}
_____ back when the weight _____ .
_{39(spring)} _{40(remove)}

In addition to the 33 vertebrae and 23 discs, the back also

_____ 31 pairs of spinal nerves, 140 muscles, ligaments,
_{41(contain)}

tendons, and cartilage. The complexity of the back _____
_{42(be)}

the source of many potential types of backache. In 80 percent of the

cases, the exact cause of the pain _____ .
_{43(identify, never)}

Adapted from U.S. Food and Drug Administration. "Anatomy of a Backache," *FDA Consumer.* Washington, D.C.: GPO, 1989, 9.

F. Use the information provided below to write an article for the school newspaper about a meeting of the International Student Club. First, choose the officers of the club from the students in your grammar class. Then, fill in the other information based on your class. Finally, choose between active and passive voice as you tell where, when, and why the meeting was held, who was elected and appointed, and what was decided.

Name: International Student Club,
Time: the first and third Friday of each month, 1:00 P.M.
    Friday, October 4
Place: the Student Center, B201
Purpose: to elect officers and schedule a party

Results: President: _____

Vice President: _____

Secretary: _____

Treasurer: _____

Faculty Sponsor: _____

Date for Party: Saturday, November 9
Committee Assignments:

Food: _____

Publicity: _____

Decorations: _____

Entertainment: _____
Next Meeting: Friday, October 18

G. Working with two or three other students, arrange to do a demonstration of a simple scientific principle. As you do the demonstration, one student will write the sentences that describe your actions on the board. Each sentence should begin with the name of the person doing the action. The focus of this writing is to describe the actions of the person doing the demonstration. You should use the past time context.

H. Change the focus of the description written in exercise G, and write a description of what happened. Remove all mention of the person who did the actions. In this writing, you are making a technical report; the approved style is impersonal.

I. To practice editing someone else's written English, turn to Section Four. Study the information about editing on page 404, and then do the editing exercises on page 416.

J. For additional writing topics and the editing summary for this chapter, turn to Section Four, page 427.

CHAPTER

12

Punctuation

Overview of Punctuation Choices

Correct punctuation is important because it helps a reader to understand your meaning more exactly and more easily. Here is a summary of the types of marks that you will use most in writing. The most important of these for you to use accurately in written academic English are the period, the comma, and the apostrophe.

to show end of sentence	.	period	!	exclamation mark	?	question mark
inside sentences	,	comma	;	semicolon	:	colon
other special purposes	, apostrophe <u>underlining</u>		"quotation marks"		

The Period and Other End Marks

The period (.) is used to show the end of a sentence. In general, most sentences written for college assignments will end with a period rather than a question mark (?) or an exclamation mark (!). Be very careful to distinguish between a period (.) and a comma (,) in your handwriting.

Period
Statements end with a period.

Your classnotes should be helpful in reviewing for the final exam.

Question Mark
Questions end with a question mark.

What does "voracious" mean?

Exclamation Mark
Commands usually end with a period unless they are expressed with strong emotion. You might use an exclamation mark in less formal writing.

Turn to page 501.

Watch out!

Exclamations can sometimes end with an exclamation mark, but this mark is seldom used in formal academic writing even when strong emotion is expressed.

This is a very serious situation. The government must act immediately to deal with the problem.

You might use an exclamation mark in a personal letter or other informal writing.

What a wonderful idea!

The Comma

Commas are used only within sentences. They are never used to indicate the end of a sentence. Commas have several important uses. In the list below, the most important uses are given first. The following are not the only uses for the comma in written English, but they are the most important ones for you to know and use.

A. Commas can be used to create compound and compound-complex sentences.

Commas are used with joining words such as *and, but, or, nor, for, so,* and *yet*.

When a comma is used with a joining word to connect two simple sentences, a **compound sentence** is created. If a dependent clause is included, a **compound-complex** sentence is formed. See Chapter One for more information on sentence types.

compound sentence
English is a required course, but I would rather take French.

compound-complex sentence
The foreign student advisor assists students who are not legal residents of the United States, and the financial aid advisor assists students with resident status.

B. Commas can be used to mark the end of introductory elements.

Commas are used to show the end of elements such as adverbial clauses and introductory phrases.

After the lecture was over, the professor asked for questions.

After the lecture in the auditorium, the class went to the library.

Walking across the campus, Sean met two friends.

C. Commas can be used to separate items in a series.

Commas separate lists of the same kind of items. Do not place a comma after the last word in a series.

> Every student in this class is taking a reading, writing, and math course.

> We concentrated on discussing ideas, outlining, and summarizing in class yesterday.

D. Commas can be used to separate parts in dates and addresses.

Commas separate the day's number from the year. They also separate the city from the state or country, and they set off the state or country as shown in these examples.

> He moved from Tehran, Iran, in August 1985.
> He moved to Miami, Florida, on August 22, 1985.
> On August 22, 1985, he moved to Miami, Florida.

E. Commas can be used to indicate transitional words and expressions.

The following transitional words and expressions help unify your writing and should be set off with one or two commas as appropriate.

also	in fact
for example	nevertheless
furthermore	on the other hand
however	therefore
in addition	thus

> There are students from several countries in my class; in fact, there are students from seven different countries.

> The college needs a better system for registration. For example, I stood in the registration line for four hours yesterday.

> I wanted to register early in the morning; my advisor, however, was not available until in the afternoon.

F. Commas can be used to separate nonrestrictive relative clauses from the rest of the sentence.

As is shown in Chapter Ten, nonrestrictive relative clauses are separated from the rest of the sentence by commas.

Note also the use of commas to separate the parts of numbers.

> New York City, which is the financial capital of the United States, has a population of over 7,000,000 people.

The Apostrophe

• •

The apostrophe has two uses in written English: to indicate contractions and to indicate possession.

A. Apostrophes are used to form contractions.

In speaking, contractions occur when two separate words are combined to make a single word and some sounds are left out or changed. For example, *do not* becomes *don't*, and *will not* becomes *won't*. In writing, this change in pronunciation is indicated by spelling and by the use of an apostrophe. Contractions are very popular in spoken English, and you may have difficulty in understanding native speakers until you learn contractions. In formal written English, it is often better to write the full form.

Examples of Contractions with *be*

I am = I'm	*that is = that's*	*who is = who's*
she is = she's	*there are = there're*	
they are = they're	*there is = there's*	

Examples of Contractions with *have*

I have eaten = I've eaten	*she had eaten = she'd eaten*
she has eaten = she's eaten	

Examples of Contractions with *will*

I will = I'll	*they will= they'll*

Examples of Contractions with *not*

she is not = she isn't	*he should not = he shouldn't*
they are not = they aren't	*you will not = you won't*
she was not = she wasn't	*he does not = he doesn't*
they were not = they weren't	

B. Apostrophes can be used to indicate possession.

In spoken English, there is no difference in pronunciation between *students*, *student's*, and *students'*. When you speak, the other words in the sentence tell your listener which form you mean. In writing, you use the apostrophe to show the difference.

all students
*The **students** have to pay their fees next week.*

the fees of one student
*The **student's** fees must be paid next week.*

the fees of all students
*The **students'** fees must be paid next week.*

The apostrophe is also used in some expressions of time such as these:

a day's work

five days' work

Use the following rules if a noun is **singular.** (If a noun is to be **plural,** make it **plural** first, and then follow the two rules.)

Rule #1: Nouns Without *-s* at End

If a noun does not end in *-s*, add an apostrophe and an *-s*. Notice that this rule applies to singular nouns, to noncount nouns, and to irregular plural nouns.

teacher	*teacher's*
information	*information's*
men	*men's*

Rule #2: Nouns with *-s* at end

If a plural noun ends in an *-s*, add only an apostrophe.

teachers	*teachers'*
books	*books'*

It's

The apostrophe should NOT be used to show possession with personal pronouns (*yours, his, hers, its, ours, theirs*).

incorrect
*My dictionary is several years old. ***It's** binding is broken.*

correct
***Its** binding is broken.*

It's means *it is.* My calculator does not work; it is broken.

"What's wrong with your calculator?"

*"**It's** broken."*

Practice with Commas and Apostrophes

A. In the space provided below, write the contractions for the following forms. When can you use these written contractions?

1. I am _____

2. he is _____

3. he has _____

4. are not _____

5. you are   _____

6. would not   _____

7. will not   _____

8. have not   _____

9. has not   _____

10. did not   _____

11. it has   _____

12. it is   _____

13. they are   _____

14. there is   _____

15. I would   _____

16. is not   _____

17. they have   _____

18. who is   _____

19. cannot   _____

20. let us   _____

B. In the space provided below, form the singular and plural possessives of the following words.

	Noun	Singular Possessive Form	Plural Possessive Form
Example:	book	*book's*	*books'*
1.	woman	_____	_____
2.	girl	_____	_____
3.	pen	_____	_____
4.	baby	_____	_____
5.	brother	_____	_____
6.	roommate	_____	_____
7.	anybody	_____	_____
8.	neighbor	_____	_____
9.	child	_____	_____
10.	wife	_____	_____
11.	teacher	_____	_____

C. Write one sentence for each of the comma rules illustrated on pages 303–304. It would probably be more interesting and helpful to have sentences about your own experiences and ideas. Working with another student, edit the sentences that both of you have written. After making the necessary corrections, keep the list in your Grammar Notebook for future reference.

D. Write five sentences using the apostrophe in contractions and five sentences using the apostrophe to show possession. It would probably be more interesting and useful to have sentences about your own experiences and ideas. Working with another student, edit the sentences that both of you have written. After making the necessary corrections, keep the list in your Grammar Notebook for future reference. Use these as examples when you edit your own writing.

The Semicolon

Semicolons (;) are used only within sentences. They are never used to indicate the end of a sentence. The first letter of the word following the semicolon is not capitalized. The semicolon has two important uses that you should remember.

A. Semicolons can be used to combine sentences without joining words.

Semicolons are used to connect two simple sentences that do not have the joining words *and, but, or, nor, for, so,* or *yet.*

sentence 1
English is a required course at Kansas State University.

sentence 2
It is not required at Kansas Technological Institute.

combined sentence
English is a required course at Kansas State University; it is not required at Kansas Technological Institute.

B. Semicolons can be used to combine sentences with transition words.

Semicolons are used to connect two simple sentences that have transition words such as *also, first, furthermore, however, in addition, indeed, instead, on the other hand, then,* and *therefore.*

English is a required course at Kansas State University; **however,** *it is not required at Kansas Technological Institute.*

The Colon

· ·

Colons (:) are used only within sentences. They are never used to indicate the end of a sentence. The colon has two important uses for you to remember.

A. Colons are used to set off a list or series.

Colons used this way direct a reader's attention to one or more examples or to a list.

Students should bring four items to class every day: the textbook, a dictionary, a notebook, and a pen.

Before being admitted to college, many students must take two tests: the SAT and the TOEFL.

B. Colons are used to separate numbers to give time and to punctuate the salutation on a business letter.

Class begins at 8:55 A.M.   *Dear Dr. Cole:*

Quotation Marks

· ·

A. Quotation marks are used to tell your reader that you are writing the exact words someone else said or wrote.

Among Abraham Lincoln's famous words is his definition of the United States as "of the people, by the people, and for the people."

B. Quotation marks are also used to mark the titles of short stories, poems, and articles.

"The Lottery" is a well-known short story.

Robert Frost wrote the poem "Fire and Ice."

The newspaper printed an article called "Computers Today."

C. There are always two quotation marks. Notice the capitalization and the commas in the examples.

"Be sure to outline Chapter One tonight," said the teacher.

One student said, "Let's turn in our outlines on Monday."

Another student added, "We have already turned in one outline."

Underlining

• •

A. Underlining (in handwritten or typed work) and italics (in printed work) are used to mark the titles of books, plays, magazines, and newspapers.

Underlined (handwritten or typed)	Italics (printed)	Type of Work
The Hobbit	*The Hobbit*	a book
Romeo and Juliet	*Romeo and Juliet*	a play
Newsweek	*Newsweek*	a magazine
New York Times	*New York Times*	a newspaper

B. Do not underline the title of a typed or handwritten essay, composition, or report.

Capitalization

• •

There are three important places for capital letters: the first word of every sentence, proper names, and important words in titles.

A. Capitalize the first word of every sentence.

Be sure that your handwriting clearly shows the difference between capital and small letters.

B. Capitalize proper names.

Proper names refer to specific people, places, languages, historical periods, days and months, organizations, and religions. In addition, the pronoun *I* is always capitalized, no matter where it appears in a sentence.

Be sure to always capitalize exact names like the following:

People	Places	Languages	Days, Months, Holidays
Mr. Adams	*California*	*Arabic*	*Tuesday*
President Bush	*England*	*English*	*March*
Sean Moreland	*Thailand*	*Japanese*	*Fourth of July*
Sara Reynolds		*Urdu*	*Halloween*

Oceans	Rivers	Mountains
the Atlantic Ocean	*the Amazon River*	*the Rocky Mountains*
the Mediterranean Sea	*the Mississippi River*	*Mount Everest*

C. Do NOT capitalize general nouns that are not proper nouns.

a person	a state	a language
a day	a holiday	a river
a president	a country	a college

While this example means a specific place, the writer did not use the proper noun that names the college.	*The college is closed during national holidays.*
In the second example, the writer used the proper noun that is the name of the college.	*Dalton College is closed during national holidays.*
The writer does not give the name of a particular language, but is referring to any second language.	*Learning a second language is difficult.*
The writer used the proper noun that is the name of a particular language.	*Learning German is difficult.*

D. Do NOT capitalize the names of seasons.

fall   winter   spring   summer

I started college last spring.
He plans to graduate next summer.

E. Capitalize the major words in a title.

Titles of books, plays, magazines, newspapers, poems, short stories, and essays are proper names of publications.

book
The Invisible Man

play
Death of a Salesman

magazine
Sports Illustrated

newspaper
New York Times

poem
"The Three Ravens"

short story
"The Pit and the Pendulum"

essay
"The Great Society"

Practice Using Capital Letters

A. Copy the following sentences on another sheet of paper. Then, ask a classmate to look at your handwriting and answer the two questions.

> When I first came to the United States, I did not speak any English. At that time, I had to depend on my brother who had been studying in Texas since November. There were many times when we both wanted to know more about American culture and American English.

Which letters should be capitalized? _____

Which letters need to be written more clearly? _____

B. Where is the missing capital letter in the two sentences below? Why is it important to the reader to know if the writer wanted the second sentence to begin with *Because* or *I*? Written English is hard to understand when there are missing capital letters and missing periods and commas.

> My easiest class is calculus, and my hardest class is composition because I don't like to write I sometimes do not do my homework.

C. Reread the examples given in section E on capitalization on page 311. After rereading the examples, work with another student in your class to make the rule for writing titles more specific. Write your answer in the space provided here.

1. What must you do in addition to capitalizing the major words in a title?

   _____

2. When should an article (*a, an, the*) be capitalized in a title?

   _____

3. How are the first four titles different from the last three titles?

   _____

. . . .

Practice with Punctuation

A. On a separate sheet of paper, write the following paragraph using your neatest penmanship. Be sure to distinguish between capital letters and small letters in your handwriting. After you have finished writing, exchange paragraphs with another student who will check your handwriting to see if your capital letters are different from your small letters and are correctly written.

Before I came to the United States, I studied English in Vietnam. After moving to New York City, I started night classes at Martin Luther King Senior High School in Queens. Then, on January 1, I moved to Washington, D.C., and started college at Georgetown University on February 11. After I graduate, I plan to live in Norman, Oklahoma, with my brother Pon.

B. Working with another student, decide whether the following words and expressions should be capitalized. Circle each letter that must be capitalized. Then, fill in the blanks in the statements at the end of the word list.

1. washington
2. november
3. monday
4. robert kingston
5. *othello* (a play)
6. fall
7. nile river
8. french
9. clarkston high school
10. pacific ocean
11. rocky mountains
12. mississippi river
13. asia
14. college
15. dr. m. l. johnson

16. summer
17. *the theatre of revolt* (a book)
18. halloween
19. chemistry
20. "the killers" (a short story)
21. university of texas
22. ms. sonya alvarez
23. miami, florida
24. english literature
25. kansas state university
26. united states
27. chinese
28. north dakota
29. 500 north main street
30. los angeles

a. _____ letters in the above list should be capitalized.

b. _____ expressions in the above list need the article *the*.

313

C. Match the words and expressions in exercise B to the following reasons for capitalization by writing each word in the appropriate space. Be sure to write the words using capital letters.

1. Cities/States/Countries _____

2. Continents _____

3. Days/Months/Holidays _____

4. Languages _____

5. Mountains _____

6. Proper Names _____

7. Rivers/Oceans _____

8. Schools _____

9. Street Addresses _____

10. Titles _____

D. In the space provided below, write at least one proper noun for the following general nouns. To make this list useful, you should select words that you think you might use in your own writing. Use these examples when you edit your writing.

Examples of Proper Nouns and Capitalization

1. a city _____

2. a state _____

3. a country _____

4. a language _____

5. a building _____

6. a university _____

7. a river   _____

8. a month   _____

9. a holiday   _____

10. a continent   _____

11. an ocean   _____

12. a mountain   _____

13. an island   _____

14. a lake   _____

15. a street   _____

16. a book   _____

17. a short story   _____

18. a county   _____

19. a teacher   _____

20. a magazine   _____

E. To practice editing someone else's written English, turn to Section Four. Study the information about editing on page 404, and then do the editing exercises on pages 421–423.

CHAPTER

13

Nouns, Adjectives, and Personal Pronouns

CHAPTER ORGANIZATION

Noun Phrases

In each of these examples, the basic noun is *book*; other words are added to make the meaning of *book* more exact.

the book

the geography book

the expensive geography book

the beautiful but expensive geography book

the beautiful and useful but expensive geography book

Personal pronouns are words like *I, me, my, mine, she, her, hers,* and others. They are often used to replace or to refer to nouns and noun phrases.

***My** geography book cost $60. **It** is required for the geography class that **I** am taking this term.*

Structure of Noun Phrases

Nouns are words like *book, education,* and *university.* In Chapter Nine, the relationship between nouns and articles is explained. In this chapter, you will investigate the structure of **noun phrases** and will learn about ways to use **adjectives** effectively.

Nouns are seldom used alone. Usually, they are combined with other words to make **noun phrases.** These combinations can be very short or extremely long.

Order of Words in Noun Phrases: (determiner or article) + (adjective) + (noun) + noun

Noun phrases, of course, always have a noun. In front of the noun, you can add determiners, adjectives, and other nouns to build your exact meaning. (The parentheses in the rule mean that the word is possible but not always required. For some nouns, you must have a determiner; for others, no determiner is possible.)

Noun

The noun phrase in the first example is simply a noun. A noncount noun without an article is used for generic meaning.

*I like **music**.*

Article + Noun

In the next example, the noun phrase is made of an article plus a noun. Generic meaning is meant. The writer means "I need one of those kinds of things."

*I need **a pencil**.*

Article + Adjective + Noun

The third example shows a noun phrase with an article, an adjective, and a noun. The meaning is indefinite; the writer means "I ate a specific sandwich, but I know that you do not yet know what I am talking about so I begin with *a*."

*I ate **a delicious sandwich**.*

Article + Adjective + Noun + Noun

The fourth example includes all categories with article + adjective + noun + noun. The noun phrase is indefinite (and specific).

*I bought **a new computer disk**.*

Article + Noun + Phrase or Clause

Noun phrases can also be modified by prepositional phrases and by relative clauses. Both of these noun phrases are definite in meaning because information has been added to make the meaning clear to the reader.

*I like **the students in my dormitory**.*

*I like **the book that I got for my birthday**.*

Nouns Modifying Nouns

English speakers frequently create noun phrases where a noun works like an adjective to modify another noun, for example, *grammar class*, *music book*, and *cheese sandwich*.

Most of these combinations can be analyzed as a noun followed by a prepositional phrase.

a plate made of paper
a paper plate

Usually, singular nouns must be used to modify other nouns. It is usually ungrammatical to use a plural noun. English does not have plural adjectives.

incorrect
books bag

correct
I need **a book bag.**

incorrect
books bags

correct
I need **two book bags.**

incorrect
shoes store

correct
My brother manages **a shoe store.**

incorrect
shoes stores

correct
My brother manages **two shoe stores.**

Meanings of Noun-Plus-Noun Combinations

Grammarians have identified the following major categories of these noun + noun combinations. This list is not complete but only suggests the kinds of relationships you will find. There is some overlapping of these categories. Purpose and group membership, for example, are sometimes hard to distinguish.

Source or Material
The modifying noun refers to the source or material out of which something is made.

a clay tablet, a paper napkin, a lead pencil, a rubber band, plastic glasses

Use
The modifying noun gives the use to which the main noun is put.

a water glass, a tea cup, a vegetable dish, a water fountain

Location
The modifying noun gives a location or place.

a street sign, an apartment office, the university library

Direction

The modifying noun gives the direction that a street or road goes.

the Atlanta Highway, the Santa Ana Freeway, the Brooklyn Bridge

Time

The modifying noun refers to time.

a morning flight, an evening class, an afternoon appointment

Group

The modifying noun names the larger group for a whole/part relationship.

a board member, a class member, an airline pilot, a university instructor, a computer keyboard

Purpose

The modifying noun tells the purpose of the main noun.

a tiger hunt, a physics test, a chemistry class

Practice with Noun + Noun Combinations

A. Working with another student, make a list of the noun phrases that combine noun + noun in "A View of the United States in the Late Twentieth Century" on page 138. These noun phrases include *minority groups, the world economic leader, education system,* and others. Then, discuss with the whole class the meanings of these phrases using the seven categories listed above.

B. You will find that academic English uses many noun phrases that combine many nouns into one phrase, for example, *part-time faculty personnel management policies.* Using a textbook from your major field of study, make a list of 10 phrases that combine three or more nouns. If possible, work with another student who is majoring in the same area.

Select phrases that seem to be important: for example, phrases from titles of the chapters, phrases used in reviews or exercises at the end of chapters, or phrases that are printed in special print (bold, italic, etc.). Write the list of words on a separate sheet of paper. Then, analyze them by drawing a circle around the parts of the phrase that go together.

part-time faculty personnel management policies

Using Noun Phrases

Noun phrases are used in all the ways that single nouns can be used. Work with other students in your class to provide one additional example to fit each of these uses. Write your examples in the space provided here.

1. Subject of a sentence (***My chemistry class*** *is interesting.*)

2. Direct object of a sentence (*I like **my chemistry class**.*)

3. Complement of *be* (*He is **my chemistry teacher**.*)

4. Object of preposition (*This is the book for **my chemistry class**.*)

Adjectives

The Order of Words in Noun Phrases

Generally, words in front of the noun will occur in the following order if more than one is used in a noun phrase.

determiner +

sequence + number + quality or character + size + age + temperature + shape + color + origin or location +

noun +

noun

Grammarians have classified the words that come in front of nouns into these groups based on their meanings.

sequence: *first, second*

number: *one, two*

quality or character: *beautiful, happy, intelligent*

size: *tall, big, huge, short, small, tiny*

age: *old, young*

temperature: *hot, cold*

shape: *round, square*

color: *red, purple*

origin or location: *French* (*the French diplomat* = "from France")
                    central (*a central location* = "in a central
                        place")

Using Adjectives

To use adjectives effectively, you might need to expand your vocabulary.

A lower-proficiency-level student might write this sentence, using the adjective *nice*. What does *nice* mean? A more advanced student would find a more exact way to describe a favorite teacher, using adjectives such as *considerate, well-prepared, well-educated, sympathetic,* or so forth.

I had a very nice English teacher in high school.

I had an English teacher in high school who was both demanding and sympathetic.

Practice with Adjectives

A. You will probably find it useful to know what adjectives you use regularly. This information can help you decide if you need to expand your vocabulary to include more exact and varied adjectives. Analyze at least 10 pages of English that you have written recently. First, use a highlighter to mark all of the adjectives; then, make a list of the adjectives, dividing them into the categories listed above on pages 321–322 of this chapter. Note the number of times you use each adjective. Keep your list in your Grammar Notebook.

B. One method for expanding your adjective vocabulary is to learn new words in each of the meaning categories. What words do you know to describe **color** or **character**? Bring to class a popular magazine that has many advertisements. Select an advertisement that is printed in color. Tape the advertisement to a sheet of notebook paper. Then, list the words to name each of the colors in the ad, drawing a line from the color adjective to the color in the advertisement. The object of the exercise is to have a word for every color that is used in the ad. If there is a color for which you do not know the word, what methods can you use to find the information you need? Keep the picture and your list of adjectives in your Grammar Notebook to use for future reference.

C. To expand your knowledge of adjectives for **shapes,** take the same advertisement that you used in exercise B and identify all of the shapes in the picture. Keep this list in your Grammar Notebook to use when you are writing. When you look at the pictures and lists of other students in the class, add to your own list new words that you like or think will be useful.

D. Bring to class four pictures of different unknown as well as famous people. You can find these in popular magazines and in newspapers. Working with the other students in your class and using a dictionary as necessary, make a list of 10 **character** adjectives to describe each of the people. Keep this list with your other list of adjectives in your Grammar Notebook.

E. Colors are often used as symbols. In the United States, the red, white, and blue colors of the flag are associated with patriotism, so politicians often use those colors for their advertisements. Other colors are also symbolic: white for weddings, black for funerals, light blue for baby boys, pink for baby girls, red and green for Christmas. Work with other students from your culture to make a list of the uses of colors for symbolic meaning. What colors are associated with religious holidays? What colors are associated with political parties? What colors are associated with different seasons of the year? With happiness? With sadness? Share your color symbolism with the other members of your class. You might make a more effective presentation if you made a poster to illustrate the colors and their meanings, perhaps with photographs or pictures from magazines from your culture.

F. For practice with adjectives, you might enjoy doing the crossword puzzle on the next page. For each clue, write the correct word in the answer spaces either across or down as appropriate. While most of the clues refer to adjectives, a few refer to other types of words. The answers are on page 460.

Across Clues

2. The opposite of "foolish" or "silly." The elderly woman is very _____ .
4. Opposite of "young"
5. Opposite of "fast"
8. Opposite of "cold"
11. Color for brides and weddings in the U.S.
13. _____ juice (U.S. breakfast)
15. Plural of "child"
16. Precious metal (Au)
18. Opposite of "cooked" Do you like _____ meat? I like _____ vegetables.
19. Opposite of "old"
21. Color for baby boys (U.S.)
22. Opposite of "short"
24. Being away from my friends and family makes me feel _____ .
25. Color of a ruby
27. Color for baby girls (U.S.)
28. U.S. flag = red, white, and _____
29. Present tense of "wrote"
30. Opposite of "green" for fruit

Down Clues

1. Opposite of "dignified"
3. Opposite of "slow"
6. The color of a cloud on a summer day
7. Opposite of "energetic"
9. Color of a banana
10. Opposite of "trivial." I have a _____ problem.
12. Opposite of "criminal"
14. Color of ink often used by teachers to correct tests and papers
16. Color of dollar bill (U.S.)
17. Opposite of "early"
18. Opposite of "poor"
20. Color of coal
21. "Fill this out in blue or _____ ink."
23. Color of a lemon
26. Precious metal (Ag)

Review of Personal Pronouns

These pronouns are called **personal** because they are used primarily to communicate about people or about persons.

Personal pronouns are used to replace nouns and noun phrases. They help to tie sentences together in a unified whole.

The new computer that my brother bought has all of the usual features. With its software, it can quickly do computations that would have taken hours. It can also do word processing so that he can revise papers more easily and more quickly. In addition, it is a portable, so he can take it with him on business trips.

Personal Pronouns			
Subjective	**Objective**	**Possessive**	**Reflexive**
I	*me*	*my* *mine*	*myself*
you	*you*	*your* *yours*	*yourself*
he	*him*	*his* *his*	*himself*
she	*her*	*her* *hers*	*herself*
it	*it*	*its* *its*	*itself*
we	*us*	*our* *ours*	*ourselves*
they	*them*	*their* *theirs*	*themselves*

I speak English. **My** *education is important to* **me** *and to* **my** *family.*
I must earn **my** *tuition money* **myself.** **My** *success will not just be*
mine; **my** *success will also be* **my** *family's success.*

Practice with Personal Pronouns

A. Answer the following questions about the chart on personal pronouns.

1. How many different words are used to refer to *I?* _____

2. How many different words are used to refer to *you?* _____

3. How many different words are used to refer to *it?* _____

4. How many different words are used to refer to *he?* _____

5. How many different words are used to refer to *she*? _____

6. How many different words are used to refer to *we*? _____

7. How many different words are used to refer to *they*? _____

8. What do the answers to questions 1–7 imply about the difficulty of learning and using the different personal pronouns?

9. Analyze the use of the personal pronouns in the example. What part of the sentence is each personal pronoun: subject, object, possessive, reflexive?

B. Personal pronouns are used to tie sentences together and to give a more sophisticated style. To review this use of pronouns, find each pronoun in the passage titled "Cultural Differences in the ESL Classroom" on page 160. Circle the pronoun, and then draw a line to the noun or noun phrase to which it refers.

C. Personal pronouns can replace the proper names of people or things. Find the personal pronouns in the following passage, and draw a line to the noun or noun phrase to which each personal pronoun refers.

1. A special group of reptiles ruled the earth 200 million to 65 million years ago. These creatures, which are called dinosaurs, vanished a long time before people appeared. They ranged in size from the size of a chicken to over 40 feet tall and 90 feet long. Since the mid-1800s, scientists have discovered the fossil remains of many different kinds of dinosaurs. Although they have developed many theories about dinosaurs, no one knows why they became extinct.

2. For centuries, scientists have felt like prisoners on the earth, their home planet. In the past, they could only guess at the secrets of the universe and could only look at outer space from the earth. Now, a new space age is beginning. A sophisticated group of spacecraft will probe the solar system in the next decade in search of answers to their questions. After 1993, scientists will shift most science missions to expendable rockets and will be sending up more than 35 flights. They hope to discover answers to many questions that have puzzled mankind for generations.

3. Located high in the mountains of southern Peru, Machu Picchu is commonly called the last stronghold of the Incas. When Pizarro captured Cuzco, the closest city to Machu Picchu, it was the capital of a well-organized and expertly administered empire that reached from today's Argentina to Colombia. With Spaniards pursuing, many Incas fled to Machu Picchu after they abandoned Cuzco. Nothing was heard of the city until it was rediscovered in 1911. Today, many of its original buildings still exist in spite of earthquakes in 1650 and 1950.

Adapted from the following:
1. *World Book Encyclopedia*, 1988 ed., s.v. "dinosaur."   2. Cook, William J. "The Edge of Infinity." *U.S. News and World Report* (May 15, 1989): 53–54.   3. *Encyclopedia Americana*, 1983 ed., s.v. "Cuzco" and "Peru."

D. Study the example given at the bottom of the chart on personal pronouns on page 326. Work with another student to plan an example to illustrate the uses of all of the forms of one of the personal pronouns *(you, he, she, it, we,* or *they)*. Share your example with the other students in the class. After making any necessary corrections, keep your example in your Grammar Notebook for future reference.

Practice with Noun Phrases, Adjectives, and Personal Pronouns

Writers use adjectives for many purposes: for example, to make their writing more exact or to make their writing more interesting. Find the adjectives used by this ESL student. What does the writer achieve by using such words in writing on this particular topic?

Writers use personal pronouns to avoid repeating the same nouns many times and to tie their sentences together to make a unified passage. Circle the personal pronouns used in this passage, and draw a line from each pronoun to the noun to which it refers.

English often combines two or more nouns to make a noun phrase. Working with the other students in your class, make a list of the noun phrases that combine noun + noun, for example, *street light.*

The Price of Life

by Carlos Gamba

The sun was setting in the west. Its flaming rays filtered between the branches of the pine trees seemingly setting them afire in a blaze of red.

A strong man walked escorted by two guards toward the electric chair where he was going to be executed that very same evening. Steadily the last light from the long-gone sun clutched desperately at the metallic blue sky with opalescent fingers of carmine red, bright orange and faint yellow, with a green crest. His strong arms were strapped to the armrest of the chair that was made of fine Georgia pine wood. His wrists were wet with a sponge, and he was blindfolded. His heart beat wildly inside his chest as if steered by the force of a thousand wings as if a flock of imaginary birds tried to escape in anticipation of the final moment.

Then came the brutal shock! The last gasp of breath, and his contracted massive humanity lay inert. After a few moments, a doctor examined the body and declared the man dead. Outside the tall branches of the trees could not be seen any longer. Their once proud trunks were swallowed by the darkness of the night. The moon failed to show up.

Not far away from the prison walls, a small group of men fanatically cheered the news of the execution as if it were a sporting event. For them, justice had triumphed. Their position was that murderers should be put to death in order to protect the rest of society. To spare the life of such a person or the sole idea of commuting his sentence to life in prison was unthinkable. After all, what chance did the murderer give his victim? Capital punishment was an example to deter other killers from committing crimes. Besides, it was a just price to compensate the victim's survivors.

In front of the prison entrance the street lights cast long shadows over the sidewalks. Under them a group of men and women who were against capital punishment protested the execution. For them, the system had failed. After decades of capital punishment, crime was still rampant in the streets of their cities. Legalizing the death penalty was not going to deter or reduce crimes; therefore putting a man to death was no solution. It converted the executioners into legalized murderers. The only possible justification for killing another person is self-defense.

Their vigil ended in sorrow when they learned the man had been executed. They were silent while, among them, a woman cried in grief. She was the wife of the man in the chair. Now she was alone.

Sometimes law overshadows the power of reason. Still, it is for the jurist to decide what human life is worth, especially when condemning a man who, whatever crime he has committed, is in turn murdered. Until jurists can decide what human life is worth, capital punishment should be abolished as a legal way of administering justice.

14

Adverbs

CHAPTER ORGANIZATION

"Adverb" Defined

. . . .

Adverb is the name for words like *slowly, daily,* and *locally.* They are used in sentences to give information about how, when, where, and why things happen. **Adverbial** is the word used for phrases and clauses that have the same meaning as single-word adverbs.

In these three sentences, information is given about time. The first sentence has a single-word **adverb** while the second sentence has an **adverbial clause.** See Chapter Ten for more information on adverbial clauses. The third example illustrates a prepositional phrase used as an **adverbial phrase.**

adverb of frequency

*He **frequently** studies in the library.*

adverbial clause

*She studies in the library **after she has eaten lunch.***

adverbial phrase

*They study **in the afternoon.***

. . . .

Practice with Adverbs

Write answers to the following questions; use adverbs in your answers. Do not use any adverb more than one time. After editing your answers, keep them in your Grammar Notebook to use as examples.

1. How do you write English?

   I write English slowly. _____

2. How do you take tests?
3. How do you talk in class?
4. How do you speak English?
5. How do you work in groups?
6. How do you make friends?

Formation of Adverbs from Adjectives

Adverbs are frequently formed by adding -ly to an adjective.

When the adjective ends in -y, change the final -y to -i and add -ly.

adjective
*He is a **happy** person.*

adverb
*He talked **happily** about the new project.*

Be careful to use the correct form.

incorrect
He walked **quiet from the room.*

correct
*He walked **quietly** from the room.*

Practice Recognizing Adverbs and Adjectives

Circle the correct form. Then, write the word **adverb** or **adjective** above the circled word.

1. We did the exercise (completely) (complete).

2. We did the (completely) (complete) exercise.

3. We could do the exercise more (quickly) (quick) if we worked in pairs.

4. Everyone should work (carefully) (careful) during the exam tomorrow.

5. Miguel (certain) (certainly) finished the essay (quickly) (quick).

6. Read all test questions and work (systematically) (systematic) through the test.

Adverbs of Frequency

Adverbs of frequency tell how often something happens. They are often used with general truth verb forms when someone refers to habits and routines. Adverbs of frequency range from *always* (100%) to *never* (0%).

Positive Meaning

	all the time
always	Toan **always** *does his homework.*

	most days
usually = normally =	He **usually** *arrives at 7:45.*
generally =	
almost always	

	many days
often = frequently	He is **often** *the first student to arrive.*

	some days
sometimes = occasionally	He **sometimes** *arrives before his teacher.*

Negative Meaning

	not often
seldom = rarely =	He **seldom** *whispers to his friends in class.*
hardly ever =	
almost never	

	not ever
never	He **never** *gets the lowest grade on tests.*

· ·

Practice with Adverbs of Frequency

A. Write five sentences that are true about yourself, and use the following adverbs of frequency: *always, usually, sometimes, rarely,* and *never.* Then, compare answers with the other students in your class; prepare a list of the things that you *always* and *never* do.

B. On a sheet of paper, write answers to the following questions using adverbs of frequency. Then, compare your answers to those of other students in your class. After editing your answers, place them in your Grammar Notebook for future reference.

1. How often do you arrive late to class?
2. How often do you arrive early to class?
3. How often do you take a bus to class?
4. How often do you ride a bicycle to class?
5. How often do you eat breakfast (or lunch or dinner) before class?
6. How often do you go to a library to study?
7. How often do you eat lunch on campus?

8. How often do you turn your homework in on time?
9. How often do you watch the news on television?
10. How often do you read the news in a newspaper?

No and Not

No is a determiner and is used with a noun.	*There were **no textbooks** in the bookstore.*
	***No students** attended the orientation session.*
	*My cousin speaks **no English**.*
Not is an adverb and is used with a verb.	*The bookstore **did not have** any textbooks.*
	*My cousin **does not speak** any English.*
Because *not* is an adverb, it also modifies adjectives *(not much homework, not many students, not very expensive).*	***Not much homework** was assigned in our sociology class.*
	***Not many students** are majoring in physics right now.*

Practice with *No* and *Not*

A. Add *no* or *not* to the following sentences.

1. I used to think that there was ⎯⎯ difference between the words *no* and *not*.

2. Now I know that there is a difference, and I should ⎯⎯ use them in the same way.

3. I have ⎯⎯ time to explain the difference right now.

4. However, this exercise is ⎯⎯ very difficult, and by the time I

   finish it, I will ⎯⎯ have any more problems.

5. ⎯⎯ student in this class should have problems with *no* and *not* again.

6. ⎯⎯ many students agree with me on this subject.

7. Julio is ⎯⎯ taking this class.

8. He has _____ trouble with adjectives and adverbs.

9. He does _____ need help with them.

10. He has _____ problems with his writing or his grammar.

B. Put a caret ∧ to show where to place *not* in the following sentences, and then write any additional words above the space where they need to be added.

We will ∧ *take a test tomorrow.*   (not)

We ∧ *like hot ice cream.*   (do not)

1. We have studied French this term.

2. We are studying physics now.

3. We like hot ice cream.

4. We eat breakfast after lunch.

5. We will be rude if we ask many questions in class.

Word Order with Adverbs and Adverbials

Adverbs can come in many different places in sentences. In addition, sentences often have two or more adverbs or adverbials. There are two sets of rules to follow.

Order for Adverbs of Frequency
Adverbs of frequency are usually placed in front of a single-word verb or after any auxiliary. An adverb of frequency comes after a form of *be*.

He **never** studies in the library.

He has **never** studied in the library.

He is **never** in the library.

He will **never** study in the library.

Order for Negative Adverbs of Frequency
Negative adverbs of frequency are sometimes placed at the beginning of a sentence in formal spoken and written English. The adverb of frequency has an effect similar to that of making a question: the auxiliary moves in front of the subject.

Rarely has the dean met with international students.

If the verb is a form of *be*, the verb moves in front of the subject.

Rarely is *our teacher late for class.*

If there is no auxiliary, *do/does* or *did* is added.

Never did *the students express so much concern and confusion.*

This word ordering is not generally used. The more usual ordering puts the adverb of frequency in the verb phrase as explained above.

*The students **never** expressed so much concern and confusion.*

*The dean has **rarely** met with international students.*

*Our teacher is **rarely** late for class.*

Order for Other Types of Adverbs

Other types of adverbs tend to be found as illustrated in these examples.

place before manner
She walked into the library slowly.

place/manner before time
She walked into the library slowly last night.

place/manner/time before reason
She walked into the library slowly last night because she did not feel very good.

However, time adverbs and adverbials are often placed at the beginning of a sentence, especially when several other adverbs or adverbials are used.

time moved to the beginning of the sentence
Last night she walked into the library slowly.

Also, shorter adverbs tend to be placed in front of longer adverbials.

She walked slowly into the library reading room.

If two adverbs or adverbials of the same type are used, the more specific usually comes first.

She likes to study in her bedroom at home.

Problem

It is important to notice that adverbs seldom occur between the verb and the direct object. Adverbs and adverbials tend to be either at the beginning or at the end of a sentence.

incorrect

*I saw **yesterday** Pedro.

correct

I saw Pedro **yesterday**.

correct

Yesterday I saw Pedro.

. . . .

Practice with Adverbs

A. Put a caret ∧ in each of the following sentences to show where an adverb of frequency could be added. Then, answer the questions after the six sentences.

Students ∧ *never* whisper to each other during tests in this class.

1. Students stand up when answering a question in class.

2. Students use the term "teacher" when they want to talk to their teacher.

3. Students get up to sharpen pencils whenever they want.

4. Students knock on the classroom door if they arrive late.

5. Students stand up when a professor or teacher enters the classroom.

6. Students take weekly quizzes.

What adverbs of frequency should be used to describe classroom customs in this ESL class?

Sentence 1 _____   Sentence 4 _____

Sentence 2 _____   Sentence 5 _____

Sentence 3 _____   Sentence 6 _____

What adverbs of frequency should be used to describe classroom customs in your country or in your high school classroom?

Sentence 1 _____   Sentence 4 _____

Sentence 2 _____   Sentence 5 _____

Sentence 3 _____   Sentence 6 _____

B. Place each adverb of frequency in the correct position in the following sentences. Study the examples carefully.

(always)   *Tua is⌄late for class.*

(usually)   *He⌄arrives at 8:15 A.M.*

(never)   *He has⌄arrived before 8 A.M.*

1. (usually)   Ladan and Larissa study together.

2. (often)   They meet at the library after lunch.

3. (rarely)   The study tables at the library are full after lunch, and they can study quietly.

4. (usually)   They manage to find a quiet place on the second floor of the library.

5. (sometimes)   They have studied in the student center.

6. (seldom)   The student center is busy between 2:00 and 4:00 P.M.

7. (never)   They have been able to study together at night because Ladan has a night job.

8. (always)   She leaves campus at 5:45 P.M.

C. Write the correct form of the verb, and put the adverb of frequency in the correct order.

1. Ali _____ at 6:30 A.M.
   (get up, usually)

2. He _____ late for his 8 A.M. class.
   (be, never)

3. Chi Chi _____ late for class.
   (be, often)

4. Because she _____ home at 7:45 A.M., she does not have
   (leave, usually)
   enough time to get to class on time.

5. Chi Chi _____ to bed at 2:30 A.M. after the late movie
   (go, often)
   on television.

6. As a result, she _____ her homework and has a difficult
   (do, rarely)
   time in class.

7. Ali _____ in bed by 11:30 P.M.
   (be, frequently)

8. He _____ late homework so far this quarter.
   (hand in, never)

D. Rearrange the following sentences to have the usual English word order.

incorrect

*I saw yesterday Pedro.

correct

I saw Pedro yesterday.

1. Pedro has been for two years at the language center.
2. He was at his TOEFL so nervous that he hardly could think.
3. It would be not fair to announce his test scores to anyone.
4. He had taken already the TOEFL three times.
5. He must keep always trying to improve his English if he wants to go to college.
6. He goes sometimes to the language lab for help.
7. Always he speaks Spanish with his friends.
8. He has been two years here and has not improved his spoken English.
9. He needs every day to speak English.
10. Pedro thinks that he knows already enough English.

E. Write two example sentences using each of the following words at the beginning of the sentence: *seldom, rarely, never, nor,* and *neither.* Revise and edit the sentences. Then, share your sentences with the rest of your class. After making any corrections, write the sentences on a sheet of paper to keep in your Grammar Notebook for future reference. Example: *Seldom do I study later than 10* P.M.

F. Working with another student, analyze one page of a recent newspaper. List all of the adverbs that you find on that page. Compare your answers to those of other teams that have analyzed other materials. If you want to learn any of these words, add them to your list in your Grammar Notebook.

CHAPTER

15

Conditional and Hypothetical

"Conditional" and "Hypothetical" Defined

Conditional refers to a relationship in which something is necessary to cause something else to happen. If the first thing happens, the second thing is generally guaranteed to happen.

Hypothetical refers to imaginary or even impossible conditions; the things referred to generally will not or cannot happen.

Conditional and hypothetical sentences are similar because of their use of *if*-clauses. However, they are used for different purposes. This chapter explores the different meanings and purposes of conditional and hypothetical sentences.

Conditional

If oil is poured on water, the oil floats on top of the water.

Condition: You pour water on oil.

Result: The oil floats on the water.

Hypothetical

If George Washington were alive, he would be surprised at the size of the federal government.

Condition: This condition is impossible. George Washington is dead.

Purpose: The writer wants to contrast the U.S. in the 1780s with the U.S. today.

Meaning of Conditional Sentences

General Truth

Conditional sentences are often used to make general truth statements. The first three examples are about things that are generally true and not about future time or about things happening right now. Notice that *will* and *can* can be used for a general truth meaning as well as for future time. If you are not familiar with this meaning, see page 156 in Chapter Five for more information.

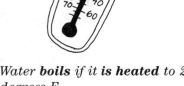

*Water **boils** if it **is heated** to 212 degrees F.*

*Water **will boil** if it **is heated** to 212 degrees F.*

*If students **study** in the library, they **can·read** in peace and quiet.*

Future Time

These conditional sentences are about future time. Remember that the *if*-clause uses simple present tense to mean future time. Also, notice that modals other than *will* can be used.

*If he **takes** physics next quarter, he **will not take** calculus.*

*If the economy **improves** next year, people **should make** more money.*

Past Time

Conditional sentences can also be about conditional relationships in the past.

*Last quarter, our teacher had this attendance rule: if we **arrived** in class more than five minutes late, he **considered** us "absent."*

Remember to use the simple past tense in the *if*-clause.

*Last year, I had a very demanding professor: if she **liked** my compositions, I **was** very pleased.*

Grammar of Conditional Sentences

Conditional sentences are made by combining an **if-clause** with an **independent clause.**

General Truth or Future Time

The verb in the *if*-clause is in the simple present tense for sentences about general truth or about future time.

general truth
*Peter is usually late to class. We are surprised if he **arrives** on time.*

future time
*We will go to the library this afternoon if we **have** enough time.*

Past Time

The verb in the *if*-clause is in the simple past tense for sentences about past time conditions.

past time
*She studied in the library if her friends **went** with her.*

Word Order

The *if*-clause often comes at the beginning of a sentence so that the condition is given first.

***If Peter arrives on time,** we are surprised.*

***If we have enough time,** we will go to the library this afternoon.*

***If her friends went with her,** she studied in the library.*

Practice with Conditional Sentences with Habitual Meaning

A. Finish the following conditional sentences. Add words of your own to make the meaning of each sentence logical and complete.

1. If I do not eat breakfast, I _____

2. If I have free time, I _____

3. If I have extra money, I _____

4. If I do not have class, I _____

5. If I need money, I _____

B. Fill in each blank with the correct form of the verb in parentheses.

1. If Hesham _____ late, he misses the bus.
   (sleep)

2. He has to leave home at 7:30 A.M. if he _____ to class.
   (walk)

3. If he goes to the student center after class, he usually _____
   (watch)

   television.

4. If he does not watch television, he _____ with his friends.
   (talk)

5. He goes to the cafeteria if he _____ lunch on campus.
   (eat)

6. He usually _____ campus at 3:30 P.M if he finishes his
   (leave)

   homework.

C. Write conditional sentences to answer the following questions about how you habitually handle these situations. Your sentences should be meaningful, and the verb forms should be correct. After editing your answers, put them in your Grammar Notebook to use as examples.

1. What do you usually do if you are tired but are unable to sleep?

   If I am tired but am unable to sleep, I usually watch TV.

2. What do you usually do if you are worried about something?
3. What do you usually do if you wake up too late for breakfast?
4. What do you usually do if you need money?

5. What do you usually do if you do not know the meaning of a word?
6. What usually happens if you are late to class?

D. With other students in your class, discuss your answers to question 5 in exercise C. Make a list of all of the ways in which different people find the meanings of new words.

E. With other students in your class, discuss your answers to question 6 in exercise C. Make a list of all of the different ways in which this situation is handled in various countries and schools.

. . . .

Practice with Conditional Sentences with Future Time Meaning

A. Finish the following conditional sentences. Add words of your own to make the meaning of each sentence logical and complete.

1. If I get an A in this class, _____

2. If we have an exam next week, _____

3. I will graduate next year if _____

4. Next quarter, I will _____

   if _____

5. Next year, I will _____

   if _____

B. Fill in each blank with the correct form of the verb in parentheses.

1. If Moussa gets more speaking practice this quarter, he _____
   (be)
   able to speak better.

2. If I _____ time tomorrow, I will finish my essay.
        (have)

3. If Chana goes to college next year, she _____ a scholarship.
                                        (have)

4. If Magid finishes his homework, he _____ to the movies
                                      (go)
   tonight.

5. If you _____ me at 4:00 P.M., I _____ you a ride
   (meet)   (give)
   home.

6. If Ivan _____ fewer hours this quarter, he _____
   (work)   (have)
   more time to study.

C. Write conditional sentences to answer the following questions. Your sentences should be meaningful, and the verb forms should be correct. After editing your answers, put them in your Grammar Notebook to use as examples.

1. What will happen if you do not do your homework tomorrow?
2. What will happen if you miss class tomorrow?
3. What will you do if you have a question about your homework tonight?
4. What will you do if you get an A on your next test?
5. What will you do if you leave your billfold at home tomorrow?

D. With other members of the class, discuss your answers to question 3 in exercise C. What different ways do people have for dealing with problems with their homework?

Modal Auxiliaries in Conditional Sentences

· ·

The basic independent clause in a conditional sentence can use *will* or another modal. Other modals that are frequently used in conditional sentences include *can, may, might, must,* and *should.*

Will for Certainty
Will can be used to mean future time certainty or for general truth certainty. The first example is about future time. The second example is about general truth; it gives a library rule.

future time
*If he comes to school tomorrow, we **will go** to the library together.*

general truth
*If a student damages a library book, he or she **will be billed** for the cost of replacing the book.*

Other Modals for Less Certainty
The other modals are used to make the results seem less certain.

future time/certainty
*If the teacher assigns a test for next Monday, we **will** study on Sunday.*

future time/obligation

*If the teacher assigns a test for next Monday, we **should** study on Sunday, but we already have plans to go out of town.*

future time/slight probability

*If the teacher assigns a test for next Monday, we **might** study on Saturday so that we can have a party on Sunday. But we might study on Sunday, too.*

Practice with Modals in Conditional Sentences

A. Discussion Assignment: Do you exercise on a regular basis? What kinds of exercise do you enjoy? Is exercise important for students? Why or why not?

Grammar Assignment: Put square brackets [ ] around each conditional sentence in this article. What modal auxiliary verbs are used in the main clause of each conditional sentence?

The Benefits of Exercise

[1]Regular exercise can help maintain strong muscles, keep joints flexible, and lower the risk of a heart attack. [2]If you want to maintain a healthy body, you should burn more than 300 calories each day through muscular activity. [3]Burning less than 300 calories a day may harm the

muscles and promote the storage of body fat. [4]Furthermore, to maintain strong muscles, your muscles should work at more than half their maximum tension at least every other day. [5]If you lift things, such as sacks of groceries or several textbooks, you will keep your muscles strong. [6]Also, your body joints should move through their maximum range of motion twice a week to keep the connective tissues flexible. [7]For example, if you swing your arms around to stretch them to their full range of movement, you will keep the connective tissues flexible. [8]To make exercising beneficial, your heart must also be accelerated above 110 beats per minutes for at least five minutes each day. [9]If you walk or climb stairs or carry something an average of five minutes each hour, you will probably lower your risk of heart attack. [10]As a further benefit to exercising, if you are physically active, you will probably be able to eat more without gaining weight than a person who weighs the same and is not as physically active. [11]However, you should see a doctor immediately if you experience extreme fatigue, pains in your chest, or a shortness of breath.

Adapted from *Encyclopedia Americana*, 1983 ed., s.v. "exercise."

B. Discussion Assignment: At what times do you eat during the day? Do you eat snacks? If so, when do you snack? What is a calorie? Why do some people count calories?

Grammar Assignment: Put square brackets [ ] around each conditional sentence in this article. What modal auxiliary verbs are used in the main clause of each conditional sentence?

Calorie Salary

[1]Jennifer Anderson, an assistant professor in the Department of Food Science and Human Nutrition at Colorado State University, says that snacking is easy for adults if they obey the "calorie-salary rule." [2]Adults should determine their daily "salary" or allowance of calories and thus make sure they "spend" no more than that salary each day.

[3]For example, if you know that you will be eating lots of food at a party, you should eat low-calorie foods the rest of the day. [4]Or, if you

eat a large lunch, you should balance out the extra calories with a low-calorie supper. [5]If you find yourself eating more calories than usual in a day, you can increase your physical activity. [6]Exercise helps to burn up extra calories.

Adapted from U.S. Food and Drug Administration. Public Health Service, Department of Health and Human Services. "The 'Grazing of America': A Guide to Healthy Snacking." *FDA Consumer,* vol. 23, no. 2. Washington, D.C.: GPO, 1988.

C. Write five conditional sentences to illustrate your ideas on how to be a good student. For things that you are absolutely sure about, use *will.* For things that are possible but that you cannot promise, use *can.* For things that you advise, use *should.* After you have edited the sentences for grammar, share your ideas with the rest of the class. On a sheet of paper record the sentences that you think are the best ideas about being a good student. Keep that list in your Grammar Notebook for future reference. Example: *If you read your assignments before class, you will understand the teacher's lectures better.*

. . . .

Practice with Conditional Sentences

A. Write meaningful conditional sentences to answer the following questions. After you are satisfied with the meaning, edit them carefully to have the correct verb forms. Then, keep them in your Grammar Notebook to use as examples.

1. What will you do if you do not understand a question on the final examination?
2. Generally, what happens if students do not understand questions on examinations?
3. What will happen if you do not pay your fees and tuition next quarter?
4. What usually happens if people do not pay their debts?
5. What will happen if you lose your dictionary?
6. What can you do if you have trouble understanding a teacher's instructions?
7. What will happen if you drive at 75 MPH inside the city limits?
8. What will you do if your car runs out of gas on the highway?

B. Fill in each blank with the correct form of the verb in parentheses, and indicate the time meaning of the sentence. Discuss the completed sentences with the rest of your class. How can you tell whether each sentence is about general truth or future time?

Time

1. If the weather *is* _____ nice next
   Saturday, we will go on a picnic.   *future* _____
   (be)

2. If it _____ next Saturday, we will cancel
   (rain)
   the picnic.   _____

3. If you _____ not arrive on time, you will
   (do)
   miss the food.   _____

4. If you _____ in the sun a long time, you
   (sit)
   will get a sunburn.   _____

5. The teacher will explain the answer to you if you

   _____ her.   _____
   (ask)

6. If Suha decides to join the international club, she

   _____ an application tomorrow.   _____
   (fill out)

7. We will get there in time for class if the bus

   _____ on time.   _____
   (be)

8. Fahid will get angry at himself if he _____
   (make)
   that mistake again.   _____

9. If there are any mistakes on my paper, my teacher

   _____ them.   _____
   (find)

10. Julio _____ angry if anyone
    (get)

    _____ anything about his accent.   _____
    (says)

11. If I _____ every week, my mother and
    (not, write)
    father get very upset.   _____

12. We _____ late for class if the bus is late.   _____
    (be)

C. Discuss the following chains of sentences with other students in
your class. What are the relationships among the sentences? Notice that
the first set of sentences is about future time; the second set of sentences is about general truth.

If the university raises its tuition, many students will transfer to other schools. If many students transfer to other schools, the university will have fewer students and will lose money. However, if the university does not raise its tuition, it will not make enough money to pay its bills. Either way, the university will lose.

If students learn to type, they can turn in papers that are easy to read and easy to prepare. If students' papers are easy to read, teachers are usually very pleased with the students. If teachers are pleased with students, they often give better grades. Thus, if students learn to type, they might improve their grades. Certainly, they spend less time preparing the final drafts of the papers.

D. Working with another student, select one of the following statements. Then, write a chain of sentences like those in exercise C. Share your paragraph with the rest of the class, and discuss the logic of your ideas.

1. If people smoke cigarettes all of their lives, ...
2. If the university raises its TOEFL requirement, ...
3. If parents do not listen to their children, ...
4. If children do not respect their parents, ...
5. If a business cheats its customers, ...

Meaning of Hypothetical Sentences

Hypothetical sentences are used to discuss things that are not true or did not happen; **hypothetical** events are **imaginary** events. Hypothetical meaning is often used in academic study to test or evaluate ideas and information. Hypothetical sentences can be about scientific generalizations (**general truth**) or about past time.

General Truth
In these sentences, untrue situations are used as part of a discussion of problems.

general truth
*If he **spoke** Spanish, he **could take** a job in Venezuela, but he **does not speak** Spanish, so he **cannot have** that job.*

Notice the use of simple past tense in the *if*-clause.

general truth
*If the library **opened** at 7:00 A.M., I **would study** before class, but it **does not open** until 8:00 A.M., and my class **begins** at 8:15 A.M.*

Past Time

Hypothetical statements are often made about past time events that did not happen. The *if*-clause is always used to state something that did not happen. The main clause tells the results. What happened? 1. Roberto did not read the instructions carefully. 2. Roberto did not understand the research assignment. 3. His grade was not as good as it might have been.

past time

*If Roberto had read the instructions carefully, he **might have understood** the research assignment and made a better grade.*

What happened in this situation? 1. People did not believe the news reports. 2. An energy crisis occurred. A past time event influenced another past time event.

past time

*If people **had believed** the news reports, the energy crisis **would have been avoided**.*

Past Time Influences Present Time

Past time events can, of course, influence present time events.

*If I **had saved** more money last year, I **would not have** so many financial problems now.*

Hypothetical statements are not always about bad things, just about things that did not happen or that are not true. What happened? 1. She listened to her doctor. 2. She is alive and well today.

*If she **had not listened** to the doctor, she **would be** dead. She **is** alive and well today.*

Grammar of Hypothetical Sentences

• •

For general truth hypothetical statements, the verb in the *if*-clause is the simple past tense. The main clause usually uses *would* + verb; however, other modals can also be used for different meanings.

Thomas Edison died long ago.

general truth

*If Thomas Edison **were** alive, he **would love** computers.*

He does not have a good
education.

general truth

*If he **had** a good education, he
might have a better job.*

Two different past time meanings occur with hypothetical sentences.
The past time influenced something in the past. Or, the past time event
influences something in the present. In both situations, the **if-clause** uses
the past perfect to mean "past time and not true."

Past Time
When the past time *if*-clause
influenced a past time event, the
main clause uses a modal + *have*
+ past participle.

past time influenced past time

*If I **had been** wiser about my
finances, I **would not have had** so
many problems last year.*

past time influenced past time

*If Jose **had gone** to the party, he
might have met my brother.*

**Past Time Influences
Present Time**
When the past time *if*-clause
influences the present, the main
clause uses modal + verb. The
modals that can be used for
hypothetical meaning include
could, might, and *would.*

past time influences present time

*If I **had eaten** breakfast this
morning, I **would not be** hungry
now.*

past time influences present time

*If the government **had prevented**
air pollution in the past, we **could
breathe** cleaner air today.*

Were in Hypothetical *If*-Clauses

· ·

In formal spoken and written English, the form of *be* in a hypothetical *if*-clause is *were* for all subjects. Some grammarians call this use of
were the **subjunctive.**

General Truth
Notice that the usual rules of
subject-verb agreement do not
apply.

*If they **were** here, we could leave.*

*If he **were** here, we could leave.*

*If I **were** you, I would buy a better
dictionary.*

*If Thomas Edison **were** alive, he
would love computers.*

Practice with Hypothetical Sentences for General Truth Meaning

A. Finish the following hypothetical sentences. Add whatever words of your own that will make the meaning of each sentence logical and complete.

1. If I had more time, *I would learn to play the piano.* _____

   But *I work and take three classes.* _____

2. If I had a scholarship, _____

   But _____

3. I would not take this course if _____

   But _____

4. I would buy a computer if _____

   But _____

5. If I wrote better, _____

   But _____

B. Fill in each blank with the correct form of the verb in parentheses.

1. If Djohan came to class more often, he *would learn* (learn) more.
   But *he does not come to class very much, and he does not learn very much.*

2. He _____ more progress if he studied more.
   (make)

   But _____

3. Shinji _____ better if he had more practice.
   (speak)

   But _____

4. If he attended every class, he _____ a better student.
   (be)

   But _____

5. If Mahmoud _____ here now, he would help us.
      (be)

   But _____

6. We would speak better if we _____ more conversation
                               (have)

   practice.

   But _____

    C. Write hypothetical sentences to answer the following questions. The sentences should be meaningful. After you are satisfied with the meaning, edit the sentences carefully to have the correct verb forms. Then, put the corrected sentences in your Grammar Notebook to use as examples.

1. What would happen if you came to class late every day?
2. What would you do if you found a lot of money?
3. What would happen if the electricity suddenly went off in your apartment?
4. What would you do if you lost your textbook?
5. What would you do if you failed all your courses?
6. What would you do if you received a TOEFL score of 650?

    D. Give advice about what to do in the following situations, using "If I were you . . . " The sentences should be meaningful, and the verb forms should be correct. Write your advice on a sheet of paper to keep in your Grammar Notebook.

    Example: a friend has lost his textbook
    If I were you, I would buy another book.

1. a friend smokes a pack of cigarettes each day
2. a friend does not do any homework
3. a friend speaks English only in ESL class
4. a friend is thinking about cutting class
5. a friend has lost his green card
6. a friend has lost her passport

    E. With the other students in your class, discuss the answers to numbers 1, 2, 3, and 4 in exercise D. What are the limits of friendship? Is it appropriate to interfere in a friend's activities? Would your actions be different for a relative?

. . . .

Practice with Hypothetical Sentences for Past Time Meaning

A. Finish the following hypothetical sentences. Add whatever words of your own that will make the meaning of each sentence logical and complete.

1. If I had studied at another college, _____

2. If I had chosen another major, _____

3. If I had spent yesterday differently, _____

4. I would not have eaten lunch yesterday if _____

5. I would have gone to the library last night if _____

B. Fill in each blank with the correct form of the verb in parentheses.

1. If Marzieh had studied more, she _____ the course last
   (pass)
   quarter.

2. I _____ her if she had asked for help.
   (help)

3. Mauricio would have gone to the concert if he _____ about
   (know)
   the free tickets.

4. If you _____ the United States one hundred years ago, you
   (visit)
   would have found life very different from life today.

5. If Magid had finished his homework, he _____ to the
   (go)
   concert.

C. Write hypothetical sentences to answer the following questions. The sentences should be meaningful answers to the questions. After you are satisfied with the meaning, edit the sentences carefully to have the correct verb forms. Then, put them in your Grammar Notebook to use as examples.

1. What would have happened if you had overslept this morning?
2. What would have happened if you had missed your ride to school today?
3. What would you have done if you had failed your final exam?

355

4. What would you have done if yesterday had been a holiday?
5. What would you have done yesterday if you had gotten ready to pay for lunch and discovered you had no money?

D. Use a highlighter to mark all of the hypothetical sentences in the following paragraph. Then, discuss with your class what really happened to this student. Next, write a similar chain story about a bad day in your own life. Share your composition with the rest of your class.

A Bad Day

[1]Yesterday was a terrible day for Adel. [2]It was the day of the Alternate Regents' Exam: a very important writing exam for all students who have earned 70 quarter hours. [3]After students have earned 70 hours, they must take and pass a writing exam; they must write an interesting and accurate essay of 400 words in 90 minutes in order to continue taking college courses. [4]Adel's essay was too short because he arrived 45 minutes late to the exam. [5]If he had arrived on time, he would have passed the test; however, three complications prevented him from arriving on time. [6]If he had not had a flat tire, he would have arrived on time. [7]If he had set his alarm to get up earlier, he would have had extra time to fix a flat tire. [8]If he had gone to bed before midnight instead of at 4:00 A.M., he would not have slept so soundly. [9]Instead, Adel did not wake up at his usual time, his alarm did not go off, and his car had a flat tire. [10]Adel will find out the results of the exam in three weeks. [11]If he passed the examination, he will graduate. [12]If he did not pass the examination, he will have to take it again until he passes.

Wishes as Hypothetical Statements

· ·

English has an old saying about wishes: "If wishes were horses, beggars would ride." By their very nature, wishes are hypothetical; they are untrue, imaginary, and often impossible.

Wish + **Noun Clause**
The verb *wish* is followed by a noun clause. The clause is connected to the sentence by the word *that. That* is optional.

*I wish **that I spoke Spanish**.*

*He wishes **that** he knew how to type.*

He wishes he knew how to type.

Hypothetical Meaning
Like hypothetical sentences, the clause that follows *wish* uses past tense for present time and general truth statements.

wish about present time
*He wishes that he **owned** a better calculator.*

Past Time
The clause that follows *wish* uses past perfect for past time statements.

wish about past time
*I wish that I **had studied** more for the final examination.*

Could **and** *Would*
The models *could* and *would* are often used in wishes. *Could* refers to hypothetical abilities or possibilities. *Would* refers to hypothetical promises or certainties.

*She wishes that she **could speak** French.*

*I wish that the teacher **would postpone** the test.*

Were
In formal English, the noun clause uses *were* without change for subject-verb agreement. Grammarians call this use the **subjunctive.**

formal version
*He wishes that he **were** taller.*
informal version
*He wishes that he **was** taller.*
formal version
*I wish that I **were** in Spain right now.*
informal version
*I wish that I **was** in Spain right now.*

Practice with Wishes

A. Some people think that making wishes is a waste of time. Others disagree strongly and say that wishes are the basis for creative thinking. What is your attitude toward wishes? Discuss your ideas with the other students in your class.

B. Write a list of five statements about your own wishes. Edit the list carefully for grammar, focusing especially on the verb in the clause. Then, exchange lists with another student in your class. Rewrite his or her list to make each statement use the pronoun *he* or *she* rather than *I*.

Summary of the Grammar of Conditional and Hypothetical Sentences

Verbs in Conditional Sentences

General Truth/Conditional

If + present tense, present tense

*If water **is heated** to 212 degrees F., it **boils.***

If + present tense, modal + verb

*If water **is heated** to 212 degrees F., it **will boil.***

*If students **study** in the library, they **can read** in peace and quiet.*

Future Time/Conditional

If + present tense, modal + verb

*If he **takes** physics next quarter, he **will not take** calculus.*

*If the economy **improves** next year, people **might make** more money.*

Past Time/Conditional

If + past tense, past tense

*Last quarter, our teacher had this attendance rule: if we **arrived** in class more than five minutes late, he **considered** us "absent."*

*Last year, I had a very demanding professor: if she **liked** my compositions, I **was** very pleased.*

Note: The modals most often used in conditional sentences include *can, may, must, should,* and *will.*

Verbs in Hypothetical Sentences

General Truth/Hypothetical
If + past tense, modal + verb

*If Thomas Edison **were** alive, he **would love** computers.*

*If he **had** a good education, he **might have** a better job.*

Past Time Influencing Past Time/Hypothetical
If + past perfect, modal + *have* + past participle

*If I **had been** wiser about my finances, I **would not have had** so many problems last year.*

*If he **had gone** to the party, he **might have met** my brother.*

Past Time Influencing Present Time/Hypothetical
If + past perfect, modal + verb

*If I **had eaten** breakfast this morning, I **would not be** hungry now.*

*If the government **had prevented** air pollution in the past, we **could breathe** safely today.*

Note: The modal auxiliaries most often used in hypothetical sentences include *could, might,* and *would.*

. . . .

Practice with Conditional and Hypothetical Sentences

A. Finish the following sentences. Add whatever words of your own to make the meaning of each sentence logical and complete. Discuss with the rest of your class the ways that you can tell if a sentence has conditional or hypothetical meaning.

1. If I leave now, *I will get home early.* _____

2. If I had had more money last month, _____

3. If I were you, _____

4. Last year I would have gone to _____ if _____

5. If I had started earlier, _____

6. I would have registered for more courses if _____

B. Fill in each blank with the correct form of the verb in parentheses. Pay special attention to the word order of the adverbs of frequency.

1. If Bahram does not know the answer, he _will always admit_ it right

   (admit, always)

   away.

2. Canh would have gone to the orientation meeting if he

   _____ about it.

   (know)

3. If Yoshiko makes a mistake, the teacher _____ it.

   (correct, usually)

4. If Susanna _____ a college degree, she would have a

   (have)

   better job.

5. Siamak would have had a conference with Dr. Reid yesterday if he

   _____ the meeting.

   (remember)

6. I wouldn't drink so much coffee if I _____ you.

   (be)

7. If I had gone to the meeting, I _____ for the publicity

   (volunteer)

   committee.

8. If Fisal studied more, he _____ more.

   (remember)

C. Finish the following sentences. Add whatever words of your own that will make the meaning of each sentence logical and complete. Label each sentence as "conditional" or "hypothetical." Discuss with the rest of your class the ways that you can tell if a sentence has conditional or hypothetical meaning.

Sentence	**Meaning**
1. If I were you, _I would study in the library._	_hypothetical_

2. I would have gone to the library yesterday if _____ _____

3. If you had asked me, I _____ _____

4. If I have the time, I _____ _____

5. If I had known about the test, I _____ _____

6. He would have gotten the job if _____ _____

7. If I were ten years older, I _____ _____

8. I will type the paper if _____ _____

D. Fill in each blank with the correct form of the verb in parentheses.

1. If I were you, I _____ ESL again next quarter.
   (take)

2. If I had gone to the soccer game, I _____ the lecture.
   (miss)

3. I would not have gone if I _____ it was going to rain.
   (know)

4. If it rains tomorrow, I _____ home.
   (stay)

5. I will call you next week if I _____ another volunteer.
   (need)

6. I would study French if I _____ the time.
   (have)

7. I would not have gone if I _____ about the price.
   (know)

8. If I had the time, I _____ for more than one course.
   (enroll)

E. Follow the example sentences, and write two versions of the information about Juan. The first version is conditional future time. The second version is hypothetical past time. Compare your sets of sentences to those of the other students in your class, and make any necessary corrections. Then, put your list in your Grammar Notebook to use as examples when you are writing conditional or hypothetical sentences.

If it (rain), the dean (cancel) the picnic.

Conditional Future Time: *If it rains next weekend, the dean will cancel the picnic.*

Hypothetical Past Time: *If it had rained last Saturday, the dean would have canceled the picnic.*

1. If Juan (study) harder, his test grade (be) better.
2. If he (have) time, he (watch) television.
3. He (be) happy if he (get) a good grade on the midterm test.
4. He (buy) a new calculator if he (have) enough money.
5. If he (read) the assignment, he (understand) the lecture.

F. Write hypothetical sentences to answer the following eight questions. The sentences should be meaningful, and the verb forms should be correct. After editing the sentences, keep them in your Grammar Notebook to use as examples.

> Example: What would you do if you had a holiday from school today?
> *If I had a holiday from school today, I would watch television.*

1. If you had enough money, what would you buy?
2. What would you do tomorrow if you were a millionaire?
3. Would you have gotten a better grade if you had studied more?
4. If you had more free time, what would you do?
5. Would you have learned to speak English more fluently if you had had a conversation course?
6. If you had had the time, what would you have done yesterday?

G. Fill in each blank with the correct form of the verb in parentheses. Follow the time frame directions.

1. future time conditional meaning

   If I *ask*_____ him, he *will usher*_____ at the concert.
      (ask)   (usher)

2. past time hypothetical meaning

   If I _____ a ticket, I _____ to the game.
      (buy)   (go)

3. general truth hypothetical meaning

   I _____ more if I _____ the time.
    (study)   (have)

4. future time conditional meaning

   I _____ $20 a month if I _____ the campus bus.
    (save)   (take)

5. future time conditional meaning

If I _____ your library book, I _____ it to the
    (find)   (return)

library.

6. general truth hypothetical meaning

I _____ my essay if I _____ a typewriter.
  (type)   (have)

7. past time hypothetical meaning

If I _____ that he was sick, I _____ the teacher.
  (know)   (tell)

8. general truth conditional meaning

Students _____ this course if they _____ absent
        (fail)   (be)

more than 10% of the classes.

H. Put brackets [ ] around the conditional or hypothetical sentences, and draw double lines under the verbs in each sentence. Then, label the sentences in one of the following ways:

Conditional: General Truth
Conditional: Future
Hypothetical: General Truth
Hypothetical: Past

1. The sun, like the other stars, is a giant sphere of gases. It has a diameter of 865,000 miles. The sun is 100 times larger than the earth. [If the earth were at its center, the moon would orbit about halfway between the earth and the sun's surface.]

Hypothetical: General Truth

2. Many telescopes come equipped with special filters for direct observation of the sun. If your telescope has no such protective device, you will need to buy one.

_____

3. When scientists reach an area that they think may contain fossils, they begin searching. If the scientists want to study plants or invertebrates, they split open the rocks in the area to find fossils inside them. If they want to study larger animals, they search for bone fragments.

_____

4. The first permanent English settlement in North America was established at Jamestown, Virginia, in 1607. By 1670, English settlements had been established in 12 of what later became the 13 original colonies. If Spain, Italy, or Portugal had established permanent settlements in America at that time, the native language of the United States would probably not have been English.

_____

Adapted from *World Book Encyclopedia*, 1988 ed., s.v. "colonial life in America," "fossil," and "sun."

I. Put brackets [ ] around the conditional and hypothetical sentences, and complete each sentence with the correct form of the verb in parentheses. Then, label the sentences in one of the following ways:

Conditional: General Truth
Conditional: Future
Hypothetical: General Truth
Hypothetical: Past

1. An immigrant to the United States who applies for naturalization must be at least 18 years old and a permanent resident. If the request for naturalization is approved, the person _____ (take) an oath that pledges loyalty to the United States. _____

2. The human nervous system is sometimes compared to a huge telephone system with many millions of miles of wires. If these wires were not connected to a central switchboard, they _____ (be) useless. _____

3. Amerigo Vespucci was an Italian explorer who made three trips to South America from 1499 to 1504. Vespucci later claimed that he had reached a "New World." In 1507, Martin Waldseemuller, a German mapmaker, named this newly discovered world "America" after Amerigo Vespucci. If Waldseemuller had popularized the voyages of Christopher Columbus instead of the voyages of Amerigo Vespucci, the continents of North and South America _____ (have) different names. _____

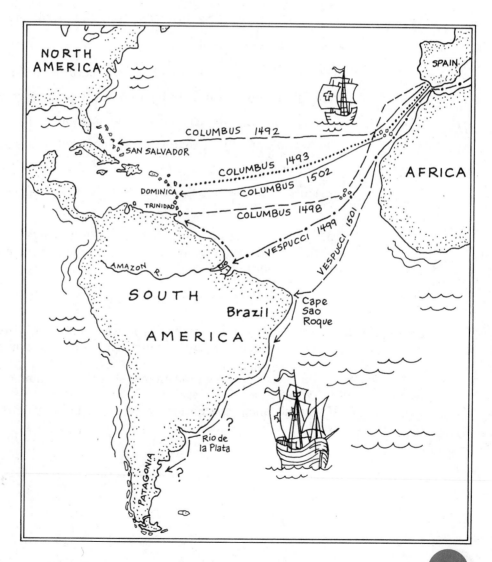

4. As air rises, it expands and becomes cooler. If enough water vapor is in the expanding air, the vapor _____ (condense) and forms clouds. _____

5. When Hernando Cortés landed on the coast of Mexico in 1519, he learned that the Aztec Indians ruled a great civilization further inland. If the Aztecs had not welcomed Cortés as a white god, he and his men _____ (not, overcome) the Aztecs so easily. The victory of Cortés led to the Spanish conquest of Central America and made Mexico one of Spain's most important areas in the New World.

_____

6. The world's supplies of petroleum and natural gas are being used up rapidly. If they continue to be used at the present rate, we _____ (exhaust) our petroleum supplies by the early 2000s. The world's supply of coal will last about 200 years at the present rate of use. _____

Adapted from *World Book Encyclopedia*, 1988 ed., s.v. "brain," "cloud," "coal," "exploration," and "immigration."

J. Write a paragraph about one of the following topics. After you are satisfied with the organization and meaning of the paragraph, edit it carefully for verb choice and form.

1. If you had a three-week vacation and unlimited funds, where would you go? Why?
2. Where would you like to be if you were not here? Why?
3. If you could relive a day in your past, what day would you choose? Why?
4. If you decide not to go to summer school next summer, what will you do? Why?
5. If you had spent last Saturday (or any other day) differently, what would you have done?

CHAPTER

16

Gerunds and Infinitives

"Gerund" and "Infinitive" Defined

English can change the form of a verb so that the verb can be used as a noun.

Gerund Defined

A verb can be changed by adding *-ing*. If the new word is used as a noun, it is called a **gerund**. In the second example, *swimming* is the subject of the sentence. In the third example, *swimming* is the complement. In the fourth example, *swimming* is the direct object.

*Juanita **swims** every weekend.*

gerund as subject
***Swimming** is her favorite sport.*

gerund as complement
*Her favorite sport is **swimming**.*

gerund as direct object
*She likes **swimming** very much.*

Infinitive Defined

A verb can also be changed by adding *to*. This combination is called an **infinitive**. As with gerunds, infinitives are used for the same sentence functions as nouns. They can be subjects, complements, and direct objects. In the second example, *to study* is the subject, and *to learn* is the complement. In the third example, *to study* is the direct object.

*We **study** in the library.*

infinitive as subject   infinitive as complement
***To study** is not **to learn**.*

infinitive as direct object
*I like **to study**.*

Uses of Gerunds and Infinitives

Gerunds and infinitives are used in sentences in many of the same ways as nouns and noun phrases.

Gerunds can be used as:
  subject
  direct object
  complement
  object of a preposition
  appositive

gerund as subject
***Preparing** for a test is hard work.*

gerund as direct object
*He likes **working** in the computer lab.*

gerund as complement
*The first step is **opening** the box.*

gerund as object of a preposition
*We look forward to **meeting** you.*

gerund as appositive
*The first step, **opening** the box, is the only easy step in the process.*

What sentence function does each
gerund have in these examples?

He enjoys **typing** on a computer.

Typing makes readable papers.

An important skill for a student is
accurate **typing.**

Infinitives can be used as:
  subject
  direct object
  complement
  appositive
  adjective modifier
  adverbial

infinitive as subject
To study is not the same as to
learn.

infinitive as direct object
I want **to study** Chinese.

infinitive as complement
Her problem is **to save** enough
money for graduate school.

infinitive as appositive
Her problem, **to save** enough
money for graduate school, seems
easy to solve if she is a good
student because she might be able
to get an assistantship.

infinitive as
adjective modifier
His problem is **easy to solve.**

infinitive as adverbial
(reason)
She came here **to study medicine.**

What sentence function does the
infinitive have in each of these
sentences?

I like **to exercise** in the gym after
class.

My plan is **to take** classes in the
morning, **to study** in the library
in the afternoon, and **to study** at
home in the evenings.

To live is to learn.

Practice with Uses of Gerunds and Infinitives

A. In the appropriate space, identify the sentence function of the
underlined gerund or infinitive.

1. Writing (a) is an important result of education.
2. A person who has learned to write (b) can communicate with people over time and distance and keep ideas ready to use (c).
3. Writing (d) provides a permanent record of information.
4. Students use handwriting (e) to record and organize (f) the ideas that they hear in lectures and classrooms.
5. Later, they can use their notes to study (g).
6. Children usually begin to write (h) in kindergarten or first grade.
7. Sometimes, children learn to write (i) even before entering (j) school.

(a)   *subject*
(b) _____
(c) _____
(d) _____
(e) _____
(f) _____
(g) _____
(h) _____
(i) _____
(j) _____

B. Use a highlighter to mark all of the gerunds and infinitives in the following paragraphs. Then, write its sentence function above each gerund or infinitive.

1. Good nutrition includes eating the proper amount of food each day. Overeating can lead to obesity, a condition which puts extra strain on the heart and increases a person's chances of getting such diseases as diabetes and heart disease. Many people try to lose weight quickly by following one of many fad diets. However, these diets can be dangerous.

2. The main goal for readable handwriting consists of good letter formation. The letters *a, e, r,* and *t* seem to cause problems for many writers. Too much space between letters and irregular slanting of letters may also result in poor handwriting. In general, a person who wants to write more legibly should correct these common problems before handing in an assignment.

Gerunds as Direct Objects

The following commonly used verbs usually take gerunds rather than infinitives as their direct objects:

anticipate	*finish*	*postpone*
appreciate	*go*	*practice*
avoid	*(dis)like*	*quit*
be worth	*imagine*	*recommend*
can(not) help	*involve*	*spend money*
consider	*mind*	*spend time*
delay	*miss*	*suggest*
dread		
enjoy		

In the example, note that the gerund is the direct object of *avoid*. Of course, these verbs can have other kinds of words as direct objects.

noun phrase as direct object

*He avoided **his friends** because he was too tired to talk.*

gerund as direct object

*He avoided **studying** in the library.*

. . . .

Practice with Gerunds as Direct Objects

A. Fill in each blank with the gerund form of the verb in parentheses.

1. I am considering _____ history next quarter.
   (take)

2. Majid avoided _____ to the writing lab.
   (go)

3. Do you mind _____ me your pen?
   (loan)

4. The college is considering _____ ESL classes in the evening.
   (hold)

5. Juan enjoys _____ accounting.
   (study)

6. Maria postponed _____ the TOEFL.
   (take)

B. Write sentences using the gerund form of the verb in parentheses. Add whatever words of your own that will make the meaning of each sentence logical and complete.

1. I cannot help (worry) _____

2. I would never consider (go) _____

3. I suggest (take) _____

371

4. I do not spend time (review) _____

5. I avoid (spend) _____

6. My advisor recommended (take) _____

C. Finish the following sentences with a gerund and any other words of your own that will make the meaning of each sentence logical and complete.

1. I avoid _____

2. I miss _____

3. I am considering _____

4. I do not mind _____

5. I enjoy _____

6. I cannot avoid _____

D. Write sentences using gerunds to answer the following questions. The sentences should be meaningful, and the verb forms should be correct. After editing the sentences, keep them in your Grammar Notebook to use as examples.

1. What do you recommend doing to understand English better?
2. What did you enjoy doing last weekend?
3. What did you finish doing last week?
4. What did you avoid doing last night?
5. What are you going to practice doing tonight?

E. Discuss with the rest of your class the answers that they gave to number 1 in exercise **D.** Develop a list of suggestions for improving your English. Write that list on a sheet of paper to keep in your Grammar Notebook.

F. Discussion Assignment: What are the Summer and Winter Olympic Games? Where are they held? Have you ever watched them on television? Have you ever attended the Olympics? What events do you enjoy watching?

Grammar Assignment: Read the following paragraph, and put a double line under all the complete verbs; then, put a circle around the gerunds. Answer the questions after the paragraph when you have finished marking the gerunds.

The Olympics

[1]Amateur athletes from nations around the world compete in events every four years during the Summer and Winter Olympic Games. [2]The event that requires the greatest overall ability in the Summer Games is the pentathlon. [3]This event involves competing in horseback riding, fencing, shooting, swimming, and cross-country running. [4]Athletes who compete in these events know the importance of training. [5]They avoid gaining weight, and they exercise daily to build up their strength. [6]Some athletes spend time concentrating on their weaker areas; others train equally in all areas. [7]During their practice sessions, contestants anticipate winning the gold medal for the pentathlon. [8]Preparing for the pentathlon requires great personal sacrifice, and few people enjoy training many hours every day for years. [9]On some days, athletes must dread training, but with the chance of getting a new world's record and winning a gold medal, they persevere.

Adapted from *Encyclopedia Americana*, 1983 ed., s.v. "Olympic Games."

1. The following prepositions are followed by gerunds: _____

   _____

2. The following verbs are followed by gerunds: _____

   _____ _____ _____ _____

   _____

3. The following gerund is used as the subject: _____ .

4. An infinitive appears in sentence # _____ .

Prepositions Followed by Gerunds

Prepositions are followed by nouns, noun phrases, or gerunds. The following preposition combinations are often followed by gerunds. Turn to Appendix E for a more complete list of prepositions combined with verbs and adjectives.

Preposition + Noun or Gerund

Notice that a preposition can be followed by a noun or by a gerund.

*I am afraid of **snakes.***

*I am afraid of **stepping** on a snake.*

*My mother is famous for **her kindness.***

*My mother is famous for **helping** people.*

To as a Preposition

To is sometimes used as a preposition.

*We **are used to studying** in the library.*

*I **am looking forward to meeting** you.*

Used To and Be Used To

Do not confuse *used to* with *be used to*. These phrases have very different meanings.

Used to refers to actions and habits in the past. These things are over and are no longer possible. Notice that *used to* is followed by the simple dictionary form of the verb.

*I **used to study** with my sister, but she lives in Alaska now.*

*Maria **used to live** in Mexico; now she lives in Canada.*

Be used to refers to habits. This verb is usually followed by a gerund. It can be used for all possible verb forms, but is especially common in simple present tense for present time habits.

*I **am used to getting up** early; it does not bother me.*

*My roommate **is used to sleeping** late; getting up early is a problem for him.*

*I **am used to studying** in the library.*

Practice with *Used To* and *Be Used To*

A. Fill in each blank with the correct form of the verb in parentheses.

1. Mansoo used to _____ in Albuquerque.
   (live)

2. Now, he is used to _____ in Boston.
   (live)

3. He used to _____ the constant desert heat.
(hate)

4. Now, he is used to _____ in snow and ice.
(drive)

5. In Albuquerque, he used to _____ 20 hours a week.
(work)

6. Now, he is used to _____ 40 hours a week.
(work)

7. He used to _____ with his family in Albuquerque.
(live)

8. In Boston, he is used to _____ alone.
(live)

B. Discuss with your class ways to learn how to use words and phrases that are similar in form but very different in meaning. How can you remember the differences between *used to* and *be used to*? How can you learn to use these words correctly? Do any of your classmates have mnemonic devices that help them to remember the differences?

C. Write five sentences about things that you used to do before you moved to the city where you now live. Share those sentences with the other students in your class. Discuss ways that all of your lives have changed.

D. Write five sentences about things that you are used to doing every day. Share those sentences with the other students in your class. Make a list together of the things that all of you are used to doing.

Practice with Prepositions and Gerunds

A. Fill in each blank with the correct preposition. After you have completed the exercise, turn to Appendix E for a list of these preposition combinations to use in checking your answers.

1. I do not plan __*on*__ studying until this weekend.

2. Elaheh is tired _____ studying irregular verbs.

3. He was prevented _____ parking in the student parking lot because he did not have the correct parking decal.

4. We are interested _____ hearing about the final exam.

5. Ju is thinking _____ transferring to Stanford University.

6. He insisted _____ helping me with the project.

7. We are looking forward _____ attending the workshop on student services.

8. I am tired _____ studying ESL.

B. Add the correct preposition and gerund form of the verb in parentheses.

1. Pragnesh constantly worries _about passing_ this course.
                                      (pass)

2. Dr. Jones does not approve _____ after midnight.
                                 (study)

3. Manis is afraid _____ his job as a student assistant.
                      (lose)

4. The bad weather prevented the team _____ last Saturday.
                                          (play)

5. Sotheara was proud _____ her essay in two hours.
                         (finish)

6. Kooknam is capable _____ her essay in one hour.
                         (complete)

7. Marie is sorry _____ your calculator.
                     (lose)

8. She will be responsible _____ it.
                              (replace)

9. Uriel is interested _____ English.
                          (learn)

10. I am tired _____ about his problems.
                  (hear)

C. Write sentences to answer the following ten questions. The sentences should be meaningful, and the verb forms should be correct. After editing your answers, keep them in your Grammar Notebook to use as examples.

1. How is studying in college different from studying in high school?
2. What are you afraid of doing?
3. What are you sorry about doing?
4. What are you interested in doing this weekend?
5. What are you lazy about doing?
6. What are you prevented from doing?
7. What are you good at doing?
8. What are you used to doing now that you did not do 10 years ago?
9. What do you look forward to doing?
10. What are you tired of doing?

D. Discuss with the other students in your class their answers to questions 9 and 10 in exercise C.

Infinitives as Direct Objects

Some verbs cannot have gerunds as their direct object. Instead, these verbs must have infinitives. The following verbs should be followed by infinitives:

afford	*deserve*	*intend*	*offer*	*promise*
agree	*expect*	*learn*	*plan*	*refuse*
arrange	*fail*	*manage*	*prepare*	*seem*
attempt	*hesitate*	*need*	*pretend*	*want*
decide	*hope*			

Like gerunds, infinitives can be used in many of the same ways that nouns are used.

noun phrase as direct object
He wants *a new dictionary*.

infinitive as direct object
He wants *to go* to the library.

Note that the correct example uses an infinitive. Using a gerund is wrong.

correct
He wants *to learn* Arabic.

incorrect
*He wants *learning* Arabic.

Practice with Infinitives as Direct Objects

A. Finish the following sentences with an infinitive and any other words of your own that will make the meaning of each sentence logical and complete.

1. We have decided *to hold our meeting next Monday at 2:30.* _____

2. I would like _____

3. I hope _____

4. I expect _____

5. I attempted _____

6. I want _____

B. Write sentences with infinitives to answer the following questions. The sentences should be meaningful, and the verb forms should be correct. After editing them, keep your answers in your Grammar Notebook to use as examples.

1. What grade do you expect to get on the next test?
2. What do you plan to major in?
3. What would you refuse to do?
4. How many hours do you need to study tonight?
5. What have you decided to do next summer?
6. How do you intend to improve your spelling?

C. Find out what other students gave as their answers to numbers 2 and 6 in exercise B. Discuss similarities and differences in the answers that were given by the entire class.

Infinitives and Adjectives

Infinitives frequently follow adjectives. Sometimes grammarians call the infinitive the complement of the adjective because it is necessary to complete the meaning of the adjective.

Note that many of these uses have sentences that begin with *it*. In this use, *it* does not have any meaning but is just serving to be sure there is a word in the subject position.

*It is **easy to check out** a book in the university library.*

*It seems **excessive to require** four textbooks for one course.*

Practice with Adjectives and Infinitives

A. Fill in each blank with the correct form of the verb in parentheses.

1. It is sometimes hard <u>*to think*</u> in English.
   (think)

2. It is difficult _____ the pronunciation of some Americans.
   (understand)

3. I am eager _____ my pronunciation.
   (improve)

4. My math teacher was delighted _____ her students.
   (help)

5. It is easy _____ to type.
   (learn)

6. Our physics teacher thinks it is reasonable _____ a quiz
   (give)
   every Friday.

7. I can always find a writing lab tutor who is willing _____

(help)

me.

8. I am content _____ at this school for six more months.

(stay)

B. Finish the following sentences with an infinitive and any other words of your own that will make the meaning of each sentence logical and complete.

1. Everyone was unhappy *to hear about the test.* _____

2. We are prepared _____

3. The students were disappointed _____

4. I am surprised _____

5. Ali is lucky _____

6. I am pleased _____

C. Working with another student, make a list of five activities that are easy to do at your school. For example, *it is easy to buy supplies in the bookstore.* Compare your list to those of other students in your class. If you do not agree with each other, discuss any changes that need to be made to have an accurate list of activities.

D. Working with another student, make a list of five activities that are difficult or impossible to do at your school. For example, *it is impossible to cash a personal check.* Compare your list to those of other students in your class. Discuss any of these problems that you think the school needs to solve for its students. Prepare a letter in which you first explain the problem, and then make positive suggestions about solving the problems. After you have agreed on the wording of the letter and have edited it carefully, arrange to send it to an appropriate official of the school.

E. Discussion Assignment: How does it feel when you cannot communicate with another person? Is failure to communicate more of a problem for a tourist or for a refugee? Why?

Grammar Assignment: Use a highlighter to mark all of the infinitives in this article. Then, answer the questions after the article.

Needs of Refugee Children

[1]Language is the first obstacle. [2]It is very difficult and frustrating to live in a world where you cannot understand others or make yourself understood. [3]One four-year-old boy, a member of the city of Spokane's only refugee family from Romania, was particularly difficult in class. [4]He simply cried and cried the whole time that he was in Head Start, and his teachers were unable to comfort him or to find out why he was so troubled. [5]Each time a new adult came into the room, he would run to the person and talk and talk—and then cry and cry. [6]A translator could not be found through local universities or the language bank. [7]Finally, through a letter to the newspaper, a woman was located who spoke the boy's language. [8]She volunteered to work with the boy. [9]After spending some time with him, she asked him why he cried so much. [10]He answered, ''Because the people here don't have ears.''

Note: Head Start is a U.S. government program to provide underprivileged children with preparation for attending school.

Adapted from Broughton, Connie. ''Serving Refugee Children and Families in Head Start.'' *Children Today*. Washington, D.C.: GPO, 1989, 6–10.

1. Sentence 2 has _____ example(s) of adjective + infinitive.

2. Sentence 4 has _____ example(s) of adjective + infinitive.

3. Sentence _____ has an infinitive as its direct object.

4. In Sentence 7, is *to* a preposition or is it part of an infinitive? Circle the correct answer.

F. Discussion Assignment: How did people communicate with each other thousands of years ago? Why was the printing press important to the development of written communication? What will communication be like in the future?

Grammar Assignment: Read the following paragraph, and put a double-line under all the complete verbs; then, put a box around all the infinitives. Answer the questions after the paragraph when you have finished marking the infinitives.

Communication

[1]The first human beings did not have the opportunity to write and record their ideas on paper; instead, they used sounds and gestures to

communicate with each other. [2]Paintings and drawings were the first steps toward a written language. [3]When the Egyptians discovered how to make a paper-like material, they recorded their history on it with hieroglyphic symbols. [4]About 1500 B.C., people in the Middle East invented the alphabet. [5]The Greeks modified it, and the Romans borrowed it from the Greeks. [6]Written communication began to improve, but everything was copied slowly by hand. [7]Centuries later, Johannes Gutenberg invented the printing press which had the ability to copy a page of print quickly many times. [8]As time passed, the telephone, telegraph, radio, and television were developed. [9]Today, computers and satellites are available to send information around the world quickly. [10]In the future, methods of communication will continue to improve when people need to send and receive information faster and more efficiently.

Adapted from *World Book Encyclopedia*, 1988 ed., s.v. "communication" and "handwriting."

Examine the verbs you have identified:

1. Passive verbs appear in sentence #s _____

2. Past tense verbs appear in sentence #s _____

3. Present tense verbs appear in sentence #s _____

4. Future time meaning appears in sentence # _____

5. Infinitives appear in sentence #s _____

Infinitives and *Too*

The word *too* is used to intensify the meaning of an adjective. It often means that there is some problem because of an excessive amount of the adjective.

The basic pattern is *too* + adjective + infinitive.

*He is **too tired to study**; he will just eat dinner and go to bed.*

*She is **too young to go** to school; she is only three years old.*

ESL students can confuse English speakers by using *too* incorrectly; *too* often means there is a problem.

incorrect
*John is too happy because he passed the test.

English speakers use the word *very* to mean "a lot of this."

correct
John is very happy because he passed the test.

. . . .

Practice with Infinitives and *Too*

A. Finish the following sentences using *too* and an infinitive. The sentences should be meaningful, and the verb forms should be correct.

1. The midterm exam was <u>too</u> long <u>to finish</u>.

2. Five miles is _____ far _____

3. The math problem is _____ difficult _____

4. Last night, I was _____ tired _____

5. The article was _____ boring _____

6. It is _____ late _____

7. Yesterday's class was _____

8. This school is _____

B. Decide whether *too* or *very* is more appropriate to make a logical sentence. Write the correct word in the blank space.

1. My algebra teacher talks _____ fast to understand.

2. The midterm examination was _____ long to complete. I did not finish it.

3. The final examination was _____ difficult. As a result, most of the students failed.

4. The final examination was _____ difficult. However, most of the students passed.

5. This novel is _____ long to read in one weekend.

6. The movie I saw on television last night was _____ exciting. I really enjoyed it.

7. "I am _____ happy to meet you."

8. The new book about Muhammad Ali's health is _____ sad.

Infinitives and *For*

Compare these two examples that use an adjective + infinitive.

The first sentence is a statement of general truth.	*Algebra is easy to learn.*
In the second sentence the meaning has been made more specific: Jose is the learner.	*Algebra is easy **for Jose** to learn.*
Notice that object forms of pronouns are used because the pronoun is the object of a preposition.	*Algebra is easy **for him** to learn but not **for me.***

Practice with Infinitives and *For*

Finish the following sentences using the preposition *for* and an infinitive. Add whatever words of your own that will make the meaning of each sentence logical and complete.

1. Yesterday's lesson was difficult *for me to understand.* _____

2. These exercises are easy _____

3. Some courses are difficult _____

4. It is good _____

5. The new computer is hard _____

6. _____ is dangerous _____

7. _____ is interesting _____

8. _____ is expensive _____

Infinitives and *In Order To*

In order to answers the adverb question "Why?"	*I took the computer class **in order to learn** WordPerfect.*
In order to can be omitted as in the second example.	*I took the computer class **to learn** WordPerfect.*

Practice with Infinitives and *In Order To*

Write sentences with infinitives to answer the following questions. The sentences should be meaningful, and the verb forms should be correct. You can use either form given in the example. After comparing your answers to those of other students in the class, make any necessary changes. Then, put the list in your Grammar Notebook.

1. Why are you taking this course?

   I am taking this course in order to improve my English.

   I am taking this course to improve my English.

2. Why did you come to this city?
3. Why did you go to the bookstore yesterday?
4. Why did you close the classroom door?
5. Why do you go to the student center every day?
6. Why should you come to class tomorrow?

How, When, Where + Infinitive

How, when, and *where* are often followed by infinitives.	*I would like to know **how to type**.*
	*I never know **when to listen** and **when to take** notes.*
	*I cannot remember **where to go** for the next meeting.*

Practice with Infinitives and *How, When, Where*

Write one sentence for each of the following: **how** to do something, **when** to do something, and **where** to do something. Share those three sentences with the other students in your class. After making any needed changes, write the sentences on a sheet of paper to keep in your Grammar Notebook.

Verbs That Can Have Either a Gerund or an Infinitive as Direct Object with No Meaning Difference

The following verbs can be followed by either a gerund or an infinitive without any difference in meaning:

begin	*hate*	*love*	*prefer*
continue	*like*	*neglect*	*start*

There is no important difference in meaning between these two sentences.

*She **began to study** for the test yesterday.*

*She **began studying** for the test yesterday.*

Practice with Verbs That Can Have Either a Gerund or an Infinitive as Direct Object with No Meaning Difference

Write sentences to answer the following questions. Read the questions carefully to determine if they are asking for gerund or infinitive answers. The sentences should be meaningful, and the verb forms should be correct. Share your sentences with other students in your class. Then, make any needed corrections, and put your answers in your Grammar Notebook.

1. What did you hate doing as a child?
2. What will you begin to do next semester?
3. What are you going to start doing next weekend?
4. What are you going to continue to do in this class?
5. What did you like doing as a child?
6. What did you neglect to do last night?

Verbs That Can Have Either a Gerund or an Infinitive as Direct Object with Different Meanings

The following verbs can be followed by either a gerund or an infinitive. However, the sentences have different meanings.

forget	*remember*	*stop*

Forget

Often an infinitive refers to something that occurs after the action of the main verb. In the first example, first I forgot, and then as a result I did not indent. The first result was no indention for the paragraph. Another result was a lower grade.

I forgot to indent my paragraph. My teacher gave me a lower grade because of this mistake.

Often a gerund refers to something that occurs before the action of the main verb. In the second example, I put salt in the soup. Then, I forgot about doing it. The result is too much salt in the soup.

I forgot putting salt in the soup when I added more salt. The soup was terrible because it was too salty.

Remember

The gerund sentence is about recalling the past.

Maria remembers to indent her paragraphs.

Maria remembers going to the store yesterday.

When investigators are trying to get people to remember the past, they ask questions using the gerund.

Do you remember locking your car doors?

Do you remember cashing the check?

Do you remember copying your friend's research paper?

Stop

First, he stopped; then he smoked.

While walking across campus, he stopped to smoke a cigarette.

He stopped an activity that he had done before.

He stopped smoking because it made him sick.

Practice with Verbs That Can Have Either a Gerund or an Infinitive as Direct Object with Different Meanings

A. Fill in the blanks with the gerund or infinitive form of the verbs in parentheses. Read carefully for the correct meaning.

1. Majid stopped _____ to the writing lab. (He no longer goes
   (go)
   there.)

2. He began _____ in the student center instead.
   (work)

3. He prefers _____ in the student center rather than
   (study)

   _____ (study) in the writing lab.

4. Khanh forgot _____ his dictionary to class yesterday. (He
   (bring)
   did not bring the book.)

5. He remembered _____ it on the chair near his front door.
   (put)
   (He put it there yesterday.)

6. Luckily, he remembered _____ it today. (He has his
   (bring)
   dictionary with him today.)

B. Write sentences to answer the following questions. Read the questions carefully to determine if they are asking for gerund or infinitive answers. The sentences should be meaningful, and the verb forms should be correct. After editing your sentences, keep them in your Grammar Notebook to use as examples.

1. What have you stopped doing lately?
2. What did you remember to do last night?
3. What do you plan to begin doing differently?
4. What did you forget to do today?
5. What do you like to eat for lunch every day?
6. When did you stop using a bilingual dictionary?

C. With the other students in your class, discuss the very different meanings of these two sentences. Can you think of ways to act out the events in these sentences?

1. On the way to the library, he stopped to talk with his friends.
2. Because of differences in political ideas, he stopped talking with his friends.

Causative Verbs

· ·

In many situations, we cause other people to do work for us or to act for us. English has a small group of words that can be used in sentences to express this relationship in which one person causes and another person acts. These verbs are *have, get, make, let,* and *help.*

Formation

The verb takes a complete sentence as its direct object. The verb of the embedded sentence is either an infinitive or an infinitive without *to*. The teacher caused something; the students attended a lecture.

*The teacher **had** the students **attend** a lecture yesterday.*

*The teacher **got** the students **to attend** a lecture.*

Have and *Get*

These two verbs have similar causative meanings. However, their grammar is different. *Have* is more formal. Notice the difference in their grammar.

*Every day at the beginning of class, the teacher **has** Juan **close** the door.*

*Every day at the end of class, the teacher **gets** Maria **to open** the door.*

The verb in the direct object does not change for subject-verb agreement because it is an infinitive either with or without *to*.

*Every Saturday, his mother **has** Pepe **take** her to the grocery store.*

*Every Saturday, their mother **has** Pepe and Maria **take** her to the grocery store.*

Passive Sentences

Both *have* and *get* can take passive sentences in their direct objects. The passive verb is the past participle.

active sentence
*I **had** the mechanic **repair** my car.*

active sentence
*I **got** the mechanic **to repair** my car.*

passive sentence
*I **had** my car **repaired**.*

passive sentence
*I **got** my car **repaired**.*

Make

Make carries the meaning of "cause through force"; the force can be physical, moral, political, or legal. The verb is the simple dictionary form (the infinitive without *to*). No passive is possible.

*The teacher **makes** the students **take** a quiz every Friday.*

*The university **makes** students **buy** medical insurance.*

*The teacher **made** Juan **rewrite** his research paper.*

Let

Let means "allow" or "give permission." The verb in the direct object is the simple form without *to*. The student asked to leave class early. The teacher gave permission.

*The teacher **let** the student **leave** class early.*

Help

With this verb, the subject of the sentence is involved in the action. In contrast to *have, get,* and *make,* the subject is more than a causer. The verb in the object is usually the simple form without *to*. However, if the subject of the embedded sentence is complex, *to* may be used. Passive sentences are rare.

*The librarian **helped** the student **find** information for her research paper.*

*The student who sits next to me in my grammar class **helped** me **to understand** our homework assignment.*

Feel, Hear, See, and Watch

These verbs are causative in meaning and have grammar similar to *have* and *make.*

*Standing on the beach, Juan **could feel** the wind **blow.***

*I **heard** the teacher **ask** the question, but I did not know the answer.*

*On the way home from school, I **saw** an accident **happen.***

*The teacher **watched** the students **take** the test.*

· ·

Practice with Causative Verbs

A. Finish the following sentences, and pay special attention to the causative patterns. Write the correct form of the verb in parentheses.

Advisement and Registration

1. My advisor wanted me _____ Grammar IV next term.
   (take)

2. He helped me _____ the advisement form.
   (fill out)

3. He didn't make me _____ another pronunciation course.
   (take)

389

4. He let me _____ between morning and afternoon classes.
(choose)

5. I asked the registrar for permission _____ an extra course
(take)
next term.

6. The registrar had me _____ an overload request when I
(submit)
paid my fees.

7. The business office makes students _____ their fees as soon
(pay)
as they register.

8. Although my money has not arrived from my parents yet, I got my

roommate _____ me enough money for my fees.
(loan)

9. My roommate also found a friend _____ me a ride to class
(give)
every morning.

10. This friend will let me _____ him for the rides at the end of
(pay)
the month.

B. Write sentences to answer the following six questions. The sentences should be meaningful, and the verb forms should be correct. After editing your answers carefully, keep them in your Grammar Notebook for future reference.

1. Do you let friends copy your homework assignments? Why or why not?
2. Did your parents make you wash the dishes after dinner? Why or why not?
3. Do you help friends who need money? Why or why not? How?
4. What did your teacher make you do the first day of class?
5. What has your teacher helped you do so far this term?
6. What has your teacher let you do that is different from what teachers let you do in other schools?

C. Finish the following sentences. Add whatever words of your own that will make the meaning of each sentence logical and complete. Practice using causative patterns.

1. I often let _____

2. I always help _____

3. I never make _____

4. I sometimes get _____

5. I usually have _____

· ·

Practice with Gerunds and Infinitives

A. Fill in each blank with the infinitive or gerund form of the verb in parentheses.

1. Lina wants _____ to Syria.
   (return)

2. She is too busy _____ her homework.
   (do)

3. She is spending her time _____ for presents for her family
   (shop)
   and friends.

4. She is excited about _____ home.
   (go)

5. Adel appreciated _____ from his host family.
   (hear)

6. He delayed _____ an apartment.
   (find)

7. He spent a great deal of time _____ for the right place to
   (look)
   live.

8. His friends enjoyed _____ him.
   (help)

9. He is excited about _____ in.
   (move)

10. We expected _____ early.
    (finish)

B. Fill in each blank with the infinitive or gerund form of the verb in parentheses.

1. I promise _____ the money as soon as possible.
   (return)

2. Genene avoids _____ each night as long as possible.
   (study)

3. He finished _____ the research paper about 2:00 A.M.
   (write)

4. I expect _____ for New York at 7:00 A.M. tomorrow.
   (leave)

5. Colleen refused _____ me any more money.
   (loan)

391

6. Karen considered _____ to night classes next quarter.
   (change)

7. She promised _____ in school even though she works full-
   (stay)
   time.

8. Our teacher may postpone _____ the test until next week.
   (give)

9. I need _____ several hours before I take a test.
   (study)

10. I will practice _____ gerunds and infinitives in sentences.
    (use)

C. Fill in each blank with the infinitive or gerund form of the verb in parentheses.

1. I finished _____ the novel *Moby Dick*.
   (read)

2. Tuan suggested _____ together tonight.
   (study)

3. Thanh refused _____ with the rest of the class.
   (study)

4. He wanted _____ supper before we studied.
   (eat)

5. For awhile, we considered not _____ with the group.
   (eat)

6. He offered _____ anyone who did not understand the
   (help)
   lesson.

7. I am excited about _____ for that class.
   (register)

8. I do not recommend _____ all night the night before an
   (study)
   exam.

9. He seemed _____ the application process.
   (understand)

10. Sonia promised _____ the book next week.
    (return)

D. Fill in each blank with the gerund or infinitive form of the verb in parentheses.

1. I would recommend _____ History 211 after you finish
   (take)
   _____ History 210.
   (take)

2. My friend offered _____ me $50.
   (lend)

3. After the answer was explained, the student began _____ the process.
(understand)

4. Kiyomi has discovered that she enjoys _____ research.
(do)

5. The teacher asked us to continue _____ until we have learned the concept.
(review)

6. She plans _____ us to review everything again.
(ask)

7. We will finish _____ before we begin a new lesson.
(review)

8. I want to stop _____ now.
(write)

E. Choose the correct answer(s), and write the letter(s) in the blank.

1. Shinji likes *a or b*
   a. to golf   b. golfing

2. Ivan continues _____ because he needs the extra money.
   a. to work   b. working

3. He hoped _____ a Pell Grant, but he wasn't selected.
   a. to get   b. getting

4. When he works, he needs _____ classes at night.
   a. to take   b. taking

5. He prefers _____ classes during the day.
   a. to take   b. taking

6. He began _____ for a night job, but he was unsuccessful.
   a. to look   b. looking

7. He hates _____ late to class on the days that he must work late.
   a. to arrive   b. arriving

8. He plans _____ a little money from every month's wages.
   a. to save   b. saving

9. He wanted _____ a full-time student last year.
   a. to be   b. being

10. He decided _____ for a bank loan.
   a. to apply   b. applying

F. Finish the following sentences using the gerund or infinitive form of the verb in parentheses. Add whatever words of your own that will make the meaning of each sentence logical and complete.

1. Griselda is going to the library _to check out two history books._
   (check out)

2. _____ passive voice was difficult.
   (learn)

3. Several students were not prepared _____
   (pay)

4. _____ in English has been difficult for me.
   (write)

5. _____ took two hours.
   (find)

6. _____ requires a lot of attention.
   (listen)

7. Hossein needs _____
   (buy)

8. I will delay _____
   (take)

9. I intend _____
   (ask)

10. I plan _____
    (begin)

G. Circle the gerunds, and draw a box around the infinitives in the following sentences; then, explain the rule for the use of each gerund or infinitive.

1. Orville and Wilbur Wright made the world's first successful airplane flight after studying the writings of other aviation pioneers and after experimenting with gliders, kites, and wind tunnels.

   RULE: A gerund is used _after a preposition._ _____

2. The Bureau of Immigration used Ellis Island as a United States immigration location for more than 60 years. During that time, officials at the island processed over 12 million immigrants. The Bureau of Immigration began using this site in 1892.

   RULE: A gerund is used _____

Restored Great Hall of Ellis Island

3. Immigration is the act of moving permanently to another country. The act of leaving one's own country is called emigration. Adapting to a different life is called assimilation. Immigrants who are not completely assimilated may have problems when they must choose between old habits and new ways. In addition, problems may arise between parents and children because youngsters often adjust faster than their parents.

RULE: A gerund is used _____

A gerund is used _____

4. In many schools, students learn to use computers. This method is called computer-assisted instruction (CAI). In a typical CAI class, each student sits at a computer terminal. The computer presents instructions on the screen, and the student responds by typing answers on the keyboard.

RULE: An infinitive is used _____

A gerund is used _____

5. Computers are often divided into two groups according to the jobs that they perform: general-purpose computers and special-purpose computers. A general-purpose computer is capable of handling many kinds of jobs and is not restricted to a particular use. A special-purpose computer performs a specific job for a particular user.

RULE: <u>A gerund is used   </u>

Adapted from *World Book Encyclopedia*, 1988 ed., s.v. "computer," "Ellis Island," "immigration," and "Wright Brothers."

H. Circle the gerunds, and draw a box around the infinitives in the following sentences; then, explain the rule for the use of each gerund or infinitive.

1. Geology is the study of the earth. Geologists attempt to explain how the earth was formed and how it changes. Geologists also contribute to space exploration by advising scientists about potential lunar landing sites.

RULE: _____

RULE: _____

2. The earth is probably at least 4½ billion years old. Scientists learn the age of rocks by measuring the amount of radioactive isotopes in the rocks. They can approximate the age of a rock by comparing the amount of uranium and lead in the rock.

RULE: _____

3. A glacier is a huge mass of ice that moves slowly over land. Glaciers begin to form when more snow falls during the winter than melts or evaporates during the summer. The ice eventually becomes very thick and starts to move slowly under the pressure of its own weight.

RULE: _____

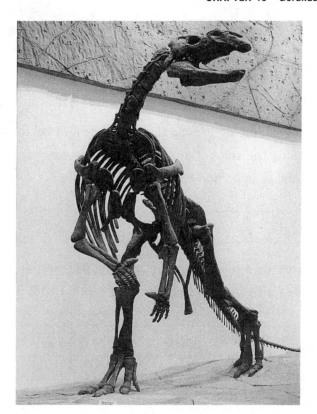

Mutaburasaurus (Australian
dinosaur)

4. Scientists have many ways of learning about dinosaurs. Studying
   dinosaur fossils is one way. Scientists also learn about dinosaurs by
   observing animals that have similar traits to those of dinosaurs.

   RULE: _____

   RULE: _____

5. One of the main tasks of geographers is to identify and record the
   location of places, of earth features, and of human population. They
   also want to know about the types of animals and plants that live
   there.

   RULE: _____

   RULE: _____

6. The early settlers in America faced serious problems and suffered severe hardships. But, many had important reasons for risking the dangerous voyage across 3,000 miles of ocean.

   RULE: _____

7. Experts usually determine the adequacy of a person's diet by examining the amount of calories and protein that it provides. Protein is needed to build and maintain body cells.

   RULE: _____

   RULE: _____

8. The body uses food to produce energy. The protein in food generally provides the energy that a person needs to maintain life.

   RULE: _____

   RULE: _____

Adapted from *World Book Encyclopedia*, 1988 ed., s.v. "colonial life," "dinosaur," "earth," "food," "geography," "geology," and "glacier."

I. Discussion Assignment: Have you chosen a college major yet? What is it? Why did you choose it? When you were a child, what did you want to grow up to be? Have you changed your mind?

Grammar Assignment: Read the following paragraph, and put a double line under all the complete verbs; then, put a circle around the gerunds and a box around the infinitives. Answer the questions after the paragraph when you have finished marking the gerunds and the infinitives.

Choosing a Career

[1]Have you ever dreamed of being an airplane pilot or a deep-sea diver who is searching for lost treasure? [2]Daydreaming about careers is fun, and many young people do it frequently. [3] It is never too early to start preparing for career decisions. [4]The key is you: your interests, your abilities, and your goals. [5]You will want to make a good match between the things that you want and like to do and the things that a job requires. [6]Exploring careers involves exploring yourself, identifying your talents, and examining your strengths and weaknesses.

Divers making an
underwater archeologic
survey

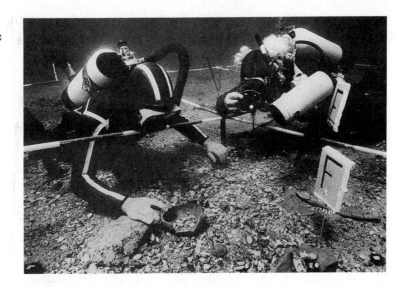

⁷Exploring careers also means finding out as much as you can about types of work in order to see what suits you best. ⁸Taking the time to explore the world of career opportunities does not guarantee job satisfaction, but it helps. ⁹You will probably work for most of your adult life, and your job will take a great deal of your time. ¹⁰The amount of time that you are likely to spend working is a good reason to give some careful thought to your career. ¹¹A person who works full-time for 35 years will spend over 70,000 hours at work. ¹²Making a good career decision is important.

Adapted from U.S. Department of Labor. Bureau of Labor Statistics. *Exploring Careers.*
Bulletin 2001. Washington, D.C.: GPO, 1979, 2.

Answer the following questions:

1. Gerunds are used as subjects in sentence #s _____

2. Gerunds are used after special verbs in sentence #s _____

3. Gerunds are used after prepositions in sentence #s _____

4. List the special verbs that precede gerunds in these paragraphs.

    _____ _____ _____ _____

5. Infinitives appear in sentence #s _____

6. A progressive verb form is used in sentence # _____

J. Discussion Assignment: What are some fire safety rules that you know? What can you do to avoid becoming a burn victim?

Grammar Assignment: Read the following paragraph, and fill in each blank with the correct form of the verb in parentheses: gerund or infinitive.

Burn Victims

Children suffer a high number of scald burns. In the kitchen, they are scalded by _____ pans of hot liquids off the stove or
                                    [1](pull)
by _____ over cups of hot coffee. Hot tap water in the
      [2](knock)
bathroom can also cause serious scald burns. Tap water at 140 degrees will produce a serious burn in less than five seconds.

_____ with the hot water faucet can seriously harm a
[3](play)
young child. Children also suffer burns when their clothing catches on

fire. _____ with matches can be a deadly game if a child's
      [4](play)
clothing catches fire. _____ children the proper use of
                          [5](teach)
matches and _____ flammable liquids such as gasoline in
                [6](store)
safe places will drastically reduce the number of children as burn

victims.

Adults also receive burn injuries when flammable liquids are used

improperly. _____ gasoline as a solvent for paint brushes,
              [7](use)
_____ lighter fluid on hot charcoal when barbecuing, and
[8](put)
_____ any flammable liquid near an open flame are
[9](use)
extremely hazardous. Adults are also burned when they attempt

_____ a burning pan of hot grease from the stove instead
[10](remove)
of _____ the fire with a lid. Smokers also receive burns in
    [11](smother)
bed. _____ with a lighted cigarette occurs frequently.
      [12](fall asleep)
Adults need _____ themselves and their children from
              [13](protect)
_____ victims of fire.
[14](become)

Adapted from "Emergency Treatment of Burns," Shriners Burn Institute brochure, undated.

K. Discussion Assignment: What do astronomers do? Have you ever used the sun or the stars as directional guides?

Grammar Assignment: Read the following paragraph, and answer the questions following the paragraph.

Astronomy

Astronomy involves [1]**studying** the stars, planets, and other objects in the universe. Astronomers observe the locations and motions of heavenly bodies and record their observations. Some astronomers, who are called observational astronomers, specialize in [2]**observing** the sun, planets, and stars through telescopes. Others are theoretical astronomers, who use the principles of physics and mathematics in [3]**determining** the nature of the universe. Astronomy is an old science. It began in ancient times with the observation that the heavenly bodies go through regular cycles of motion. Since then, the study of these cycles has been useful in [4]**keeping** time, **marking** the arrival of the seasons, and **navigating** accurately at sea. During the day, a variety of storms and other activities can be seen on the surface of the sun. However, the sun is too bright [5]**to observe** safely without [6]**using** special equipment. Sunlight also makes the sky too bright [7]**to see** other stars and planets during the day.

Adapted from *World Book Encyclopedia*, 1988 ed., s.v. "astronomy."

Explain why the following gerund or infinitive was chosen:

1. *studying: <u>A gerund is used after the verb</u>* involve. _____

2. *observing:* _____

3. *in determining:* _____

4. *keeping, marking, navigating:* _____

5. *to observe:* _____

6. *using:* _____

7. *to see:* _____

L. One of the reasons for studying English and for attending school is to make changes in your life. Think about the changes that you would like to make during the next year, and discuss those changes with another student in the class. Then, write a paragraph about the resolutions and changes you want to make over the next twelve months. Consider using the following verbs: *decide, hope, intend, need, plan, promise,* and *want.* After you have revised the paragraph to have the meaning that you want, edit it carefully. Focus your editing on the gerunds and infinitives in the paragraph. Use the editing method taught in Section Four.

M. Write a paragraph about the ways that you study. Do you work best by yourself or in a group? Do you work best in a quiet place or with music and conversation around you? Do you work best while you are sitting at a desk or on a sofa? Consider using the following verbs: *anticipate, avoid, delay, enjoy, expect, like, practice,* and *spend time.* Before you write, discuss your study methods with other students in your class as a way of clarifying your ideas. After you have revised the paragraph to have the meaning that you want, edit it carefully. Focus your editing on the gerunds and infinitives in the paragraph. Use the editing method taught in Section Four.

N. Space is provided on page 459 in the Grammar Journal for you to analyze your use of gerunds and infinitives.

O. To practice editing someone else's English, turn to Section Four. Study the information about editing on page 404, and then do the editing exercises on pages 420–421.

SECTION

FOUR

Editing Written English

Learning How to Edit
Practicing the Editing Process
Editing Your Own Written English

Learning How to Edit

In this section, you will learn to use an editing method to help you make your written English more accurate. There are five stages in the writing process:

1. thinking and planning
2. writing
3. revising
4. editing
5. rewriting and proofreading

In writing, experienced writers first think and plan; next, they write the first draft(s) to get their ideas down on paper. Then, they revise what they have written and examine the organization and the support of their ideas. After that, they edit what they have written. When experienced writers edit, they examine each sentence and each word. They try to identify and correct errors in sentence structure, grammar, vocabulary, punctuation, and spelling. The final stage of the writing process is the preparation of the final copy; this final stage involves proofreading the material to be sure that there are no careless typing or handwriting mistakes. In this text, we will concentrate on editing, rather than on proofreading.

When experienced writers edit, they usually have two tasks in mind:

1. They want to find any mistakes that they have made so the mistakes can be corrected.
2. They want to make the correct sentences even better, sometimes using sentence-combining for sentence variety.

The editing practice in this section will not enable you to find and correct all the problems in everything you write, but it will help you concentrate your attention on problem areas that high-intermediate ESL students should be aware of. There are two reasons why you should carefully edit your writing:

1. Readers may not understand your meaning if your writing is not clear.
2. Mistakes are annoying and distracting to readers. They may think that you are either more careless or less intelligent than other writers who have learned to edit more carefully.

There are 12 common writing problems that high-intermediate and advanced ESL students have. These 12 common writing problems have been ranked in the chart on page 405 so that you can tell which problems are more serious than others.

Focus on Editing

The editing process in this book uses numbers to identify writing problems. The 12 numbers, which represent problem areas common to ESL writers, have been divided into the three editing stages shown. Using the numbers will help you focus on your individual areas of weakness, and editing in stages will help you concentrate on editing priorities.

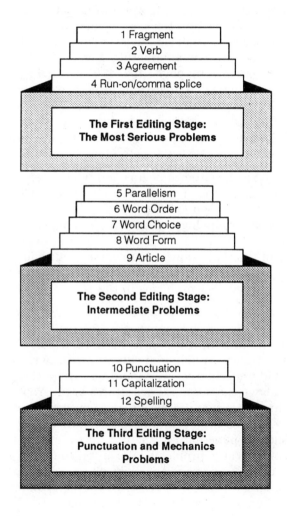

1 Fragment
2 Verb
3 Agreement
4 Run-on/comma splice

**The First Editing Stage:
The Most Serious Problems**

5 Parallelism
6 Word Order
7 Word Choice
8 Word Form
9 Article

**The Second Editing Stage:
Intermediate Problems**

10 Punctuation
11 Capitalization
12 Spelling

**The Third Editing Stage:
Punctuation and Mechanics
Problems**

Benson, Beverly, and Patricia Byrd. *Improving the Grammar of Written English: The Editing Process.* Belmont, California: Wadsworth Publishing, 1989.

Editing by the Numbers

There are three stages in this editing system. The most serious problems are at the top; intermediate, often long-term problems are in the middle; and surface problems of punctuation and mechanics are at the bottom. The relative importance of each problem is shown by its position.

To help you edit better, we have assigned a number to each problem and provided examples for each number (pages 408–410). The numbers help you concentrate on specific areas of grammar and remind you to edit specifically for certain items each time you write. By remembering that the most serious problems have the lowest numbers, you know that you should concentrate on eliminating them first. These numbers and the symbols (described on pages 407–410) will help you in editing your own writing, editing a classmate's writing, and understanding your teacher's editing comments.

Applied English Grammar concentrates on the first three areas of the editing system described above. The other nine areas are briefly covered in this book. This text will help you

1. recognize when a sentence begins and when it ends;
2. identify when groups of words are not sentences but fragments;
3. find the parts of a sentence;
4. use the basic terminology of English grammar to discuss the parts of sentences;
5. understand the time frames that control your choice of verbs;
6. recognize and correct incorrect verb forms and spelling mistakes;
7. recognize and correct problems in the 12 editing areas.

In this section, you will practice editing for a specific kind of problem in each exercise. To become more effective as an editor, you should read your own paragraphs several times, each time looking for a different problem area. To help you edit your own writing better, your instructor will underline mistakes and will write the number of the type of problem above the mistakes or in the margin. You are responsible for understanding what you did wrong and for correcting the mistakes. However, when you are beginning to write, do not worry about editing problems such as punctuation, spelling, or even verb forms. You can go back and correct these problems later after you have gotten your ideas down on paper. If you spend time editing too soon, you may (1) forget what you wanted to say or (2) restrict yourself to only the words you can spell and only the same kinds of sentences.

EDITING SYMBOLS		
Symbol	**Description**	**Sample Sentences**
∧	Add a letter, word, phrase, or punctuation	I want to take several computer course. ˢ I want to take ᵃ philosophy course. I want ₜₒ ₜₐₖₑ several art courses After finishing his math test, he went to his English class.
X	Omit a letter, a word, or a phrase	She entered the classroom. She entered into the classroom. She entered through the door the classroom.
↶	Move this word or phrase	The teacher yesterday gave a test. The teacher in class yesterday gave a test.
/	Delete capital or punctuation	The student attended all the lectures. The student attended all the lectures.
∼	Reverse letters	thier
⊬	Begin a paragraph	Use this symbol to identify where an existing paragraph should be separated to form two paragraphs.
✓	Identify a problem	There is a problem here. Come back to this sentence later and rewrite it.

THE FIRST EDITING STAGE: THE MOST SERIOUS PROBLEMS

Number	Problem(s)	Sample Sentences
1	Fragment	*The students did well on the exam. Because they had studied. correct The students did well on the exam because they had studied.
2	Verb 2a Tense	*He is a student since 1985. correct He has been a student since 1985.
	2b Form	*Students must decided which college to attend. correct Students must decide which college to attend.
3	Agreement 3a +s	*The teacher discussed their three assignment. correct The teacher discussed their three assignments.
	3b Subject/Verb	*The man with the math books come from Brazil. correct The man with the math books comes from Brazil.
	3c Noun/Pronoun	*Each student should hand in their paper. correct Each student should hand in his or her paper.
4	Run-On	*The students took a test yesterday two students were absent.
	Comma Splice	*The students took a test yesterday, two students were absent. correct The students took a test yesterday; two students were absent. *or* correct The students took a test yesterday, but two students were absent.

THE SECOND EDITING STAGE: INTERMEDIATE PROBLEMS		
Number	**Problem(s)**	**Sample Sentences**
5	Parallelism	*Jose attends the university because of its low tuition, its good reputation, and to live in a big city. correct Jose attends the university because of its low tuition, it good reputation, and its location.
6	Word Order	*In my country, only those people can be given such titles who have graduate degrees. correct In my country, only those people who have graduate degrees can be given such titles.
7	Word Choice	*After class I usually take lunch at home. correct After class I usually eat lunch at home. *or* correct After class I usually have lunch at home. *There activity fee is expensive. correct Their activity fee is expensive. *The university is surrounded from tall trees. correct The university is surrounded by tall trees.
8	Word Form	*From the least to the most importance, the three . . . correct From the least to the most important, the three . . .
9	Article	*Students need a best explanation possible. correct Students need the best explanation possible.

THE THIRD EDITING STAGE: PUNCTUATION AND MECHANICS PROBLEMS		
Number	**Problem(s)**	**Sample Sentences**
10	Punctuation 10a Comma	*Before I came to the United States several friends had studied here.
		correct Before I came to the United States, several friends had studied here.
	10b Apostrophe	*I am attending college with my brothers help.
		correct I am attending college with my brother's help.
11	Capitalization	*I have a Computer science test and an English test on monday.
		correct I have a computer science test and an English test on Monday.
12	Spelling	*At ESL centers, courses in listening, speaking, reading, and writting are taught.
		correct At ESL centers, courses in listening, speaking, reading, and writing are taught.

Practicing the Editing Process

Suggestions for Editing Past Time

1. Use simple past tense forms most of the time.
2. Use past perfect, past progressive, or some modal forms for special reasons. Time expressions are usually needed.
3. Check for subject-verb agreement with past progressive forms.
4. Check for correct irregular verb forms and spelling.

Editing Assignment: Read each paragraph, and underline each subject with one line and each verb with two lines. (This has been done for you in the first paragraph.) Review the suggestions above. Then, put an X through each incorrect form, and write the correction above it.

A. A Trip to the Zoo

¹My father used to take my sister and me to interesting places like the zoo, the museum, or the library each week. ²One Sunday when I am six years old, he decided to take us to the zoo. ³We park our car, buy our tickets, and headed toward the elephant area. ⁴We stand next to the fence near a very huge elephant with a long trunk and big body. ⁵I feed him peanuts and touch his trunk. ⁶Then, we went to the lion area and see many lions, tigers, and leopards in large cages. ⁷Finally, we went to the reptile area, and we see different types of poisonous snakes. ⁸The zoo is very busy that day, but I am too busy with the animals to notice the people. ⁹We saw many strange animals at the zoo that day, and for many years after our trip, the zoo is my favorite place to visit.

B. Simón Bolívar

¹Simón Bolívar had Spanish blood even though he liberated five nations from Spanish domination. ²As a young boy, he live in Venezuela, but he did not study in a public school; his parents hired a private tutor for him. ³This teacher taught Bolívar about revolutions in other countries. ⁴These teachings start his dream of fighting against Spain. ⁵Later, when he visit Spain and France and hear about the French Revolution, he decide to return to South America and to fight against the Spanish rule. ⁶Of the five countries that Simón Bolívar liberate, one country needs a president. ⁷Therefore, the other leaders elect him as the first president of my country, and they give him the title of "Liberator." ⁸They also name my country after him: Bolivia.

C. Getting My Driver's License

¹Last Saturday, I finally got my driver's license. ²However, last Saturday was the second time that I attempt the test. ³Four weeks ago, I

take the test for the first time, but I did not drive very much before I took the test that day. ⁴During the first test, I was so nervous that I did everything wrong. ⁵My driving frighten the examiner, and I fail the driving test. ⁶After this unforgettable experience, I begun to practice with my uncle as my teacher. ⁷He teached me patiently until I drove calmly and carefully. ⁸With his help, I improve. ⁹Before I take the test a second time, I practice everything several times. ¹⁰Then, last Saturday morning, I walk into the testing center, pass the test, and left with my license.

Suggestions for Editing for Subject-Verb Agreement

1. Add -*s* to the verb of a singular count noun or noncount noun subject.
2. Look behind the verb when a sentence begins with *there* or *here.*
3. Expect exceptions to occur with amounts of time, money, or distance; *either/or* and *neither/nor;* and indefinite pronouns *(anybody, each, everybody, nobody, somebody).*
4. Be sure that *do, have,* and *be* follow the agreement rules.

Editing Assignment: Read each paragraph, and underline each subject with one line and each verb with two lines. (This has been done for you in the first paragraph.) Review the suggestions above. Then, put an X through each incorrect form, and write the correction above it.

A. Study Methods

¹I recommend three study methods. ²Studying in the college library is a good idea because the library is quiet. ³I do all of my homework in the library, and a student do not need to worry about a place to go between classes. ⁴In addition, there is many interesting books, magazines, and newspapers to read when a student want to take a break from studying. ⁵Whenever I am not in class, I usually go to the library to study. ⁶Another good technique is reading at home every night. ⁷I read many newspapers and magazines at home to improve my reading speed and comprehension. ⁸I need to be able to read better and faster before I take

a history or psychology course. [9]Every <u>student</u> <u>need</u> to read as much as possible at school and at home. [10]However, these two <u>methods</u> <u>is</u> not enough. [11]<u>I</u> also <u>want</u> to write better. [12]A graduate or undergraduate <u>student</u> <u>need</u> to write well. [13]Therefore, <u>I</u> <u>practice</u> writing every night at home. [14]<u>I</u> <u>do</u> my homework assignments, and when <u>I</u> <u>finish</u> my homework, <u>I</u> <u>write</u> in my journal. [15]If a <u>student</u> <u>follow</u> my suggestions, <u>I</u> <u>promise</u> better grades.

B. Studying in the United States

[1]Most international students come to the United States for three reasons. [2]They come because the United States have a variety of colleges and universities. [3]In some countries, getting into college are very difficult, and students must go outside the country if they want to go to college. [4]For example, if a student want to go to college in my country, he have to take a very difficult exam. [5]This exam is given once a year, and if a student do not pass it, he has to wait until the next year. [6]In the United States, a student have several choices, and a student can usually find a college to attend. [7]An international student also come to the United States to study because English is the first language here. [8]English is a world language, and many companies in other countries requires a knowledge of English. [9]Finally, a degree from the United States are popular in other countries, and a student who graduate from a college or university in the United States can get a good job in most countries. [10]American colleges and universities has the newest equipment and books in their laboratories and libraries, and international students come to the United States for these benefits.

C. Assignment for this paragraph: put a check mark above plural markers for nouns, such as *many, several,* and *two.* Then, add an *-s* to each noun that should be made plural. Also, look for any other nouns that should be made plural. (Singular-count nouns need an article, and plural-count nouns need *-s.*)

413

Ways to Learn English

[1]There are many way to learn English. [2]First, watching TV is a good way to learn English because you can see and listen to all different kind of situation. [3]Also, people in commercials speak very clearly. [4]Second, talking to American is a good way to learn English because you can practice your new grammar and vocabulary word, and you might learn some new word to use next time. [5]Third, reading a book is one of the best ways to learn English. [6]English is used by Americans in different way: talking and writing. [7]So, if you read a book, you can recognize a difference between spoken and written English. [8]If you read a book, you can learn more vocabulary and grammar. [9]Also, traveling is one of the best way to learn English. [10]You are forced to communicate in English if you want to say or do something. [11]I hope that these tip help you.

Suggestions for Editing Modal Auxiliaries

1. Do NOT use *to* with modals.
2. Do NOT use *-s* for subject-verb agreement.
3. Do NOT put two modals in the same verb phrase.
4. Do NOT add *-ed*.
5. Check for the correct form in the correct time frame:
   [modal + *have* + past participle] for past time
   [modal + verb] for future time or general truth
6. Check for the correct meaning. Should the meaning be stronger or weaker?

Editing Assignment: Read each paragraph, and underline each modal with two lines. Review the suggestions above. Then, put an X through each incorrect form, and write the correction above it. Would you want to change any of the modals to have a stronger or weaker meaning?

A. Driving Safely

[1]To drive safely in a big city during rush hour, inexperienced drivers should to follow my advice to always drive carefully. [2]In rush hour traffic, they should be alert and watch out for cars traveling in front of,

behind, and beside them. [3]In big cities, people drive very fast, and there are many drivers who could caused accidents. [4]Drivers are often in a hurry, and some will exceed the speed limits and will pass cars when they should to stay in their lanes. [5]These drivers might to cause accidents. [6]In addition, inexperienced drivers might read the exit signs carefully. [7]Some intersections can be very confusing, and they might be in the wrong lane and unable to exit. [8]In fact, they should probably checked a map before they got on the highway. [9]Finally, they might slow down on curves because they are very dangerous, and they could lose control of their cars. [10]Driving can be a dangerous experience, but with my advice, inexperienced drivers should be able to drive safely in a city.

B. Preparation

[1]If a friend of mine plans to study in the United States, he <u>should learn</u> about this country and its language before he arrives. [2]Since most people in the United States speak only English, my friend <u>must have to be able to understand</u> some basic English when he arrives. [3]There are many English language sources in Ethiopia. [4]He <u>can to learn</u> a lot in school, especially if he goes to an American school. [5]There, he <u>will have</u> a good chance to practice his English with native speakers. [6]In addition to this, he <u>can visited</u> the United States culture center where he <u>might have learned</u> more. [7]He <u>should know</u> a little about the United States before he arrives here. [8]Besides the language problem, my friend <u>should face</u> a weather problem in this country. [9]In my country there is no winter season with cold weather like in Montana, New York, or Michigan. [10]Therefore, he <u>must to bring</u> some warm clothes which <u>can to help</u> him to keep warm if he moves to the northern parts of the United States. [11]These two pieces of advice <u>will help</u> my friend prepare for life in this country.

Suggestions for Editing for Passive Sentences

1. Use a passive verb only
   a. if the doer of the action is unknown or unimportant or
   b. if the subject of the passive sentence is the main topic of the discussion.
2. Add a form of the verb *be* to the past participle.
3. Use the appropriate form of *be* for the time frame.
4. Use only a transitive verb.
5. Omit the *by*-phrase if the information is not specific or not important.

Hint: If a second verb form follows a *be* verb, that verb form will either be an *-ing* verb OR a past participle.

correct	correct	incorrect
*is **studying***	*is **studied***	**is study*

Once you recognize this situation, think about the meaning and check the subject to see if you want a progressive verb form or a passive verb form.

Editing Assignment: Read each paragraph, and underline each verb with two lines. Review the suggestions above. Then, put an X through each incorrect form, and write the correction above it.

A. My College

[1]My college was build in 1964, and it is locate two miles from my apartment. [2]It has several classroom buildings in addition to an administration building, a gym, and a library. [3]The administration building is on a hill and is easily seeing from the highway. [4]Behind the administration building, there are four classroom buildings in a row. [5]My classes are locate in the English building and in the mathematics building: these buildings are connect to each other by a walkway with a roof over it. [6]The gym was build four years ago, and a new library was start last year. [7]The old library building will become another classroom building when the construction of the new library is finish. [8]A computer building is plan for next year, but I will not be here when it is finish. [9]Although the buildings on campus were build at different times, each new building was design to match the others.

B. The DeKalb Farmer's Market

[1]I work at the biggest market in Georgia: the DeKalb Farmer's Market. [2]It is locate on Ponce De Leon Avenue in the city of Decatur. [3]The large parking lot is usually completely fill on Saturday and Sunday. [4]There are two entrances to the market; one is call the north entrance, and the other is call the south entrance. [5]A customer service office can be found beside each entrance. [6]Besides customer service, there are many departments in the market: bakery, seafood, meat, dairy, fruit, vegetables, and staples. [7]The fruits and vegetables are locate near the south entrance, and the meat, seafood, and dairy products are place near the north entrance. [8]In the front of the store between the north and south entrances, 65 cash registers to serve customers can be find. [9]The market is crowd with shoppers six days a week, and almost 10,000 people shop at the market every day. [10]The DeKalb Farmer's Market is a marvelous place to visit and an excellent place to buy food.

Suggestions for Editing for Determiners and Articles

Editing for Articles		
Noun	**Meaning**	**Article**
singular-count	indefinite	*a/an*
	definite	*the*
	generic-1	*a/an*
	generic-2	*the*
plural-count	indefinite	*some*
	definite	*the*
	generic-3	no article
noncount	indefinite	*some*
	definite	*the*
	generic-5	no article
proper		no article
		the

1. Singular-count nouns must have a determiner. Most of the nouns that you write are singular-count nouns. Therefore, if you can edit for these effectively, you can greatly improve your accuracy in written English.
2. Only one determiner can be used with any one noun.

Editing Assignment: Read each paragraph, and review the chart on page 417. Then, examine the nouns to see if any articles or determiners need to be added for the correct meaning. If a word needs to be added, put a ∧ (*caret*) where the word is needed, and write the correct word above it.

A. King Sae Jong

¹King Sae Jong was very wise Korean <u>king</u> who influenced <u>history</u> of Korea. ²He lived in fifteenth <u>century</u>, and became its king at <u>age</u> of seven when his father died. ³He was very wise <u>leader</u> and improved both the arts and the sciences. ⁴When he assumed power, Korean <u>people</u> were under <u>rule</u> of <u>China</u>, and they used Chinese <u>alphabet</u>. ⁵Because Chinese <u>alphabet</u> was so hard to learn, Sae Jong invented Korean <u>alphabet</u>. ⁶His <u>letters</u> are based on sound, and it is easy to learn to spell using new <u>alphabet</u>. ⁷He was also great <u>scientist</u> and invented rain <u>gauge</u> to measure <u>amount</u> of rainfall and water <u>clock</u> to record automatically <u>time</u> of day and changes in seasons. ⁸Because of his <u>love</u> for learning, he established several very important learning <u>institutions</u> during his lifetime.

B. Jeong Hee Park

¹Jeong Hee Park was son of Korean farmer. ²He grew up in southern part of Korea and taught at private school during World War II. ³He went to Japanese military academy in 1943 and became major in Japanese army in 1947. ⁴Korean government hired him as military advisor in 1950. ⁵Park and his troops did not agree with president of Korea, and they decided to form new government. ⁶Park did many good things during year that he ruled Korea. ⁷However, when he extended length of his term as president, revolution resulted, and he was assassinated by one of his advisors. ⁸Because of his achievements, many Koreans today remember him as hero.

Suggestions for Editing for Prepositions

> 1. Check the preposition combination lists in Appendix E.
> 2. Review the relationship meanings for prepositions in Chapter Eight.
> 3. Keep a list of preposition combinations that you have used incorrectly.
>   Review this list when you are editing your writing. Put this list in your
>   Grammar Notebook with the other words that you are trying to learn.

Editing Assignment: Read each paragraph, and put parentheses around the prepositional phrases. Review the suggestions above. Then, put an X through each incorrect preposition, and write the correction above it. Some prepositions should not be changed because they are correct.

A. My History

[1]I was born on Taichung, Taiwan, in January 4, 1971. [2]My native language is Chinese, but now I am learning English at Atlanta, Georgia. [3]I have been living at the United States for five years; I spent one year at Florida and the other years at Georgia. [4]I graduated in Clarkston High School in 1990. [5]I now live at Atlanta on 1229 Rockbridge Road. [6]Like many Chinese immigrants, my father worked on a Chinese restaurant for one year until he was able to open his own restaurant on January. [7]I am the youngest child in the family. [8]Besides studying English, I would like to learn other languages, such as French, Spanish, and German, and I would like to travel to many countries. [9]During my leisure time, I enjoy swimming, ice skating, and jogging.

B. The Influence of Jomo Kenyatta on My Life

[1]I was born on a small village near Mount Kilimanjaro in December 12, 1963. [2]At that same day, Kenya became independent to the British government. [3]When I was a young boy, my parents moved to Nairobi, the main city on Kenya. [4]I attended school there and studied the history of my country. [5]I enjoyed history and learned for the achievements of Jomo Kenyatta. [6]Although he was born poor, Kenyatta realized the

importance for a good education. [7]As a young boy, he attended a mission school and pressured his teachers to teach him as much as possible. [8]He later moved to England and studied to the London School of Economics. [9]He believed that Kenya should be a free nation, and during the fifteen years he lived at London, he tried to convince the British government to grant freedom to Kenya. [10]Kenyatta realized his dreams on the day that I was born. [11]He was known as the "Lion of Kenya" and the "Father of Kenya." [12]After my studies at the United States, I plan to return to my native land.

Suggestions for Editing for Gerunds and Infinitives

1. Use a gerund after a preposition.
2. Use gerunds with the following expressions (*to* is a preposition):

be accustomed to + gerund	*get used to* + gerund
be opposed to + gerund	*look forward to* + gerund
be used to + gerund	*object to* + gerund

Editing Assignment: Read each paragraph, put parentheses around each prepositional phrase and underline each gerund and infinitive. Review the suggestions above. Then, put an X through each incorrect form, and write the correction above it. The first sentence is edited as an example.

A. Test Taking

[1]Test taking is part (of going) (to college), and knowing how taking tests successfully is important. [2]Students should always get a good night's sleep the night before a test and arrive at the test several minutes early. [3]After the instructor has passed out the test, the instructions should be read carefully. [4]Next, students should establish a time schedule for answer the questions and should avoid to spend all of the test time to think about difficult questions. [5]Students can often skip harder questions and return to them if there is enough time at the end of the test session. [6]When they have a choice between several questions,

students should always read all of the choices determining the best one. [7]Students ought to write neatly, to answer all of the questions, and, if there is time, to reread the test before to turn it in.

B. The Library

[1]A library is a good place (for study). [2]There are three kinds (of study areas) (in the library) (at my university): classrooms, round tables for students who want to sit together and work, and separate desks for students who want to work alone. [3]The university library has hundreds of books. [4]I can find the book that I want by look in the card catalogue for the title or the author of the book. [5]The library also has cabinets with microfilm copies of newspapers and magazines, microfilm readers, and copy machines. [6]Students can spend time to read current newspapers and magazines in the reading room and can finish to type their papers in the typing room. [7]Librarians at the reference desk assist students in locate information which can be checked out at the circulation desk. [8]Many students enjoy read current newspapers and magazines during their free time between classes. [9]The library is the best place for study quietly, and I plan to continue go to the library every day.

Suggestions for Editing for Punctuation and Capitalization

---

1. Check for the following:
   a. Each sentence should begin with a capital letter and should end with a period or a question mark as appropriate.
   b. Use apostrophes where needed with possessive nouns.
   c. Make sure your periods (.) look different from your commas (,).
   d. Check every compound sentence for FANBOYS.
2. Look carefully for any errors that you have made frequently in other writing.

Editing Assignment: Read each paragraph, and edit for punctuation in A and capitalization in B. Put an X through any mistake; use a ∧ (*caret*) to indicate that something should be added. Then, add the correct form above the caret. For each paragraph, work with the other students in your class to make a list of the punctuation and capitalization rules that you followed to make the corrections.

A. My First Day

[1]I will never forget my first day in the United States. [2]I felt very happy when I saw my husband and my cousin at the airport. [3]After we had talked with each other for several minutes I looked for servants to carry my luggage. [4]However my husband told me that we had to do everything for ourselves in the United States. [5]I was surprised and tried to understand this strange new life. [6]While we were driving home I noticed that there were no pedestrians on the road. [7]I didnt see any public transportation vehicles either. [8]In my country public transportation is used by most people who travel. [9]After arriving home I looked at my watch and was surprised to see how late it was. [10]It was 9:00 at night but it was still light outside. [11]At 10:00 the man who lived in the next apartment knocked on the door. [12]He was an American. [13]While he was talking to my husband I listened to the conversation but I could hear only a few words clearly. [14]Because of the mans American accent I didnt understand very much. [15]My cousin told me that it would take me a long time to understand peoples conversations in English. [16]Whenever I think about my first day in the United States I always remember my three surprises.

B. Frustrations

[1]before i left india, i had thought my transition to life in the united states would be easy. [2]i knew that the main Language in the united states was english, and i knew that I could speak english. [3]I assumed that my knowledge of the American Language would be enough to communicate with americans. [4]I soon discovered that I was wrong. [5]I had a bad experience at kennedy airport in new york city. [6]I arrived on sunday, april 27, at 7:30 P.M. and did not know where to go after I got off the plane. [7]I knew that i had to go through u.s. customs and that I

had to get on a different plane that would take me to miami, florida. [8]I asked some americans in the Airport for help, but they spoke so fast that I could not understand what they had said to me. [9]as a result, I got lost and missed the flight to miami. [10]I felt very frustrated because i could ask questions in english, but i could not understand the answers. [11]finally, I found someone who understood me, and he made a reservation for me on the next flight. [12]I had never expected to be in this situation before i left india. [13]I now sympathize with others who are in a strange Country and cannot understand the language.

Editing Your Own Written English

In the exercises earlier in Section Four, you edited someone else's ideas, sentences, and paragraphs, and you edited for one kind of problem at a time. You edited paragraphs, rather than isolated sentences, and corrected any problems that you identified.

By this time, you should be familiar with this systematic approach to editing and should be familiar with the types of problems to look for. The rest of this section provides you with suggested writing topics that will give you practice in writing and in editing what you have written.

The techniques that you practiced in the sentence-combining exercises in Chapter Ten can be useful here in improving and adding variety to your sentences. We suggest that you read what you have written or what someone else has written to see if any sentences are very short and simple or very long and confusing. If you find several short sentences, you may have avoided some grammar mistakes, but the writing may be boring. If you find long, confusing sentences, the passage probably will not be understood. A writer needs to read, reread, and reread a passage and then rewrite any parts that are not clear. Working with an editing partner on these assignments can be helpful in identifying sentences to make better. You might want to check to see if the sentences are all compound or if they are a combination of sentence types. Being aware of variety in sentence types and sentence length is the mark of a good writer and editor.

In addition, as you edit your writing, complete an **Editing Summary** for each writing assignment. It is important to establish the habit of examining your writing carefully and systematically each time you write. Then, you can become a more informed writer because you know the areas of potential danger: the areas you should always edit for. Writing frequently and editing systematically are two skills that will help you continue to improve your written English.

Writing Focused on the Past Time Frame

A. Write a paragraph of 10–12 sentences on one of the following topics. After you have read the paragraph to make sure that everything is explained clearly, underline each verb. Then, edit the verbs for meaning, form, and spelling.

1. Write a paragraph that tells about a pleasant (or unpleasant) experience that happened to you during registration.
2. Write a paragraph that tells about a funny, surprising, embarrassing, exciting, or frightening experience (at school). Be sure to tell your reader the "when, where, why, how, and who" involved in your experience.
3. Write a paragraph that tells about how you applied for and/or registered at your school. Be sure to tell your reader about any documents and tests required.
4. Write a paragraph about an important event in the history of your country. Be sure to tell your reader the "when, where, why, how, and who" involved in the event.

B. After you have finished your paragraph, exchange paragraphs with another student, and read each other's papers. With your partner's help, make a record of the things you learned about your writing.

Editing Summary

1. How many regular verbs did you use? _____

2. How many irregular verbs did you use? _____

3. What verb forms did you use? _____

4. What kinds of mistakes did you find?

   meaning?   yes/no

   form?   yes/no

   spelling?   yes/no

5. How many simple sentences did you use? _____

   How many compound sentences did you use? _____

   How many complex sentences did you use? _____

   How many compound-complex sentences did you use? _____

Writing Focused on the General Truth Time Frame

A. Write a paragraph of 10–12 sentences on one of the following topics. After you have read the paragraph to make sure that everything is explained clearly, underline each verb. Then, edit the paragraph for agreement.

1. Write a paragraph in which you explain a basic scientific principle, for example, the expansion of water when it freezes.
2. Write a paragraph in which you explain how to prepare for a test.
3. Write a paragraph in which you explain some aspects of U.S. life which you especially like (or dislike).
4. Write a paragraph in which you explain some basic principle of business.
5. Write a paragraph in which you describe an object or place. You might consider describing a book, a pen, a calculator, or a credit card. Places such as the library, the cafeteria, or the student center provide plenty of details.

B. After you have finished your paragraph, exchange paragraphs with another student, and read each other's papers. With your partner's help, make a record of the things you learned about your writing.

Editing Summary

1. How many agreement mistakes did you find? _____

2. What kinds of mistakes did you find?

   missing -*s* on verb   yes/no

   added -*ed* on verb   yes/no

   missing -*s* on noun   yes/no

3. How many simple sentences? _____

   How many compound sentences? _____

   How many complex sentences? _____

   How many compound-complex sentences? _____

Writing Focused on the Modal Auxiliaries

A. Write a paragraph of 10–12 sentences on one of the following topics. After you have read the paragraph to make sure that everything is explained clearly, underline each verb. Then, edit the paragraph for appropriate choice and form of verbs, especially modals.

1. Write a paragraph in which you give someone else advice about something that you know about well. You might consider advice about a person's health, advice about choosing a school, advice about choosing an apartment or a car, advice about the first day on a new job, advice about learning English, or advice about any other topic of your choice.

2. Write a letter to a friend who is planning to spend one month traveling in the United States. Give this friend advice and recommendations about such topics as cities to visit, methods of transportation, and places to see.

3. Write a paragraph in which you identify a problem that exists at your institution or in your city and indicate how to solve that problem.

B. After you have finished your paragraph, exchange paragraphs with another student, and read each other's papers. With your partner's help, make a record of the things you learned about your writing.

Editing Summary

1. How many modal mistakes did you make? _____

2. What kinds of modal mistakes did you find?

   meaning?   yes/no

   form?   yes/no

   spelling?   yes/no

3. What kinds of verb mistakes did you find?

   meaning?   yes/no

   form?   yes/no

   spelling?   yes/no

   agreement?   yes/no

4. How many simple sentences did you use? _____

   How many compound sentences did you use? _____

   How many complex sentences did you use? _____

   How many compound-complex sentences did you use? _____

Writing Focused on Passive Sentences

A. Write a paragraph of 10–12 sentences on one of the following topics. After you have read the paragraph to make sure that everything is explained clearly, underline each verb. Then, edit the paragraph for appropriate and correct use of active and passive voice.

1. Describe how to do something, such as studying for an exam, registering for class, checking a book out of the university library, or getting a visa. Briefly describe the steps involved in this process.
2. Describe what changes should be made to improve the educational system of your country or the educational system of the school you are currently attending.
3. Describe what changes have been made in your country (or the United States) in the past 10 years.

B. After you have finished your paragraph, exchange paragraphs with another student, and read each other's papers. With your partner's help, make a record of the things you learned about your writing.

Editing Summary

1. How many passive verbs did you miss? _____

2. What kinds of passive mistakes did you find?

   meaning?   yes/no

   form?   yes/no

   spelling?   yes/no

3. What kinds of active verb mistakes did you find?

   meaning?   yes/no

   form?   yes/no

   spelling?   yes/no

   agreement?   yes/no

4. How many simple sentences did you use? _____

   How many compound sentences did you use? _____

   How many complex sentences did you use? _____

   How many compound-complex sentences did you use? _____

Additional Topics for General Editing Practice

A. Write a paragraph of 10–12 sentences on one of the following topics. After you have read the paragraph to make sure that everything is explained clearly, underline each verb. Then, edit the paragraph for appropriate and correct use of verbs and any other editing problem indicated by your instructor.

1. Explain why you are going to school at this particular time and at this particular place.
2. Describe a childhood experience that taught you something about yourself or about life.
3. Explain a quality in yourself that you would like to change. You might want to tell why you want to change this quality or characteristic or how you plan to change it.
4. Describe the best course you have ever taken.
5. Describe a place that is special to you.
6. Describe the steps a person must complete to get a visa to or from your country or the United States.
7. Explain why you chose your major.
8. Explain why you would (or would not) advise your children to go to college.
9. Discuss the major adjustments that ESL students face when they study at universities in the United States.
10. Discuss expectations for university students in your country. You might consider what students expect when they go to a university or what parents or teachers expect of students.
11. Discuss why you would or would not like to own your own business.
12. Discuss what you plan to be doing in 10 years.

B. Answer the following 10 questions before you exchange papers with a classmate or hand your paper in to your instructor.

Editing Questions

1. Did I make any verb mistakes?   yes/no

2. Did I make any agreement mistakes?   yes/no

3. Did I make any passive mistakes?   yes/no

4. Did I write any fragments?   yes/no

5. Did I make any article mistakes?   yes/no

6. Did I make any preposition mistakes?   yes/no

7. Did I make any punctuation mistakes?   yes/no

8. Did I make any capitalization mistakes?   yes/no

9. Did I make any spelling mistakes?   yes/no

10. Did I use sentence variety?   yes/no

Number of simple sentences   _____

Number of compound sentences   _____

Number of complex sentences   _____

Number of compound-complex sentences   _____

C. After you have finished checking your paragraph to answer the 10 questions in Section II, exchange paragraphs with another student, and read each other's papers. With your partner's help, make a record of the things you learned about your writing.

Editing Summary

1. How many verb mistakes did I make?   _____

2. How many agreement mistakes did I make?   _____

3. How many passive mistakes did I make?   _____

4. How many fragments did I write?   _____

5. How many article mistakes did I make?   _____

6. How many preposition mistakes did I make?   _____

7. How many punctuation mistakes did I make?   _____

8. How many capitalization mistakes did I make?   _____

9. How many words did I misspell?   _____

D. Using the information from sections B and C, summarize what you have learned about your English grammar. First, list things that you do well, and then list areas that you need to improve.

1. Things I do well: _____

_____

_____

2. Things I need to improve: _____

_____

_____

E. Using the information from sections B and C, revise your paragraph. Share the revised paragraph with your partner, and discuss the changes that you have made.

F. Using the information from sections B and C, discuss with your class ways an individual can make his or her written English grammar more accurate.

SECTION

FIVE

●●●●●●●●●●●●●●●●●●●●●●●●●●●●●

Appendices and Lists

A. Linking Verbs
B. Joining Words with Similar Meanings
C. Alphabetized List of Irregular Verbs
D. Traditional Definitions for the Modal Auxiliary Verbs
E. Prepositions

●●●●●●●●●●

Appendix A: Linking Verbs

Linking verbs connect (link) a subject to a complement (a word that renames or describes the subject).

Be
Linking verbs include all of the forms of *be*. Notice that *be* is used as the verb (rather than as an auxiliary).

subject + *be* + complement
My computer is expensive.

I am a student.

The students were in the lab before class.

Have Been
Notice that perfect forms of *be* can have complements.

subject + verb + complement
I have been unhappy since I got my grades.

John has been in the library since lunch.

Senses
Linking verbs also include verbs related to the senses such as *feel, look, smell, sound,* and *taste.*

The final examination looked easy.

Other Verbs
Linking verbs include other verbs such as *appear, become, grow, prove, remain,* and *seem.*

subject + verb + complement
Irregular verbs seem easy to learn.

He grew unhappy because of his academic problems.

Here is an alphabetized list of all of the linking verbs given above:

am	*prove*
appear	*remain*
are	*seem*
become	*smell*
feel	*sound*
grow	*taste*
is	*was*
look	*were*

Appendix B: Joining Words with Similar Meanings

Coordinating Words

Simple Sentence,   *and*
                    but
                    or
                    nor   Simple Sentence
                    for
                    so
                    yet

and	=	gives additional information
but	=	gives contrasting information
or	=	gives an alternative
nor	=	gives another negative
for	=	gives a reason
so	=	gives a result
yet	=	gives contrary information

He has a small calculator, but he really needs a much better one for his engineering class.

Some transition words and subordinating words have meanings similar to coordinating words. While these words have similar meanings, they are used in different ways.

Meanings	Coordinating Words	Transition Words	Subordinating Words
Addition	*and*	*also* *furthermore*	
Contrast	*but*	*however* *in contrast* *on the contrary* *on the other hand*	*although*
Alternatives	*or*	*instead*	
Reason/Result	*for*	*as a result* *consequently* *then* *therefore*	*because*
Time	—	*first, second* *consequently* *next* *then*	*after, before* *when, while*

coordinating word

She has a small calculator, **but** *she really needs a much better one for her engineering class.*

transition word

She has a small calculator; **however,** *she really needs a much better one for her engineering class.*

subordinating word

Although *she has a small calculator, she really needs a much better one for her engineering class.*

Appendix C: Alphabetized List of Irregular Verbs

You should know the meaning and spelling of all of these irregular verbs. It would seem wise for you to take time to test yourself to find out which of these forms you do not yet know. Then, use whatever method of memorization you prefer to add these words to your written vocabulary.

Base Form	Simple Past	Past Participle	*-ing* Form
arise	arose	arisen	arising
awake	awoke	awoke/awaked	awaking
be	was/were	been	being
bear	bore	borne	bearing
beat	beat	beaten	beating
become	became	become	becoming
begin	began	begun	beginning
bend	bent	bent	bending
bet	bet	bet	betting
bid	bid	bid	bidding
bind	bound	bound	binding
bite	bit	bitten	biting
bleed	bled	bled	bleeding
blow	blew	blown	blowing
break	broke	broken	breaking
breed	bred	bred	breeding
bring	brought	brought	bringing
build	built	built	building
burn	burned/burnt	burned/burnt	burning
burst	burst	burst	bursting
buy	bought	bought	buying
cast	cast	cast	casting
catch	caught	caught	catching
choose	chose	chosen	choosing
cling	clung	clung	clinging
come	came	come	coming
cost	cost	cost	costing
creep	crept	crept	creeping
cut	cut	cut	cutting
deal	dealt	dealt	dealing
dig	dug	dug	digging
dive	dived/dove	dived	diving
do	did	done	doing
draw	drew	drawn	drawing

(continued)

435

Base Form	Simple Past	Past Participle	*-ing* Form
drink	drank	drunk	drinking
drive	drove	driven	driving
eat	ate	eaten	eating
fall	fell	fallen	falling
feed	fed	fed	feeding
feel	felt	felt	feeling
fight	fought	fought	fighting
find	found	found	finding
fit	fit	fit	fitting
flee	fled	fled	fleeing
fling	flung	flung	flinging
fly	flew	flown	flying
forget	forgot	forgotten	forgetting
forgive	forgave	forgiven	forgiving
forsake	forsook	forsaken	forsaking
freeze	froze	frozen	freezing
get	got	gotten	getting
give	gave	given	giving
go	went	gone	going
grind	ground	ground	grinding
grow	grew	grown	growing
hang	hung	hung	hanging
have	had	had	having
hear	heard	heard	hearing
hide	hid	hidden	hiding
hit	hit	hit	hitting
hold	held	held	holding
hurt	hurt	hurt	hurting
keep	kept	kept	keeping
kneel	knelt	knelt	kneeling
knit	knit/knitted	knit/knitted	knitting
know	knew	known	knowing
lay	laid	laid	laying
lead	led	led	leading
leap	leapt	leapt	leaping
leave	left	left	leaving
lend	lent	lent	lending
let	let	let	letting
lie	lay	lain	lying
light	lit	lit	lighting
lose	lost	lost	losing
make	made	made	making
mean	meant	meant	meaning
meet	met	met	meeting
mow	mowed	mowed/mown	mowing
pay	paid	paid	paying

(continued)

Base Form	Simple Past	Past Participle	*-ing* Form
prove	proved	proved/proven	proving
put	put	put	putting
quit	quit	quit	quitting
read	read	read	reading
rid	rid	rid	ridding
ride	rode	ridden	riding
ring	rang	rung	ringing
rise	rose	risen	rising
run	ran	run	running
saw	sawed	sawed/sawn	sawing
say	said	said	saying
see	saw	seen	seeing
seek	sought	sought	seeking
sell	sold	sold	selling
send	sent	sent	sending
set	set	set	setting
sew	sewed	sewed/sewn	sewing
shake	shook	shaken	shaking
shave	shaved	shaved/shaven	shaving
shear	sheared	sheared/shorn	shearing
shine	shone	shone	shining
shoot	shot	shot	shooting
show	showed	showed/shown	showing
shrink	shrank	shrunk	shrinking
shut	shut	shut	shutting
sing	sang	sung	singing
sink	sank	sunk	sinking
sit	sat	sat	sitting
sleep	slept	slept	sleeping
slide	slid	slid	sliding
sow	sowed	sowed/sown	sowing
speak	spoke	spoken	speaking
speed	sped	sped	speeding
spend	spent	spent	spending
spin	spun	spun	spinning
split	split	split	splitting
spread	spread	spread	spreading
spring	sprang	sprung	springing
stand	stood	stood	standing
steal	stole	stolen	stealing
stick	stuck	stuck	sticking
sting	stung	stung	stinging
strike	struck	struck/stricken	striking
string	strung	strung	stringing
swear	swore	sworn	swearing
sweep	swept	swept	sweeping

(*continued*)

Base Form	Simple Past	Past Participle	-ing Form
swell	swelled	swelled/swollen	swelling
swim	swam	swum	swimming
swing	swung	swung	swinging
take	took	taken	taking
teach	taught	taught	teaching
tear	tore	torn	tearing
tell	told	told	telling
think	thought	thought	thinking
throw	threw	thrown	throwing
thrust	thrust	thrust	thrusting
understand	understood	understood	understanding
wake	woke	woken	waking
wear	wore	worn	wearing
weave	wove	woven	weaving
weep	wept	wept	weeping
win	won	won	winning
withdraw	withdrew	withdrawn	withdrawing
wring	wrung	wrung	wringing
write	wrote	written	writing

Appendix D: Traditional Definitions for the Modal Auxiliary Verbs

You will often find these words used to define the modal auxiliary verbs. Some students like to memorize these definitions, so they are presented here with sample sentences for convenient review.

Modal	Traditional Definition	Present/Future	Past
can	ability	*I can type.*	*I could type faster when I was in typing class.*
	request	*"Can I borrow a pen?"*	
	permission	*"You can borrow my pen."*	
	possibility	*"You can take calculus in the spring if you want to."*	

(continued)

Modal	Traditional Definition	Present/Future	Past
could	past ability		I could type 50 WPM when I was taking typing.
	request	"Could you take a message?"	
	possibility	That answer could be right.	The test could have been even harder.
may	request (formal)	"May I leave early?"	
	permission (formal)	"You may leave early."	
	probability	Suwan was tired yesterday; he may be tired again today.	Suwan may have worked the night shift last night.
might	slight probability	Suwan might be sick.	Suwan might have gotten a bad cold.
shall	polite questions	"Shall we begin?"	
	formal future	In class today, we shall discuss management theory.	
should	advice	Students should study every night.	I should have studied last night.
	expectation	The bus should be here at 10:00.	The bus should have been here by now.
must	necessity	Students must pay tuition.	Students had to pay tuition last quarter.
	logical deduction	Mary had a fever. She is absent now. She must be sick.	She must have had a bad night.
will	intention or promise	I will study this weekend.	
	future time certainty	We will have a test on Friday.	

(continued)

Modal	Traditional Definition	Present/Future	Past
would	past time habit		*Last year, we would study together every weekend.*
	conditional	*If I were you, I would use my dictionary more often.*	
	polite question	*"Would you please loan me a pen?"* *"Would you mind loaning me a pen?"* *"Would you like a new pen?"*	
	preference	*I would rather study math than English.*	*I would rather have studied math than English.*
		I would like a new calculator.	*I would have liked a new calculator.*

Appendix E: Prepositions

	I. Alphabetized List of Common Prepositions		
aboard	below	in	through
about	beneath	inside	throughout
above	beside	into	to
across	besides	like	toward
after	between	near	under
against	beyond	of	underneath
along	by	off	until
among	down	on	up
around	during	out	upon
as	except	over	with
at	for	past	within
before	from	since	without
behind			

II. Verb + Preposition Combinations

account for
accuse (someone) of
adapt to
add to
agree on (something)
agree to (something)
agree with (someone)
apologize for (something)
apologize to (someone)
apply for
approve of
argue with (someone)
argue about (something)
arrive at
ask for
become of
believe in
belong to
blame (someone) for (something)
blame (something) on (someone)
borrow from
care about
care for
catch up with
come from
comment on
communicate with
compare with
complain about
compliment (someone) on
congratulate on
concentrate on
consent to
consist of
convince (someone) of (something)
decide between

decide on
depend on
(dis)approve of
dream about, of
excuse (someone) for
explain (something) to
get along with
get back from
get rid of
get through with
get used to
happen to
have confidence in
have influence over
have an opportunity for
have patience with
have a reason for
hear about
hear from
hear of
insist on
introduce to
invite (someone) to
keep for, from
keep on
laugh about
laugh at
learn about
listen for
listen to
look at
look for
look forward to
object to
participate in
pay for

plan on
prefer to
prepare for
prevent from
provide for
provide (someone) with
recover from
refer to
relate to
rely on
remind (someone) of
search for
see about
send for
separate from
show up at
spend (money) on
stop from
substitute for
subtract from
succeed in
take advantage of
talk about
talk over
talk to
thank (someone) for
think about
think of
throw away
vote for
wait for
waste (money) on
wish for
work for
worry about

III. Verb + Adjective or Noun + Preposition

be absent from	be guilty of
be accustomed to	be happy with, about, for
be acquainted with	be incapable of
be afraid of	be in charge of
be angry with, at	be in danger of
be appropriate for	be in favor of
be ashamed of	be innocent of
be aware of	be interested in
be capable of	be in touch with
be certain of	be jealous of
be committed to	be known for
be composed of	be lazy about
be concerned about	be made of, from
be content with	be married to, by
be dedicated to	be opposed to
be delighted at, with	be out of date
be devoted to	be out of order
be different from	have patience with
be disappointed with, in, by	be patient with
be divorced from	be polite to
be done with	be prevented from
be dressed in	be proud of
be engaged to	be relevant to
be enthusiastic about	be responsible to, for
be envious of	be satisfied with
be equal to	be scared of, by
be essential to	be sensitive to
be excited about	be sorry about, for
be faithful to	be suitable for
be familiar with	be sure of, about
be famous for	be surprised by, at
be fed up with	have a talent for
be finished with	be terrified of
be fond of	be thankful for
be friendly to, with	be tired of, from
be frightened by, of	be used to
be generous about	get used to
be glad about	be useful for
be good at	be uneasy about
be grateful for, to	be worried about

S E C T I O N

S I X

The Grammar Journal

**A Record of My English Grammar and
My Plans for Change**

Name: _____

School: _____

Term: _____

Name/Number of Course: _____

Diagnostic Test Record Sheet

Date I Took the Diagnostic Test _____

Put an X through the numbers of the items you missed on the diagnostic test.

Look at the areas with the highest number of mistakes. You need to concentrate on improving these areas.

Problems Tested	Item Number				
Fragment	1	2	3	4	5
Verb					
Time framework	6	7	8	9	10
to + base form of verb	11	12	13	14	15
do + base form of verb	16	17	18	19	20
modal + base form of verb	21	22	23	24	25
have + past participle	26	27	28	29	30
passive	31	32	33	34	35
conditional	36	37	38	39	40
-ing	41	42	43	44	45
Subject-Verb Agreement	46	47	48	49	50
	51	52	53	54	55
Preposition	56	57	58	59	60
Article	61	62	63	64	65

What I Learned from the Diagnostic Test

1. _____
2. _____
3. _____
4. _____
5. _____
6. _____
7. _____
8. _____

Ways to Improve My English Grammar

1. _____
2. _____
3. _____
4. _____
5. _____
6. _____
7. _____
8. _____
9. _____
10. _____

My Learning Styles

A. Write a paragraph that describes the steps that you took to learn the poem "Fire and Ice." The topic sentence for this paragraph is given. Add the sentences needed to describe your process.

To learn the poem "Fire and Ice," I took several steps.

_____

_____

_____

_____

_____

_____

_____

_____

_____

_____

_____

_____

B. Circle the one best answer for the following statement.

Based on this learning experience, I think that my preferred learning style is

a. visual   b. auditory   c. kinesthetic

d. a mixture of visual and auditory

e. a mixture of visual and kinesthetic

My Learning Styles

A. Write a paragraph that describes the steps that you took to learn the map of the university given on page 19. The topic sentence for this paragraph is given. Add the sentences needed to describe your process.

To learn the map, I took several steps. First I _____

_____

_____

_____

_____

_____

_____

_____

B. Circle the one best answer for the following statement.

Based on this learning experience, I think that my preferred learning style is

a. visual   b. auditory   c. kinesthetic

d. a mixture of visual and auditory

e. a mixture of visual and kinesthetic

My Strategies for Learning English

A. I know that I need to learn a lot of new words. Here are the steps that I am taking to select those words and to learn them.

1. _____

_____

2. _____

_____

3. _____

_____

4. _____

_____

B. From talking with other students in the class, I realize that other people are doing some activities that I am not doing. Here are some changes that I could make.

1. _____

_____

2. _____

_____

3. _____

_____

4. _____

_____

Self-Analysis of Irregular Verbs

First, study the irregular verbs listed in Appendix C to find out which irregular verbs you have trouble spelling or which verbs you do not know. Then, answer these questions to find out more about your knowledge of English irregular verbs and about what you need to learn.

1. I use the following 10 irregular verbs frequently.

a. _____   f. _____

b. _____   g. _____

c. _____   h. _____

d. _____   i. _____

e. _____   j. _____

2. Although I know their meaning, I have trouble spelling the following verbs from Appendix C.

a. _____   f. _____

b. _____   g. _____

c. _____   h. _____

d. _____   i. _____

e. _____   j. _____

3. I plan to learn the following verbs that are new to me.

a. _____   f. _____

b. _____   g. _____

c. _____   h. _____

d. _____   i. _____

e. _____   j. _____

4. In order to use these irregular verbs correctly, I plan to do the following:

a. _____

b. _____

c. _____

Self-Analysis of Verbs

Highlight or circle each phrase that describes your problems with verbs.

1. I had the following problems with verbs on the diagnostic test.
   a. wrong form
   b. wrong spelling
   c. used regular spelling for an irregular verb
   d. did not follow subject-verb agreement
   e. did not use the right word for the meaning I wanted

2. I had the following problems with verbs on the diagnostic writing.
   a. wrong form
   b. wrong spelling
   c. used regular spelling for an irregular verb
   d. did not follow subject-verb agreement
   e. did not use the right word for the meaning I wanted

3. I have had the following problems with verbs while doing the exercises in the textbook and in writing the assigned paragraphs.
   a. wrong form
   b. wrong spelling
   c. used regular spelling for an irregular verb
   d. did not follow subject-verb agreement
   e. did not use the right word for the meaning I wanted

4. In order to improve my use of verbs, I plan to do the following:

   a. _____

   b. _____

   c. _____

Self-Analysis of Subject-Verb Agreement

Carry out the instructions for exercise A on page 109, and complete this journal entry.

1. I used the correct verb with both singular and plural subjects
   a. in the diagnostic test (items 46–55) _____ Yes _____ No
   b. in the diagnostic writing _____ Yes _____ No
   c. in three paragraphs I have written recently _____ Yes _____ No

2. I had problems in the following areas:
   a. spelling

Misspelled	Correct	Misspelled	Correct
_____	_____	_____	_____
_____	_____	_____	_____
_____	_____	_____	_____
_____	_____	_____	_____

   b. subject-verb agreement
      (1) singular subject but no -s on verb _____ Yes _____ No

      incorrect
      The student take many classes. Number of errors: _____

      (2) plural subject but -s on verb _____ Yes _____ No

      incorrect
      The students takes many classes. Number of errors: _____

      (3) noncount subject but no -s on verb _____ Yes _____ No

      incorrect
      This news seem important. Number of errors: _____

      (4) use of simple present tense when another verb form should have been used _____ Yes _____ No

      incorrect
      They study irregular verbs yesterday. Number of errors: _____

3. To deal with any problems that I have with subject-verb agreement, I plan to do the following:

   a. _____

   b. _____

   c. _____

Self-Analysis of Present Progressive

    Use the information from the diagnostic test, the diagnostic paragraph, and any other writing that you have done recently to answer the following questions. Check *No* or *Yes* to answer the questions. If the answer is *Yes,* circle DT (diagnostic test), DP (diagnostic paragraph), and OW (other writing) as appropriate.

1. I had problems with

    a. present progressive   ____ No ____ Yes (DT   DP   OW)

    b. present tense   ____ No ____ Yes (DT   DP   OW)

    c. stative   ____ No ____ Yes (DT   DP   OW)

2. These problems included the following:

    a. the wrong verb form   ____ No ____ Yes (DT   DP   OW)

    b. the wrong verb spelling   ____ No ____ Yes (DT   DP   OW)

    c. regular spelling for an
       irregular verb   ____ No ____ Yes (DT   DP   OW)

    d. subject-verb agreement
       mistakes   ____ No ____ Yes (DT   DP   OW)

    e. the wrong word for the
       meaning I wanted   ____ No ____ Yes (DT   DP   OW)

3. I have problems with stative verbs because _____

_____

_____

4. I have problems with subject-verb agreement because _____

_____

_____

Self-Analysis of Modals

Use the information from the diagnostic test, the diagnostic paragraph, and any other writing that you have done recently to answer the following questions.

1. I had problems with modals

   a. in the diagnostic test (items 21–25)   ____ Yes   ____ No

   b. in the diagnostic writing   ____ Yes   ____ No

   c. in three paragraphs I have written recently   ____ Yes   ____ No

2. These problems included

   a. using *to* with a modal   ____ Yes   ____ No

   b. adding *-s* for subject-verb agreement   ____ Yes   ____ No

   c. putting two modals in the same verb phrase   ____ Yes   ____ No

   d. adding *-ed*   ____ Yes   ____ No

   e. using the wrong meaning   ____ Yes   ____ No

3. I use the following modals frequently.

   _____ _____ _____ _____ _____

4. I seldom use the following modals.

   _____ _____ _____ _____ _____

5. I avoid using some of the modals because _____

   _____

6. To deal with any problems that I have with modals, I plan to do the following:

   a. _____

   b. _____

   c. _____

Self-Analysis of Questions

Analyze the questions that you wrote for the introductory exercises in First Steps together with any other questions that you have written this term. Select one major error to analyze in the first step of this self-analysis.

1. I made a mistake in the word order of a
question. _____ Yes _____ No

If *Yes,* copy below the question that you wrote using the wrong word order. Then, write the correct question.

incorrect question

* _____

correct question

_____

2. I made the following mistakes in other questions:

a. not adding *do, does,* or *did* _____ Yes _____ No

b. not using subject-verb agreement *(do/does)* _____ Yes _____ No

c. not having a subject _____ Yes _____ No

d. using the wrong question word _____ Yes _____ No

e. using the wrong form of the main verb
(*Where did he went?*) _____ Yes _____ No

3. In order to use questions correctly, I plan to do the following:

a. _____

b. _____

c. _____

Self-Analysis of Prepositions

1. Use a highlighter to mark all prepositions in the diagnostic writing sample. Notice also any prepositions that have been added by your instructor. Then, analyze any problems you had with prepositions.

   I made the following mistakes:

   a. using the wrong word   ____ Yes   ____ No

   b. leaving out a preposition when it is
      required   ____ Yes   ____ No

   c. choosing a preposition when none is
      supposed to be used   ____ Yes   ____ No

2. Use a highlighter to mark prepositions in three paragraphs that you have written recently. Notice also any prepositions that have been added by your instructor. Then, analyze any problems you had with prepositions.

   I made the following mistakes:

   a. using the wrong word   ____ Yes   ____ No

   b. leaving out a preposition when it is
      required   ____ Yes   ____ No

   c. choosing a preposition when none is
      supposed to be used   ____ Yes   ____ No

3. Look through the exercises and paragraphs you keep in your Grammar Notebook. Make a list of the verb + preposition or adjective + preposition combinations that you have repeatedly used incorrectly, for example, *get married with* rather than *get married to*.

   _____   _____   _____

   _____   _____   _____

   _____   _____   _____

Self-Analysis of Articles and Determiners

1. Analyze the problems that you had with articles and determiners in the diagnostic test and diagnostic paragraph.

   I had the following problems:

   a. I left out articles. _____ Yes _____ No

   b. I left out *a*. _____ Yes _____ No

   c. I left out *an*. _____ Yes _____ No

   d. I left out *the*. _____ Yes _____ No

   e. I used *a/an* when I should have used *the*. _____ Yes _____ No

   f. I used *the* when I should have used *a/an*. _____ Yes _____ No

   g. I used *the* when I should not have used an article. _____ Yes _____ No

   h. I had problems with *a/an* _____ times.

   i. I had problems with *the* _____ times.

2. Analyze the problems that you had with articles and determiners in the last paper that you wrote.

   I had the following problems:

   a. I left out articles. _____ Yes _____ No

   b. I left out *a*. _____ Yes _____ No

   c. I left out *an*. _____ Yes _____ No

   d. I left out *the*. _____ Yes _____ No

   e. I used *a/an* when I should have used *the*. _____ Yes _____ No

   f. I used *the* when I should have used *a/an*. _____ Yes _____ No

   g. I used *the* when I should not have used an article. _____ Yes _____ No

   h. I had problems with *a/an* _____ times.

   i. I had problems with *the* _____ times.

3. In order to use articles correctly, I plan to do the following:

   a. _____

   b. _____

   c. _____

Self-Analysis of Infinitives and Gerunds

Analyze any problems that you had with infinitives and gerunds in the diagnostic test, the diagnostic paragraph, and three paragraphs that you have written recently.

1. I had problems with infinitives. _____ Yes _____ No

    If *Yes*, I had the following problems:

    a. spelling _____ Yes _____ No

    b. use of wrong form (gerund rather than infinitive) _____ Yes _____ No

2. I had problems with gerunds. _____ Yes _____ No

    If *Yes*, I had the following problems:

    a. spelling _____ Yes _____ No

    b. use of wrong form (infinitive rather than gerund) _____ Yes _____ No

3. Look through the exercises and paragraphs you keep in your Grammar Notebook. Make a list of the verb + gerund or infinitive combinations that you have repeatedly used incorrectly, for example, *look forward to take* rather than *look forward to taking* or *enjoy play* rather than *enjoy playing*.

    _____   _____   _____

    _____   _____   _____

    _____   _____   _____

4. To deal with any problems that I have with infinitives or gerunds, I plan to do the following:

    a. _____

    b. _____

    c. _____

CROSSWORD PUZZLE ANSWERS

page 60

```
S P E N T
L
E   S   S P R E A D               F
S P E N T  W    T      F O R G O T
T    O  U  S W E P T        U
   F O U N D      O  B I T  N
S P E D  G  C  W R O T E  H A D
T    L     C A M E  K  G  O
U    L    G U P      A  U  C
C    B R O U G H T  W O N  G  O
K    L  T  H     O     C H O S E
  B L E W    T  T H R E W  T  T
     D        O  E  E
S  L     D E A L T  N  S L I D
G A V E     R  D  S A T  H
N  F E D  A      P    U
K  T  R  N      F O U G H T
  F  T O O K      K  E
   I  V       F L E W  L E D
S T O L E            D
```

page 62

```
                              K
                      B E G U N
              D    I  O  O
              B U I L T  N  W  F
                G    T  E  N    L
                B L E D       O
                L  N  F E D  W
              B  W O N      R U N
              R  W    F  U
              B R O K E N  D R A W N
              O  U  A    O L  K
              S  U  G O T T E N  L  E
              R U N G  H  E    E  E
                 N  H  T  N        N
              C A U G H T
              H    A    F
              C O M E  D R I V E N
              S       L
              D E A L T  C O S T
              N
```

page 324

```
                       S
               D I G N I F I E D
               L       A
               O L D   S L O W
         T     Y  H O T  H Y
       S   I            W H I T E
       E   R              T  L
       R  E  L    O R A N G E  L O
   C H I L D R E N    E      O
       O    G  G O L D      R A W
   Y O U N G  A R A B  I
       S    B L U E  T A L L  C
            L    E  A C H
    Y      S A D  N     C
   R E D  S  C        K
   L    P I N K
   B L U E  L
   O      V
   W R I T E
        R I P E
```

INDEX

CREDITS